MW01156091

No Place
to Hide:

Gang, State, and Clandestine
Violence in El Salvador

Laura Pedraza Fariña

Spring Miller

James L. Cavallaro

Published by the International Human Rights Clinic,
Human Rights Program, Harvard Law School

Distributed by Harvard University Press

Printed in the United States of America

The International Human Rights Clinic at Harvard Law School's Human Rights Program publishes a "Human Rights Practice Series" of books, distributed by Harvard University Press. Books in this series are designed to further interdisciplinary scholarship and practical understanding of leading human rights issues.

ISBN: 978-0-9796395-3-1

International Human Rights Clinic
Human Rights Program
Harvard Law School
1563 Massachusetts Avenue
Pound Hall 401
Cambridge, MA 02138
United States of America

617-495-9362
hrp@law.harvard.edu
http://www.law.harvard.edu/programs/hrp

Distributed by Harvard University Press
http://www.hup.harvard.edu

Printed by Signature Book Printing, http://www.sbpbooks.com

Photographs by Juan Carlos
www.juancarlosphotos.com

Table of Contents

Acknowledgments

This book was researched by students enrolled in the International Human Rights Clinic (IHRC) of the Human Rights Program at Harvard Law School under the direction of Clinical Professor and Human Rights Program Executive Director James Cavallaro over the course of seven semesters, from January 2006 to March 2009. The student researchers and contributors were Stephanie Brewer, Mark Jensen, Helen Lawrence, Timothy Mayhle, Spring Miller, Laura Pedraza Fariña, María Luisa Romero, and Molly Thomas-Jensen. Members of the Harvard Law School Student Advocates for Human Rights, including David Carpman, Virginia Corrigan, Dustin Saldarriaga, and Sara Zampierin, and IHRC clinical students, Virginia Farmer, Francesca Gesualdi, Yanyan Lam, and Natalie Zerial provided significant research and editing assistance. In February 2007, the IHRC released an earlier version of this book. Helen Lawrence assisted in the editing of this text. Michael Jones designed the cover, formatted the text and oversaw the production of this book. Anne Berndtson, Helen Lawrence, and Ada Sheng assisted in the proofreading of several drafts, with the collaboration of Emma Kohse.

The 2007 report, by the same title, benefited from drafting and coordination by Spring Miller and James Cavallaro. Laura Pedraza Fariña, who has been involved in the project since 2008, coordinated the updating of existing chapters and the drafting of new chapters. The authors of this book are thus Laura Pedraza Fariña, Spring Miller, and James Cavallaro.

The International Human Rights Clinic thanks the many individuals in El Salvador who provided us with information in the course of our research. We are particularly grateful to Matthew Eisen, Rosa Anaya Perla, Sherry Stanley, Nelson Escobar, and Juan Carlos Cañas, whose assistance in coordinating research during our trips to El Salvador was invaluable.

We also thank the staff of various Salvadoran non-governmental research, advocacy, and humanitarian organizations who helped us access the information in this book. In particular, we thank staff of the Institute for Public Opinion Research of "José Simeón Cañas" Central American

University (*Instituto Universitario de Opinión Pública* at the *Universidad Centroamericana "José Simeón Cañas"* or IUDOP); the Human Rights Institute of "José Simeón Cañas" Central American University (*Instituto de Derechos Humanos* at the *Universidad Centroamericana "José Simeón Cañas"* or IDHUCA); Christians for Peace in El Salvador (CRISPAZ); Youth Movement (*Movimiento Juvenil* or MOJE); "Octavio Ortiz" Clinic (*Clínica Octavio Ortiz*); Generation XXI (*Generación XXI*); "Father Rafael Palacios" Guidance and Training Center (*Centro de Formación y Orientación "Padre Rafael Palacios"* or CFO); Ideas and Actions for Peace, Quetzalcoatl Foundation (*Fundación Quetzalcoatl, Ideas y Acciones para la Paz*); The Human Rights Office of the Archbishop of San Salvador (*Tutela Legal del Arzobispado de San Salvador* or *Tutela Legal*); Care and Support for Situations of Social Suffering (*Proceso de Atención a Situaciones de Sufrimiento Social* or PASSOS); San Bartolo Parish Human Rights Committee (*Comité de los Derechos Humanos de la Parroquia de San Bartolo*); and "Homies" Together (*Homies Unidos*).

We would like to express our appreciation to the governmental authorities who provided us with important information and insights throughout our research process. Special thanks go to Supreme Court Justice Mirna Antonieta Perla Jiménez, Judge Edward Sidney Blanco Reyes, Judge Juan Antonio Durán Ramírez, Judge Aída Luz Santos de Escobar, Judge Doris Luz Rivas Galindo, Alan Edward Hernández Portillo (Chief Prosecutor for the Special Extortion Unit), Jaime Martínez Ventura of the Office of Juvenile Justice of the Supreme Court, and Dr. Fabio Molina Vaquerano (Research Director of the National Institute of Forensic Medicine).

Finally, we are deeply grateful to the victims of and witnesses to violence in El Salvador who spoke with our researchers. The report would not have been possible without the valuable information they shared with us.

Executive Summary

Almost two decades after the civil war in El Salvador came to an end, violence and insecurity continue to shape the daily lives of many Salvadorans. Much of this violence stems from the proliferation of youth gangs, insufficient and abusive state responses to gangs, and the crimes of clandestine groups. This book examines the phenomenon of youth gangs and documents human rights violations associated with gang violence as well as the corresponding Salvadoran governmental responses. Our examination is situated in the context of an assessment of the current state of the rule of law in El Salvador.

The war in El Salvador during the 1980s was one of the bloodiest and most brutal in a region gripped by civil conflicts throughout that decade. The Salvadoran conflict gained worldwide notoriety for the prevalence of human rights abuses, most notably those committed by death squads, which operated with the apparent acquiescence of state authorities, terrorizing civilian populations. Unfortunately, as discussed in Chapters I and II, efforts since the war to build functioning democratic institutions in El Salvador have largely failed to overcome the legacies of institutional incapacity and politicization. Current levels of violence are extraordinarily high. El Salvador's homicide rate is one of the highest in the world, and is more than double the average for Latin America, a region with high levels of violence by global standards. Continued political polarization, weak judicial and law enforcement institutions, and the persistence of extrajudicial violence seriously undermine citizen security and the rule of law in El Salvador.

Violent street gangs have grown rapidly in this fractured and dysfunctional socio-political context. The deportation of tens of thousands of Salvadorans from the United States since the late 1990s (a consequence of forced emigration of Salvadoran families during the civil war years and subsequent changes to U.S. immigration laws) helped spur the growth and development of these gangs, a process we describe in Chapter III. Since 2003, and as a result of particularized political conditions and law enforcement responses in El Salvador, the dynamics of the gang phenomenon have evolved. The two major rival gangs—the Mara Salvatrucha and the Mara 18, both of which have U.S. roots and a

U.S. presence—engage in brutal battles for control of neighborhoods and communities throughout the country. Gangs' methods of recruitment, and the sanctions they impose on members who demonstrate disloyalty or who attempt to withdraw from active gang life, are increasingly violent. Active and former gang members report that it is increasingly difficult, if not impossible, for young people to escape the pressure of gang recruitment or to leave a gang. In this increasingly violent, male-dominated environment, women are a particularly vulnerable group. Female gang members play a subordinate role within the gang hierarchy and are often subjected to physical and sexual abuse by male gang members. Gangs frequently use extortion to gather funds and solidify territorial control. Moreover, gangs' increasingly sophisticated organizational structures render them more likely to be able to carry out threats against those who refuse to comply with their demands.

The primary governmental response to the gang phenomenon, which has relied heavily on repressive law enforcement-military tactics, mass arrests, and profiling youth and alleged gang members, has been ineffective and even counter-productive. Governmental responses to the gang phenomenon are explored in greater depth in Chapter IV. Homicide rates have soared since 2003, when former President Francisco Flores launched the *Mano Dura* (Iron Fist or Firm Hand) crackdown. Meanwhile, the government's focus on anti-gang efforts has distorted the complex nature of violence in El Salvador. Impunity is the norm for the vast majority of homicides in El Salvador. In the past several years, the political roots of violence in El Salvador have become increasingly visible. Frequent, violent clashes between street protesters and police are one manifestation of the relationship between political polarization and violence in El Salvador, and spikes in unexplained, brutal homicides in periods prior to national elections are another.

Human rights organizations and civil society observers emphasize that a large percentage of homicides in recent years bear the mark of death squad executions. Clandestine groups that act much like the death squads that terrorized the country during its extended civil conflict have targeted alleged gang members or other criminal suspects and, increasingly, political leaders. They have operated with impunity and are thought to have ties to police forces. Indeed, several credible reports indicate that clandestine structures operating within El

Salvador's National Police and in alliance with the private sector have been responsible for at least a portion of these extrajudicial killings. There is also evidence that organized criminal networks have been operating with growing sophistication and impunity in El Salvador. The relationship between these organized criminal networks and the upper tiers of gang hierarchies is uncertain, as is the role of state actors in these activities, but the effect on Salvadoran citizens—a deepening sense of fear and insecurity—is clear.

In the midst of this social and political conflict, individual Salvadorans living in poor and marginalized communities have no place to hide: they are targeted by violent actors on all sides. Young people and other residents of areas with a gang presence, active gang members, and inactive gang members are targeted for threats, abuses, and even killings by gangs, police, and clandestine actors like death squads.

This book is based on fact-finding visits to El Salvador in March through April and August through September 2006; October 2007; March and October 2008 and January 2009; as well as months of follow-up research prior to and after these trips. It draws extensively on interviews with current and former gang members and other victims and witnesses of violence in El Salvador, as well as with staff of non-governmental organizations (NGOs) and governmental officials. Throughout the book, we complement our analysis of gang, state, and clandestine violence in El Salvador with narrative excerpts from interviews with victims and witnesses. To protect the safety of confidential sources, we refer to them only by pseudonyms and initials.

Methodology

This book examines the phenomenon of youth gangs in El Salvador and documents human rights violations associated with the Salvadoran government's reactions to it. The book presents information on youth gangs and state responses in the context of a broader analysis of the rule of law and generalized conditions of violence in El Salvador almost twenty years after the end of the civil war.

This book contains the results of six fact-finding visits to El Salvador (conducted in March through April and August through September 2006; October 2007; March and October 2008; and January 2009), as well as months of follow-up research both prior to and after these trips. Researchers interviewed more than one hundred representatives of non-governmental organizations (NGOs), academics, law enforcement officials, judges, attorneys, prisoners, former and active gang members, youth, and others affected by violence in El Salvador.[1] The titles of all those intereviewed were those held at the time of the interview. In many cases, during the production of this book, some individuals changed their affiliation. In addition to these formal interviews, we spoke with scores of youth and community members affected by violence in El Salvador. While in El Salvador, our researchers traveled across the country, visiting poor urban neighborhoods, community centers, churches, prisons, juvenile detention centers, government offices, courthouses, and NGOs. Our research team consulted a range of other individual and institutional sources from the United States as well.

Chapter I outlines the historical context of violence in El Salvador, while Chapter II focuses on the lasting impact of the civil war that divided El Salvador for over a decade, emphasizing its consequences for the development of Salvadoran institutions. Chapter III presents an overview of the gang phenomenon in the country, including an account

---

[1] This book draws extensively on interviews with current and former gang members and other victims and witnesses of violence in El Salvador. To protect the safety and confidentiality of these sources, we refer to them by pseudonyms and initials. Unless otherwise noted, all translations of Spanish text and interview notes are ours.

of how gangs function, recruit, and interact with local communities. Chapter IV describes the range of state responses to gang violence. Finally, Chapter V investigates the resurgence of clandestine violence in post-conflict El Salvador. Chapters III, IV, and V include transcripts and excerpts from interviews with victims and witnesses of gang, police-related, and clandestine violence in El Salvador, grouping these first-hand accounts by class of victim.

Chapter I:
The History of Violence
in El Salvador

*"We often leave home not knowing
whether we'll come back."*

- Two Mara Salvatrucha gang members, in San Salvador
(October 13, 2008)

El Salvador is one of the most violent countries in Latin America.[2] Its homicide rate in 2007 stood at 60.9 per 100,000 residents and 115.8 per 100,000 male residents,[3] more than twice the average rate for Latin America.[4] As a result, El Salvador ranks among the most violent countries worldwide (see Table 1 and Figures 1a and 1b, pp. 3-4).[5] Many observers attribute El Salvador's high rates of violence to

---

[2] JULIO JACOBO WAISELFISZ, MAPA DE LA VIOLENCIA: LOS JÓVENES DE AMÉRICA LATINA [A MAP OF VIOLENCE: LATIN AMERICAN YOUTH] 17, Table 2.1.3 (2008), *available at* http://www.ritla.net/index.php?option=com_docman&task=doc_download&gid=541. The report relies upon 2002 data collected by the World Health Organization (WHO). Honduras, a country estimated to have high levels of violence, was not included in the study as standardized data were unavailable.

[3] Corte Suprema de Justicia, Instituto de Medicina Legal (IML) "Dr. Roberto Mansferrer," Unidad de Estadísticas Forenses [Supreme Court, National Institute of Forensic Medicine, "Dr. Roberto Mansferrer," Forensic Statistics Unit, hereinafter Forensic Statistics Unit], 4 BOLETÍN SOBRE HOMICIDIOS [HOMICIDES BULLETIN], Sept. 2008, [hereinafter BOLETÍN SOBRE HOMICIDIOS 2007].

[4] BOLETÍN SOBRE HOMICIDIOS 2007, *supra* note 3. According to the Pan American Health Organization (PAHO), the estimated 2000-04 homicide rate for Latin America was 25.3 per 100,000 residents. PAN AMERICAN HEALTH ORGANIZATION, OFFICE OF THE ASSISTANT DIRECTOR, HEALTH ANALYSIS AND STATISTICS, HEALTH SITUATION IN THE AMERICAS: BASIC INDICATORS 2006 5, Mortality Indicators Table (2006), *available at* http://www.paho.org/English/DD/AIS/BI-brochure-2006.pdf. The estimated 2003-05 homicide rate for Latin American males was 43.1 per 100,000 male residents. PAN AMERICAN HEALTH ORGANIZA-TION, OFFICE OF THE ASSISTANT DIRECTOR, HEALTH ANALYSIS AND STATISTICS, HEALTH SITUATION IN THE AMERICAS: BASIC INDICATORS 2008 6, Mortality Indicators Table (2008), *available at* http://www.who.int/pmnch/topics/resource_event_template/en/index.html. The most recent country-specific data available from the Pan American Health Organiza-tion for El Salvador is from 2006, when PAHO estimated the national homicide rate at 63.8 per 100,000. PAN AMERICAN HEALTH ORGANIZATION, REGIONAL CORE HEALTH DATA INITIATIVE, Table Generator System, *available at* http://www.paho.org/English/SHA/core-data/tabulator/newTabulator.htm. Homicide rates in Latin America are among the highest in the world, more than twice the average rate in Africa (10.1 per 100,000 inhabitants), more than triple the average rate in North America (5.6 per 100,000 inhabitants), and more than fifteen times the average rate in Europe (1.2 per 100,000 inhabitants). The data for young Latin Americans is even more dire. According to a recent report released by Brazil-ian researcher Julio Jacobo Waiselfisz, "The probability of a young Latin American being a homicide victim is 30 times greater than for a young person in Europe as a whole, and more than 70 times greater than for young people in Greece, Hungary, England, Austria, Japan or Ireland." WAISELFISZ, *supra* note 2, at 13, Table 2.1.1.

[5] WAISELFISZ, *supra* note 2, at 13, Table 2.1.1; CLAIRE RIBADO, CONGRESSIONAL RESEARCH

political and social factors associated with the legacy of the country's brutal twelve-year civil war and the centuries of repressive authoritarian rule that preceded it.[6] Weak democratic institutions, persistent political polarization, and an ineffective judicial system have undermined El Salvador's capacity to ensure the security of its citizens. In addition, the social and economic consequences of the civil war and its aftermath— including widespread proliferation of weapons, families torn apart by violence and forced migration, as well as high levels of poverty and unemployment—continue to cripple El Salvador's progress toward becoming a secure and stable democratic society.

In this chapter we provide a brief overview of the war itself, while the next chapter (Chapter II) describes the challenges Salvadoran society has faced in building the rule of law and democracy in the postwar period.

Region	Youth (15-24 yrs.) Homicide Rate	Non-Youth Homicide Rate	Total
Latin America	36.6	16.1	19.9
Caribbean	31.6	13.2	16.3
Africa	16.1	8.5	10.1
North America	12.0	4.6	5.6
Asia	2.4	2.1	2.1
Oceania	1.6	1.2	1.3
Europe	1.2	1.3	1.2

Table 1. Youth and Non-Youth Homicide Rates (per 100,000) by Region
Source: JULIO JACOBO WAISELFISZ, MAPA DE LA VIOLENCIA: LOS JÓVENES DE AMÉRICA LATINA 13, Table 2.1.1 (2008) (using most recent available data from the World Health Organization Statistical Information System and excluding countries for which no data were available after 2002).

SERVICE, CRS REPORT FOR CONGRESS, GANGS IN CENTRAL AMERICA 2 (2008), *available at* http://www.fas.org/sgp/crs/row/RL34112.pdf.

[6] *See, e.g.,* UNITED STATES AGENCY FOR INTERNATIONAL DEVELOPMENTS, CENTRAL AMERICA AND MEXICO GANG ASSESSMENT 49-50 (2006) [hereinafter CENTRAL AMERICA AND MEXICO GANG ASSESSMENT], *available at* http://www.usaid.gov/gt/docs/gangs_assessment.pdf (listing "legacy of conflict and violence" as one of the "causes and risk factors of gang activity" in El Salvador); *see also* Joaquín M. Chávez, *An Anatomy of Violence in El Salvador, in* 37(6) NORTH AMERICAN CONGRESS ON LATIN AMERICA (NACLA) REPORT ON THE AMERICAS (2004) ("Understanding the high levels of social violence and the acceptance of violent norms in Salvadoran society must begin with a consideration of the historical and cultural processes associated with violence—authoritarianism, state terror, political violence and others."). *See generally* COMISIÓN DE LA VERDAD PARA EL SALVADOR, DE LA LOCURA A LA ESPERANZA: LA GUERRA DE 12 AÑOS EN EL SALVADOR (1993) [hereinafter COMISIÓN DE LA VERDAD PARA EL SALVADOR], *available at* http://www.usip.org/library/tc/doc/reports/el_salvador/tc_es_03151993_toc.html (English version).

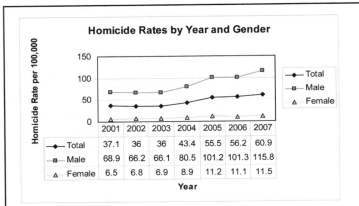

Figure 1a. El Salvador Homicide Rates by Year and Gender
Source: *Corte Suprema de Justicia, Instituto de Medicina Legal, "Dr. Roberto Mansferrer," (IML) Unidad de Estadísticas Forenses* (Supreme Court, National Institute of Forensic Medicine, Forensic Statistics Unit) (Male and female homicide rates for the years 2001, 2002 and 2003 were calculated by the authors using population data from the 1999 census, projected to the corresponding years. Population data obtained from *Dirección General de Estadísticas y Censos* (General Census Bureau), http://www.digestyc.gob.sv/.)

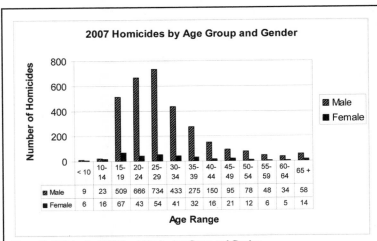

Figure 1b. El Salvador 2007 Homicides by Age Group and Gender
Source: *Corte Suprema de Justicia, Instituto de Medicina Legal, "Dr. Roberto Mansferrer," (IML) Unidad de Estadísticas Forenses* (Supreme Court, National Institute of Forensic Medicine, Forensic Statistics Unit)

A. Brief Overview of the Salvadoran Civil War

The twelve-year (1980-1991) war between the Salvadoran government and the rebel forces of the Farabundo Martí National Liberation Front (*Frente Farabundo Martí para la Liberación Nacional* or FMLN) was one of the most brutal conflicts in a region gripped by political violence during the 1970s and 1980s. The war left an estimated 75,000 Salvadorans dead and forced hundreds of thousands to flee to neighboring countries, the United States, or elsewhere.[7] Actors on both sides of the conflict committed grave abuses against civilians. Targeted killings by death squads claimed the lives of hundreds, if not thousands, of Salvadoran rural laborers (*campesinos*), students, and human rights and labor activists.[8] By January 1992, when FMLN and government representatives signed U.N.-negotiated peace accords in Chapultepec, Mexico, to put a formal end to the conflict, the war had largely destroyed the tiny country's social and political structures. The U.N.-sponsored international Truth Commission, formed in the months following the signing of the peace accords, opened its final report with a grim depiction of the violence that had consumed the country for more than a decade:

> Violence was a fire which swept over the fields of El Salvador; it burst into villages, cut off roads and destroyed highways and bridges, energy sources and

---

[7] CENTRAL AMERICA AND MEXICO GANG ASSESSMENT, *supra* note 6, at 50 ("El Salvador's civil war . . . resulted in the deaths of more than 75,000 people"); *id.*, at 45 ("By 1990, over 700,000 Salvadorans had settled in [U.S. cities] . . . ."); *see also* FEDERAL RESEARCH DIVISION, LIBRARY OF CONGRESS, EL SALVADOR: A COUNTRY STUDY (Richard Haggerty ed., 2nd ed. 1990), *available at* http://lcweb2.loc.gov/cgi-bin/query/r?frd/cstdy:@field(DOCID+sv0042 (estimating that between 1979 and 1988 more than 500,000 displaced Salvadorans reached the United States, in addition to tens of thousands more who sought refuge in neighborhing countries in the region).

[8] The U.N. Truth Commission received direct testimony regarding a total of 817 death squad victims between 1980 and 1991 and concluded that "there is no question that what have been classified as murders committed by the death squads in rural areas account for a significant proportion of all killings in El Salvador between 1980 and 1991." COMISIÓN DE LA VERDAD PARA EL SALVADOR, *supra* note 6, at 131-151.

transmission lines; it reached the cities and entered
families, sacred areas and educational centres; it struck
at justice and filled the public administration with
victims; and it singled out as an enemy anyone who was
not on the list of friends.[9]

Since 1992, El Salvador's government and its people have struggled to
overcome this legacy of violence and the impunity of the civil war years.

The roots of El Salvador's civil war included both domestic and
international factors. For centuries, El Salvador had been one of Latin
America's poorest and most deeply unequal nations, with wealth
and political power concentrated in the hands of a small elite.[10] This
inequality was reinforced by a judicial system that functioned largely
in the service of economic and political power brokers in the country,
most of whom had close ties to the military.[11] Throughout the 1970s,
popular resistance against the Salvadoran government grew. With
no access to legal avenues for advancing political change, Salvadoran
opposition movements became increasingly militant.[12]   Though
formal opportunities for electoral participation across the political
spectrum increased during the 1980s, the military continued to operate
as the dominant power in the country throughout the decade.[13] The
Salvadoran armed forces became notorious across the world for carrying
out brutal human rights abuses in the name of counter-insurgency. This

---

[9] *Id.* at 1 (all quotations from this source are taken from the English version of the report, *available at* http://www.usip.org/library/tc/doc/reports/el_salvador/tc_es_03151993_toc. html).

[10] *See* MARGARET POPKIN, PEACE WITHOUT JUSTICE 13 (2000) ("In El Salvador in the late nineteenth century, the oligarchy relied on the courts to force peasants off land that was to be concentrated in private hands to increase coffee production and to force the landless peasants to serve as cheap seasonal labor . . . . In the late 1970s, El Salvador had the most unequal distribution of incomes in Latin America.").

[11] *Id.* at 12-13; *see also* Chávez, *supra* note 6.

[12] *See* POPKIN, *supra* note 10, at 2.

[13] *Id.* at 3.

unfortunate distinction was fueled by high-profile political killings such as the assassination of San Salvador Archbishop Monsignor Oscar Romero in 1980[14] and the murders of four humanitarian church workers from the United States later that year.

By the 1980s, the Central American region had become a global ideological battleground where Cold War powers engaged in proxy battles for power and influence. Members of the Salvadoran opposition movements that became the FMLN were buoyed by the 1979 Sandinista overthrow of the Somoza regime in Nicaragua, while the Salvadoran government and its supporters in Washington grew increasingly determined to eliminate leftist forces in the country.[15] To support counter-insurgency activities, the United States funneled billions of dollars in economic and military aid to the Salvadoran government and military throughout the 1980s.[16] Although Congress conditioned military aid to El Salvador on semi-annual reports certifying that the Salvadoran government complied with human rights standards, human rights organizations charged that the United States continued to fund the Salvadoran military despite its responsibility for widespread rights abuses.[17] Indeed, the Reagan Administration certified four times that the Salvadoran government complied with human rights standards, notwithstanding "overwhelming evidence of continuing serious

---

[14] Monsignor Romero, a vocal opponent of violence and injustice, was killed by an assassin's bullet while celebrating mass in a Hospital Chapel. The U.N. Commission found that the assassination was ordered, planned, and carried out by military personnel of the Salvadoran government, operating using "death squad" procedures. COMISIÓN DE LA VERDAD PARA EL SALVADOR, *supra* note 6, at 132.

[15] *See* POPKIN, *supra* note 10, at 2-3.

[16] *Id.* at 3; BRENY CUENCA, EL PODER INTANGIBLE: LA AID Y EL ESTADO SALVADOREÑO EN LOS AÑOS OCHENTA [INTANGIBLE POWER: AID AND THE SALVADORAN STATE IN THE EIGHTIES] 27 (1992).

[17] *See, e.g.,* HUMAN RIGHTS WATCH, THE MASSACRE AT EL MOZOTE: THE NEED TO REMEMBER 3-4 (1992) (charging that "U.S. denial or willful ignorance of human rights abuses during the 1980s reflected a structural flaw in administration policy. . . . One can only speculate as to whether the war could have ended long ago had the truth about massacres like El Mozote been pursued by the U.S. government.")

violations and a total failure to investigate past violations."[18]

One of the particularly brutal features of the Salvadoran civil war was the widespread activity of "death squads"–clandestine groups that operated with varying levels of involvement or complicity on the part of state actors to carry out targeted killings of perceived enemies. In its final report, the U.N. Truth Commission for El Salvador cited the prevalence of death squads as one of the most troubling aspects of the conflict because of their roots in Salvadoran state institutions and socio-economic power structures, as well as their strong potential for re-emergence in the future. The Commission wrote in 1993:

> The death squads, in which members of State structures were actively involved or to which they turned a blind eye, gained such control that they ceased to be an isolated or marginal phenomenon and became an instrument of terror used systematically for the physical elimination of political opponents. Many of the civilian and military authorities in power during the 1980s participated in, encouraged and tolerated the activities of these groups. Although there is no evidence of latent structures for these clandestine organizations, they could be reactivated when those in high Government circles issue warnings that might trigger the resumption of a dirty war in El Salvador. Since the death squad phenomenon was the problem *par excellence* of that dirty war which ultimately destroyed all vestiges of the rule of law during the armed conflict, the Salvadoran Government must not only be ready and willing to prevent the resurgence of this phenomenon but also seek international cooperation in eradicating it completely.[19]

---

[18] POPKIN, *supra* note 10, at 49. U.S. government investigation of human rights abuses during the civil war focused on cases that received significant publicity or were particularly violent, such as the murder of four U.S. churchwomen in 1980. *Id.* at 50-57.

[19] COMISIÓN DE LA VERDAD PARA EL SALVADOR, supra note 6, at 139.

Based on its review of evidence regarding more than eight hundred alleged death squad killings in El Salvador between 1980 and 1991, which included the testimonies of civilian and military death squad members, the U.N. Truth Commission described the composition and *modus operandi* of Salvadoran death squads in its final report in the following language:

> The members of such groups usually wore civilian clothing, were heavily armed, operated clandestinely and hid their affiliation and identity. They abducted members of the civilian population and of rebel groups. They tortured their hostages, were responsible for their disappearance and usually executed them.[20]

The Commission also emphasized the blurring of lines between state and non-state actors involved in death squad activities.[21] The report concluded that ". . . even the death squads that were not organized as part of any State structure were often supported or tolerated by State institutions," and that "[f]requently, death squads operated in coordination with the armed forces and acted as a support structure for their activities."[22]

Underscoring its concerns that the death squad phenomenon could re-emerge in the future if the Salvadoran government and the international community did not take steps to address the structural and institutional context that fueled it, the Truth Commission traced

---

[20] *Id.* at 139.

[21] *Id.* at 139-141. The Commission noted that witnesses who had been members of death squads "admitted and gave details of their involvement at the highest levels in the organization, operation and financing of the death squads . . . ." *Id.* at 139. *See generally* LAUREN GILBERT, CENTER FOR INTERNATIONAL POLICY, EL SALVADOR'S DEATH SQUADS: NEW EVIDENCE FROM U.S. DOCUMENTS (1994), *available at* http://www.ciponline.org/dethsqud.txt (detailing U.S. government knowledge of death squads and individuals funding death squad activities from the United States throughout the 1980s).

[22] COMISIÓN DE LA VERDAD PARA EL SALVADOR, *supra* note 6, at 141.

the roots of state-affiliated clandestine violence in its final report.[23]
The Commission cited the formation of the National Guard in the
early twentieth century as giving impetus and informal organization
to landowners and other powerful economic interests that sought
to harness military force to exercise control over "civilian society" or
anyone who presented a challenge to their power.[24] A 1932 National
Guard-led massacre of at least ten thousand peasants in response to a
rural uprising in western El Salvador demonstrated the potency of this
loose, clandestine collaboration between military forces and powerful
economic interests. From 1967 to 1979, according to the Commission,
death squad activities in the country became more organized. In that
period, the head of the National Guard established a paramilitary
organization called ORDEN (*Organización Democrática Nacionalista* or
Nationalist Democratic Organization; this acronym also means "order"
in Spanish) whose "function was to identify and eliminate alleged
communists among the rural population."[25] After 1981, when the FMLN
launched its insurgency campaign, clandestine collaborations between
military and non-military actors to target perceived subversives and
to control the civilian population through fear became increasingly
prevalent. Over time, these structures became a central force for
violence during the war. We consider the resurgence of clandestine
forces in Chapter V.

---

[23] *Id.* at 139-41.

[24] *Id.* at 140.

[25] *Id.* at 140.

Chapter II:
The Aftermath of the War:
A Culture of Impunity and
Ineffective Institutions

*"The nation has a great weakness:
we never investigated the massacres
perpetrated during the war, and
we live through this legacy today."*

- Mirna Antonieta Perla Jiménez, Justice of the Civil
Chamber, Supreme Court of Justice of El Salvador,
in San Salvador (March 23, 2008)

U.N.-brokered negotiations brought a formal end to the armed conflict in El Salvador. Still, even after the signing of the 1992 Chapultepec peace accords, serious questions remained about how to address the underlying causes of the conflict, in particular the lack of a functioning judicial system, the limited meaningful space for political opposition in national electoral and governance structures, and the prevalence of the use of violence as a formal or informal means of exercising or challenging state policy. Unlike many other Latin American countries engaged in transition or rebuilding their political institutions through popular elections after authoritarian rule, El Salvador had virtually no experience with robust democratic politics or effective legal systems and had not arrived at a formal political consensus regarding the country's future.[26] These historical factors have generated significant obstacles to building democracy and the rule of law in post-war El Salvador. This chapter addresses challenges to the post-war construction of the rule of law in three areas: the judicial system generally, the national police, and the prison system. The weaknesses of these institutions have fostered the conditions of violence, insecurity, and lawlessness that permeate public life and that are inextricably tied to gang violence in El Salvador today.

A. Lack of Judicial Independence

1. Initial Efforts: The Post-War Reconstruction Period

An independent judiciary with sufficient resources and authority to punish abuses by the authorities and by private individuals is essential if . . . the right to life is to be restored.

Inter-American Commission on Human Rights, Report on El Salvador, 1994

---

[26] POPKIN, *supra* note 10, at 4.

El Salvador's judicial system, whose susceptibility to manipulation by powerful political and economic actors is often cited as one of the primary causes of the civil war,[27] continues to be incapable of guaranteeing the rule of law more than a decade and a half after the end of the conflict. Though domestic civil society organizations and the international community emphasized the need for judicial reform in the post-war period, institutional and political obstacles undermined the construction of a fair and effective judicial system.

One notable indication of the deeply-rooted weaknesses of the Salvadoran justice system is the fact that in the post-war period, domestic courts have rarely, if ever, investigated or prosecuted the perpetrators of human rights violations committed during the conflict.[28] The international, U.N.-sponsored Truth Commission assigned responsibility for brutal killings and rights violations to a number of high-ranking military and political leaders of the 1980s, including Roberto D'Aubisson, former president and founder of the Nationalist Republican Alliance (*Alianza Republicana Nacionalista* or ARENA) political party. However, these officials and the vast majority of lower-ranking authorities have not to date been held accountable in domestic proceedings.[29] In part, this failure to seek justice through domestic means stems from sweeping amnesty laws passed in 1992 and 1993, the latter pushed through the Legislature within days of the release of the Truth Commission Report.[30] Two months later, the Supreme Court of Justice

---

[27] *See, e.g.,* POPKIN, *supra* note 10, at 11 ("[A]buse of power by state actors and their powerful allies and a lack of legal recourse against such abuses are frequently cited among the causes of the war.").

[28] This reality stands in marked contrast to the post-authoritarian periods in Argentina and Chile, for example, where mostly after long delays, domestic courts were used, if haltingly and imperfectly, to initiate investigations and prosecutions of those responsible for human rights violations during military regimes. *See* Margaret Popkin & Nehal Bhuta, *Latin American Amnesties in Comparative Perspective: Can the Past be Buried?* 13 CARNEGIE J. OF ETHICS & INT'L AFF. 99, 108 (1999) ("Despite the extent of human rights abuses committed in El Salvador during the 1980s, El Salvador lags far behind its neighbors in addressing its past.").

[29] *See* POPKIN, *supra* note 10, at 121-23.

[30] The amnesty laws "absolved from all liability, both civil and criminal, persons who

of El Salvador declared itself incompetent to review the constitutionality of the amnesty decree, on the grounds that it was an "eminently political" act.[31] However, due to the weaknesses of the Salvadoran judicial system, and the corresponding low levels of confidence in it abroad, there was little international pressure to try those responsible for human rights abuses in domestic courts. The Truth Commission Report suggested that the Salvadoran justice system was politically and institutionally unable to address the rights violations of the war years and implied that it would have to be built anew before it would be capable of providing justice for the Salvadoran people.[32]

The 1991 domestic trial of several members of the military charged with the murder of six Jesuit priests and two women provides a poignant example of the weaknesses of the Salvadoran judicial system.[33] In 1991, the Lawyers Committee for Human Rights called the Jesuit case a "test case for the Salvadoran justice system and a potential blow to the impunity that

---

participated in any way in political crimes, common crimes related to political crimes, and common crimes committed by at least 20 persons, prior to January 1, 1992." The definition of political crimes was extremely broad; it included crimes committed "on the occasion of or as a consequence of the armed conflict, without regard to political condition, militancy, affiliation, or ideology." Decreto [Decree] No. 486/1993, Ley de Amnistía General para la Consolidación de la Paz [Law on General Amnesty for Peace], art. 4 (1993). For an extended discussion of the Salvadoran amnesty laws and an analysis of their relatively sweeping nature compared to those of other Latin American countries, *see* Popkin & Bhuta, *supra* note 28.

[31] *El Salvador: Supreme Court of Justice Decision on the Amnesty Law, Proceedings No. 10-93 (May 20, 1993), reprinted in* 3 TRANSITIONAL JUSTICE 549, 553-54 (Neil J. Kritz ed., 1995).

[32] COMISIÓN DE LA VERDAD PARA EL SALVADOR, *supra* note 6, at 190 ("El Salvador has no system for the administration of justice which meets the minimum requirements of objectivity and impartiality so that justice can be rendered reliably. This is a part of the country's current reality and overcoming it urgently should be a primary objective for Salvadorian society. The Commission does not believe that a reliable solution can be found to the problems it has examined by tackling them in the context which is primarily responsible for them. The situation described in this report would not have occurred if the judicial system had functioned properly. Clearly, that system has still not changed enough to foster a feeling of justice which could promote national reconciliation . . . .").

[33] For a detailed description of the case, see COMISIÓN DE LA VERDAD PARA EL SALVADOR, *supra* note 6, at 44-50.

continues to paralyze El Salvador."[34] The initial optimism that domestic proceedings could signal an end to the climate of impunity, however, was soon shown to have been premature. The trial revealed that there remained severe systemic barriers to conducting impartial and independent investigations into grave human rights violations and to prosecuting those responsible. Members of the Commission for the Investigation of Criminal Acts and the Honor Commission—tasked with investigating the murders—covered up the involvement of high-ranking military officials.[35] The Office of the Prosecutor interfered with the ability of prosecutors Edward Sidney Blanco Reyes and Álvaro Henry Campos Solorzano to investigate the case by forbidding them from cross-examining certain witnesses and from taking routine steps to investigate the murders. Both men would later publicly accuse the Office of the Prosecutor of blocking the investigation and would resign in protest.[36] Following his resignation, Edward Sidney Blanco Reyes began receiving death threats. Fearing for his life, he was forced to leave the country.[37]

The final ruling in the Jesuits' case came on the heels of the signing of the Mexico accords which provided for the establishment of the Truth Commission. Only two of the ten military officers charged were found guilty of murder. Although the U.N. Truth Commission would later identify several high-ranking military officers as responsible for orchestrating the

---

[34] LAWYERS COMMITTEE FOR HUMAN RIGHTS, THE "JESUIT CASE": THE JURY TRIAL (LA VISTA PÚBLICA) iii (1991).

[35] *See,* COMISIÓN DE LA VERDAD PARA EL SALVADOR, *supra* note 6, at 45; *see also* Ignacio Ellacuría, S.J. v. El Salvador, Case 10.488, Inter-Am. C.H.R., Report No. 136/99, OEA/ Ser.L/V/II.106, doc. 3 rev. ¶ 78 (1999) (accepting the Truth Commission's investigation as credible because of the "rigorous methodology" and lack of "any allegations or evidence that would cast doubt on the conclusions of the Truth Commission"); INTERIM REPORT OF THE SPEAKER'S SPECIAL TASK FORCE ON EL SALVADOR, at 6 (Apr. 30, 1990), *available at* http:// www.cja.org/cases/Jesuits_Docs/moakley_report.pdf ("The investigators have made little effort to determine whether senior military officers other than Col. Benavides might have had a role in ordering, or in covering up, the crimes.").

[36] Ellacuría v. El Salvador, *supra* note 35, at ¶¶ 87-90.

[37] Interview with Edward Sidney Blanco Reyes, Juez Quinto de Instrucción de San Salvador [Judge in the First Instance, Fifth Instruction Tribunal in San Salvador], in San Salvador (Oct. 19, 2007).

murders and present evidence of an extensive cover-up operation, the Salvadoran State never sought to bring those officers to justice.[38] Rather, the passage of the 1992-93 amnesty laws led to the release of the only two officers who had been found guilty.[39] Proceedings against fourteen members of the Salvadoran army for their participation in the Jesuit massacre were underway in Spanish courts at this writing.[40] In January 2009, President Elías Antonio Saca Gonzalez publicly charged that these proceedings do not promote the democratic development of El Salvador, a position that highlighted the continuing climate of impunity under the Saca presidency.[41]

---

[38] Ellacuría v. El Salvador, *supra* note 35, at ¶ 138.

[39] Ellacuría v. El Salvador, *supra* note 35, at ¶ 142 ("The judicial power, for its part, allowed itself to be used in a sham process that constituted a denial of justice. On the other hand, the other public powers, the Legislature and the Executive, conspired to grant amnesty to those who had been convicted, and to prevent any future investigation from ever imposing penalties for these horrible crimes against human rights. All of this affected the integrity of the proceedings and implied the manipulation of justice, as well as the obvious abuse and misuse of power, as a result of which these crimes have to this date gone completely unpunished.").

[40] The case was filed by the Center for Justice and Accountability and the Spanish Association for Human Rights, as private prosecutors under Spain's universal jurisdiction law. A detailed description of the filings is available at http://www.cja.org/cases/jesuits. shtml; *see also* Tracy Wilkinson and Alex Renderos, *In El Salvador, A New Push for Justice in Priests' Slayings*, L.A. TIMES, Nov. 13, 2008; Victoria Burnett, *Jesuit Killings in El Salvador Could Reach Trial in Spain*, N.Y. TIMES, Nov. 13, 2008, *available at* http://www.nytimes.com/2008/11/14/world/americas/14salvador.html?_r=1.

[41] Dennis Coday, *Judge to Investigate Murder of Jesuits in El Salvador*, NAT'L CATH. REP., Jan. 15, 2009, *available at* http://ncronline.org/node/3086.

2. *Current Efforts and Challenges*

There is no judicial independence in El Salvador. The judicial system has been perverted; justice is manipulated to suit political interests.

There are systematic attacks on judicial independence: through legal and institutional reforms, insults, de facto *pressures.*

Juan Antonio Durán Ramírez, Judge, Chalatenango Sentencing Tribunal, in San Salvador (March 26 and October 19, 2008)

Efforts to build a functioning judicial system in El Salvador have failed to overcome the legacy of institutional incapacity and politicization that drew the attention of international observers in the 1980s and early 1990s. Although legal reforms were a key priority in the years following the civil war, and despite some important formal advances made in the early to mid-1990s,[42] the fundamental institutional weaknesses of the

---

[42] Three key reform initiatives were designed to strengthen the judicial branch by safeguarding its capacity to act independently and impartially. First, the *Consejo Nacional de la Judicatura* [National Judicial Council or NJC] was reorganized as an independent entity with a mandate to oversee the judicial selection and training process, including by evaluating whether those selected were qualified for the post. NJC membership was expanded to include not only judges but also representatives from other sectors of society not directly connected with the administration of justice. Second, the Supreme Court selection process was amended to require the support of a two-thirds majority of the Legislative Assembly. Finally, the judicial branch was assigned an annual budget that was **not to fall below 6 percent of the national government's revenue.** *See Peace Agreement,* U.N. GAOR, 46th Sess., Agenda Item 31, Chap. III: Sistema Judicial, U.N. Doc. A/46/864-S/23501 (1992), *available at* http://www.usip.org/library/pa/el_salvador/pa_es_01161992_toc.html [hereinafter Chapultepec Peace Accords]; *see also* Fundación de Estudios para la Aplicación del Derecho [Foundation for the Study of the Application of the Law, hereinafter FESPAD], Centro de Estudios Penales de El Salvador Salvador [Center for Penal Studies, hereinafter CEPES] & Red Centroamericana de Jueces, Fiscales y Defensores por la Democratización de la Justicia [Central American Network of Judges, Prosecutors, and Defenders for the Democratization of Justice], Informe para la Audiencia sobre la Independencia Judicial en Centroamérica 5 (2004) (report prepared for the Inter-American Commission on Human Rights). Other important reforms included the passage of legislation guaranteeing criminal detainees the right to counsel in

judicial system have remained unresolved.

Rights groups, judges, and academics all agree that political pressure from the executive and legislative branches has seriously undermined institutional reforms designed to promote judicial independence, impartiality, and efficiency. A 2002 survey of judicial attitudes by the Central American Network of Judges, Prosecutors, and Defenders for the Democratization of Justice (*Red Centroamericana de Jueces, Fiscales y Defensores por la Democratización de la Justicia*) revealed that 60.8 percent of Salvadoran judges felt subject to pressure from the executive branch (see Table 2).[43] Several of the judges interviewed for this book echoed this sentiment. Supreme Court Justice Mirna Antonieta Perla Jiménez explained to our researchers that the Office of the Prosecutor has prosecuted judges for breach of judicial duty based on its dislike of their interpretation and application of the law.[44] Similarly, San Salvador Sentencing Judge Martín Rogel Zepeda remarked that judges who question the constitutionality of executive or legislative anti-gang measures have seen their opportunities for career advancement curtailed: "If you are the type of judge who questions and criticizes [executive and legislative measures] you can be sure that you will not advance in your judicial career. Those who criticize and question [executive policies] are considered a nuisance."[45]

1992, *see* POPKIN, *supra* note 10 at 227, and a new Code of Penal Procedure passed in 1996. POPKIN, *supra* note 10 at 231.

[43] FESPAD, CEPES & RED CENTROAMERICANA DE JUECES, FISCALES Y DEFENSORES POR LA DEMOCRATIZACIÓN DE LA JUSTICIA, *supra* note 42, at 7.

[44] Interview with Mirna Antonieta Perla Jiménez, Magistrada de la Sala de lo Civil de la Corte Suprema de Justicia, Corte Suprema de Justicia de El Salvador [Justice of the Civil Chamber, Supreme Court of Justice of El Salvador], in San Salvador (Mar. 23, 2008). Justice Mirna Antonieta Perla Jiménez's allegations of arbitrary prosecutions are supported by evidence of politically motivated proceedings against some judges described in Part A 2. d) in this Chapter, and are widely shared by many in the Salvadoran judicial community.

[45] Interview with Martín Rogel Zepeda, Juez Presidente del Juzgado Tercero de Sentencia de San Salvador [Presiding Judge in the First Instance, Third Sentencing Tribunal of San Salvador], in San Salvador (Jan. 21, 2009).

	Frequency	Percent	Percent
None	16	34.8	34.8
A Little	8	17.4	60.8
Average	6	13.0	
A Lot	14	30.4	
N.A.	2	4.3	4.3
Total	46	100	

Table 2. Executive Influence on Judicial Decision-Making. Survey of Judicial Perceptions

Source: FUNDACIÓN DE ESTUDIOS PARA LA APLICACIÓN DEL DERECHO, CENTRO DE ESTUDIOS PENALES DE EL SALVADOR SALVADOR & RED CENTROAMERICANA DE JUECES, FISCALES Y DEFENSORES POR LA DEMOCRATIZACIÓN DE LA JUSTICIA, INFORME PARA LA AUDIENCIA SOBRE LA INDEPENDENCIA JUDICIAL EN CENTROAMÉRICA 5 (2004) (report prepared for the Inter-American Commission on Human Rights).

(Note: The study sample included 46 judges, both at the trial and appellate levels.)

The issue of judicial independence in El Salvador has been brought to the Inter-American Commission on Human Rights (Inter-American Commission) and addressed in two of that body's thematic hearings. At the second hearing, which took place on July 20, 2007, San Salvador Sentencing Judge Leonardo Ramírez Murcia asserted that the executive threatened judicial independence by "mount[ing] a smear campaign that depicted judges as pro-criminal"[46] and by seeking to blame the judiciary for rising crime rates. Following the hearing, the Inter-American Commission cited "public insecurity and the fragility of the judicial power in the majority of the countries in the region, combined with attacks against the independence and impartiality of that power in certain countries," as "one of the most difficult barriers OAS member states faced in guaranteeing the full expression of human rights."[47]

Attempts to exert political control over judicial decision-making have been recognized in at least four contexts: (1) the judicial interpretation and application of the anti-gang law; (2) the creation of specialized tribunals and the selection and appointment of specialized judges; (3) the application

---

[46] *Institutional Threats to the Independence of the Judiciary in El Salvador,* Hearing Before the Inter-American Commission for Human Rights (2007) (statement of Leonardo Ramírez Murcia), *available at* http://www.cidh.oas.org/Audiencias/select.aspx (follow "128 Period of Sessions (July 16-27, 2007)" hyperlink; then select "Friday, July 20, 2007" from "Select a date" dropdown menu).

[47] Inter-Am. C.H.R., *Annual Report of the Inter-American Commission on Human Rights 2007,* ¶ 15, U.N. Doc. OEA/Ser.L/V/II.130 (Dec. 29, 2007), *available at* http://www.cidh.oas.org/annualrep/2007eng/TOC.htm.

of witness protection measures; and (4) proceedings to strip judges of immunity from criminal prosecution. These four areas are closely linked to executive policies designed to curb gang violence. We provide an in-depth examination of the legal framework put in place to combat gang violence in Chapter IV. The following sections focus narrowly on the impact of executive and legislative policies on judicial independence in each of these four areas.

a) Judicial Interpretation and Application of the 2003 Anti-Gang Law

Throughout his tenure, President Francisco Guillermo Flores Pérez, who held office from 1999 to 2004, maintained an antagonistic relationship with the judiciary. When judges questioned the constitutionality of his aggressive policies designed to root out gang-related violence, President Flores accused them of colluding with the opposition party[48] in what many observers considered an effort to undermine the credibility of the judiciary and pressure judges to fall in line with executive policies.[49] For example, the Adjunct Ombudsperson for Children and Youth, Luis Enrique Salazar Flores, criticized the President for attempting to draw a line between "those

---

[48] *See, e.g.*, Wilfredo Salamanca, *El Ejecutivo presentará propuesta de reforma a la Ley Antimaras*, EL DIARIO DE HOY, Nov. 6, 2003, *available at* http://www.elsalvador.com/noticias/2003/11/06/nacional/nacio16.html (President Flores told the press that "there will be no room for those judges who do not want to apply the anti-gang law, be it because they have made political deals with opposition parties or because they are against the Government." President Flores also vowed to "look for new solutions, if necessary, so that judges do not release criminal gang members."); *see also Policía pide más tiempo*, EL DIARIO DE HOY, Oct. 19, 2003, *available at* http://www.elsalvador.com/noticias/2003/10/19/nacional/nacio4.html ("President Flores complained that the legal framework allowed judges to 'protect' gang members.").

[49] *See, e.g.*, Engelberto Maldonado, *Ley Antimaras es inconstitucional, innecesaria, inaplicable e ineficaz: IEJES*, DIARIO CO LATINO, Oct. 23, 2003, *available at* http://www.diariocolatino.com/es/20031023/nacionales/nacionales_20031023_2533/?tpl=69 ("The Institute of Juridical Studies (*Instituto de Estudios Jurídicos* or IEJES) considered that the current confrontation between the Judicial and Executive branches reflects how little the Executive branch or, more specifically the Office of the Presidency, knows regarding the role of judges. . . . The flagrant encroachment of the Executive branch into the justice system is an extremely delicate issue, [according to IEJES] 'this is why a U.N. rapporteur should visit [El Salvador] to document the grave transgressions that in the current peace-consolidation process are putting our fragile democracy in danger.'").

who believe in citizen security and those who favor criminals," thereby foreclosing the possibility of constructive dialogue on criminal policies.[50]

More transparent executive branch efforts to influence judicial decisions followed the implementation of an anti-gang law, the legal arm of a broader anti-gang initiative launched by President Flores in 2003 and designed to capture and prosecute gang members aggressively (*Ley Anti Maras* or LAM I). The law criminalized gang membership, permitted juveniles to be prosecuted as adults, and provided for the imposition of fines against any person "found wandering about without an identity document in . . . any settlement, without justified cause or who is not known by the inhabitants."[51]

Following the enactment of LAM I, police forces arrested scores of individuals, predominantly tattooed youth.[52] The Office of the Prosecutor charged them with gang membership—a crime under the new law. Nevertheless, citing gross violations—including the criminalization of gang membership and the trial of juveniles as adults—of both the Salvadoran Constitution and international human rights Instruments binding in El Salvador, several judges refused to apply the provision rendering gang membership a crime. As a consequence, and because the Office of the Prosecutor could not demonstrate in the majority of cases the commission of a crime other than gang membership, these judges released most of those captured in the mass arrests by the National Civil Police (*Policía Nacional Civil* or PNC).[53]

---

[50] Luis Enrique Salazar Flores, Leyes Anti Maras: Los reveses de la Justicia Penal Juvenil en El Salvador, http://www.iidh.ed.cr/comunidades/ombudsnet/docs/docsomb_pac/el%20salvador,%20leyes%20anti%20maras.htm.

[51] Decreto [Decree] No. 158/2003, Ley Anti-Maras [Anti-Gangs Act] [hereinafter LAM I] (2003), *available at* http://www.glin.gov/view.action?glinID=93702.

[52] *See, e.g.,* Daniel Valencia, *El delito de ser marero,* EL FARO, Nov. 8, 2003, http://www.elfaro.net/secciones/noticias/20030811/noticias1_20030811.asp#; Alberto López, *Jueces sólo procesan 87 pandilleros,* EL DIARIO DE HOY, Oct. 25, 2003, *available at* http://www.elsalvador.com/noticias/2003/10/25/nacional/nacio2.html; FESPAD & CEPES, ESTADO DE LA SEGURIDAD PÚBLICA Y JUSTICIA PENAL EN EL SALVADOR 71 (2004) [hereinafter ESTADO DE LA SEGURIDAD PÚBLICA Y JUSTICIA PENAL EN EL SALVADOR 2004], *available at* http://fespad.org.sv/portal/html/Archivos/Descargas/ESPYJPES2004.pdf.

[53] *See, e.g.,* Luis Enrique Salazar Flores, *supra* note 50 (noting that by the end of 2003 the

The executive branch responded by mounting a series of public attacks on the judiciary. President Flores accused judges of protecting criminals and of having formed a "resistance block"[54] to avoid applying the law. He warned them that "the public will hold the judiciary responsible for any crimes committed by those gang members they set free."[55] President Flores swore to "rid the country of gang members" and said he was ready to impose the Firm Hand Plan (*El Plan Mano Dura*).[56] To this end, the executive created a Permanent Task Force (*Fuerza de Trabajo Permanente*), staffed by the director of the PNC and several cabinet members and mandated to ensure the application of LAM I.[57] Coordination of the Task Force's activities fell to Dr. Juan José Daboub, the Presidential Chief of Staff (*Secretario Técnico de la Presidencia de la República*) who told the press:

> The law fulfills our objective of incarcerating gang members; if some judges do not want to apply it, we,

---

PNC had captured 6,666 gang members, of which 95 percent were released for lack of adequate proof).

[54] Jaime García, *Jueces refutan acusación de incumplir ley antimaras*, EL DIARIO DE HOY, Oct. 23, 2003, *available at* http://www.elsalvador.com/noticias/2003/10/23/nacional/nacio7.html.

[55] Jaime García & Edward Gutiérrez, *Emplazan a jueces*, EL DIARIO DE HOY, Oct. 22, 2003, *available at* http://www.elsalvador.com/noticias/2003/10/22/nacional/nacio17.html; Alberto López, *Jueces piden que Órgano Ejecutivo no les presione*, EL DIARIO DE HOY, Feb. 10, 2004, *available at* http://www.elsalvador.com/noticias/2004/02/10/nacional/nac5.asp; Beatriz Castillo, *Jueces responsabilizan al Presidente Flores de cualquier agresión*, DIARIO CO LATINO, Oct. 23, 2003, *available at* http://www.diariocolatino.com/es/20031023/nacionales/nacionales_20031023_2532/?tpl=69.

[56] Daboub told Diario Co Latino that the Task Force did not contemplate making any changes whatsoever to LAM I; rather, the Task Force was created to "monitor the progress of judges and Congress [in the implementation of the anti-gang law]," and to persuade judges to do so. Beatriz Castillo, *No reformarán ley antimaras, jueces estarán obligados a implantarla*, DIARIO CO LATINO, Oct. 21, 2003, *available at* http://www.diariocolatino.com/es/20031021/nacionales/nacionales_20031021_2504/?tpl=69; *Presidente pedirá a CSJ "jueces conocedores de la ley,"* DIARIO CO LATINO, Nov. 28, 2003, *available at* http://www.diariocolatino.com/es/20031128/nacionales/nacionales_20031128_2866/?tpl=69.

[57] García & Gutiérrez, *supra* note 55.

the citizens of El Salvador, will hold them responsible
. . . Our goal is to apprehend gang members and,
together with all Salvadorans, insist that judges' first
and foremost responsibility is to the victims and not to
criminals who, once the judges set them free, go out on
the streets to kill again.[58]

Rights groups such as Amnesty International emphasized that these
statements contravene the Peace Accords, the recommendations made
by the Truth Commission, and the principle of separation of powers. Not
only do they threaten the institutional development and independence
of the judicial branch of government, but also, "may make [judges]
vulnerable by making them appear to be covering up crime, and this
could even endanger the personal safety of judges," Amnesty wrote.[59]

On April 1, 2004, the Supreme Court declared LAM I unconstitutional.[60]
The Court's president reminded President Flores that the executive branch
is obliged to follow judicial sentences.[61] Yet, one day after the Supreme
Court decision declaring LAM I unconstitutional, Congress passed a
new, temporary anti-gang law, the Law to Combat Delinquent Activities
of Special Illicit Groups or Associations (*Ley Para el Combate de las*

---

[58] Castillo, *supra* note 56.

[59] Amnesty Int'l, *El Salvador: Open Letter on the Anti-Maras Act*, Dec. 1, 2003, *available at*
http://asiapacific.amnesty.org/library/Index/ESLAMR290092003?open&of=ESL-SLV ("Amnesty International is extremely worried about the attitude and declarations of the highest
representatives of the Executive Branch against the Judicial Branch concerning the implementation of the LAM. Such intrusion goes against the Peace Accords, the recommendations of the Truth Commission and the norms and principles that regulate the separation
of powers both nationally and internationally. These recent attacks hinder the institutional
development of the Judicial Branch.").

[60] Sala de lo Constitucional de la Corte Suprema de Justicia [Constitutional Chamber of
the Supreme Court of Justice] (Dec. 52-2003/56-2003/57-2003) at Falla 16; IV, 3, B (Apr. 1,
2004), *available at* http://www.pddh.gob.sv/docs/doc00001.pdf

[61] *See* López, *supra* note 52 (The Supreme Court's President told the press: "Every authority
in the country, including the President, must abide by judicial decisions . . . we are not going
to overturn judicial resolutions simply because a different branch of the government prefers
a different interpretation of the law.").

Actividades Delincuenciales de Grupos o Asociaciones Ilícitas Especiales or LAM II), at the urging of President Flores.[62] Many judges found that it did not cure the constitutional deficiencies of LAM I and refused to apply it during the ninety-day period in which it was in effect.[63]

This confrontation between the executive and the judiciary over the legality of the anti-gang laws fueled an acrimonious relationship that continued at least until early 2009. President Saca largely continued Flores' policies, emphasizing legal reforms to facilitate the arrest and conviction of gang members. In light of judicial refusals to apply LAM I and II, President Saca resorted to maneuvers designed to circumvent judicial control and to influence judicial decisions, severely undermining judicial independence. The creation of the specialized tribunals described below is considered by many observers to be one such maneuver aimed at staffing the judicial branch with political appointees.[64]

---

[62] Decreto [Decree] No. 305/2004, Ley para el Combate de las Actividades Delincuenciales de Grupos o Asociaciones Ilícitas Especiales [Law to Combat Delinquent Activities of Special Illicit Groups or Associations] [hereinafter LAM II] (2004), *available at* http://www. glin.gov/view.action?glinID=94631.

[63] LAM II was enacted as a temporary ninety-day measure, subject to legislative renewal. The law was never renewed; rather, President Flores' successor (President Saca) introduced a new series of legal reforms under the *Súper Mano Dura* plan. Wilfredo Salamanca, *Las fallas del primer plan*, El Diario de Hoy, Aug. 31, 2004, *available at* http://www.elsalvador. com/noticias/2004/08/31/nacional/nac17.asp.

[64] Daniel Valencia, *Anteproyecto de ley contra crimen organizado no satisface a jueces*, El Faro, Nov. 6, 2006, http://www.elfaro.net/secciones/Noticias/20061106/noticias3_20061106. asp; Instituto de los Derechos Humanos de la Universidad Centroaméricana José Simeón Cañas [The Human Rights Institute of "José Simeón Cañas" Central American University, hereinafter IDHUCA], Center for Justice and International Law [hereinafter CEJIL], FESPAD, Amenazas Institucionales a la Independencia Judicial en El Salvador (2007) (report presented to the Inter-American Commission on Human Rights) (on file with authors). Although specialized tribunals were established under President Saca's government, President Flores had already called for the establishment of similar anti-gang tribunals. In an overt attempt to influence judicial decisions, President Flores told the press that those appointed must "know the anti-gang law and have the will to use it" and "share [the President's] manner of dealing with the gang problem."); *Presidente pedirá a CSJ "jueces conocedores de la ley,"* Diario Co Latino, Nov. 28, 2003, *available at* http://www.diariocolatino.com/es/20031128/nacionales/nacionales_20031128_2866/?tpl=69.

b) *The Organized and Complex Crimes Law and the Creation of Specialized Tribunals*

El Salvador's Congress approved and President Saca signed into law the Organized and Complex Crimes Law (*Ley Contra el Crimen Organizado y Delitos de Realización Compleja*) with the stated goal of addressing "the most serious crimes committed at the international and national level" by "creating a set of specialized procedures to sanction perpetrators more expeditiously and efficiently, and by establishing judges and tribunals exclusively devoted to this type of crime."[65] President Saca described the specialized tribunals as a "modern tool" to combat crime, a tool that "places El Salvador on par with First World countries."[66]

Nevertheless, several judges have criticized the specialized courts as ad hoc tribunals that threaten judicial independence and reflect an attempt by the executive to ensure sentences in line with its policies.[67] San Salvador Juvenile Court Judge Doris Luz Rivas Galindo explained that: "because judges refused to apply the anti-gang law, [the executive branch] wanted their own cadre of judges."[68] Supreme Court Judge Marcel Orestes Posadas similarly told the press that these "ad hoc

---

[65] President Saca, Remarks at the Swearing-in Ceremony of Specialized Judges (Mar. 30, 2007), *available at* http://www.casapres.gob.sv/presidente/discursos/2007/03/disc3001.html.

[66] *Id.*

[67] Aída Luz Santos de Escobar, *Para Vencer el Crimen Demandemos jueces blindados por la Constitución*, LA PRENSA GRÁFICA, Nov. 29, 2006, *available at* http://archive.laprensa.com.sv/20061129/opinion/658932.asp ("[T]he Law Against Organized and Complex Crimes . . . will deal a mortal blow to [El Salvador's] jurisdictional structure and judicial independence."); Jaime Martínez Ventura, *Anteproyecto de Ley Contra el Crimen Organizado y Delitos de Realización Compleja, Observaciones Presentadas a la Comisión Nacional de Seguridad Ciudadana y Paz Social*, *available at* http://edgardo.amaya.googlepages.com/CrimenOrganizado_AnteproyectodeLey_O.pdf (noting that the law against organized and complex crimes aggrandizes the power of the Office of the Prosecutor and erodes that of the judiciary).

[68] Interview with Doris Luz Rivas Galindo, Magistrada Presidente de la Cámara de Menores de San Salvador [Presiding Justice of the Juvenile Court of San Salvador], in San Salvador (Jan. 22, 2009).

tribunals" represented an intrusion into the system of ordinary justice and an "attempt to bring judges in line with the political agendas of certain groups, certain interests."[69]

The creation of specialized tribunals has perpetuated the existing tensions between the executive and legislative branches on the one hand, and the judiciary on the other. In addition, it has created divisions within the judiciary itself. Judges in the ordinary justice system maintain that specialized judges are political appointees, that many of them have succumbed to political pressure, and that they are accorded undeserved, special salary benefits.[70] Specialized judges note that despite being overworked they have dealt with their judicial dockets more efficiently and expeditiously than their counterparts in the ordinary judicial process.[71] Specialized Judge Ana Lucila Fuentes de Paz told our research team that specialized tribunals "are single-handedly addressing criminality in El Salvador because the majority of homicide, extortion, and kidnapping cases are concentrated in specialized tribunals."[72]

Nevertheless, evidence suggests that specialized tribunals do not fulfill the requirements of judicial independence and impartiality set forth in the Salvadoran Constitution and in international instruments such as the United Nations' Basic Principles on the Independence of the Judiciary. In particular, the judicial selection and appointment

---

[69] *Lecturas encontradas por juzgados especializados*, EL DIARIO DE HOY, Mar. 30, 2008, *available at* http://www.elsalvador.com/mwedh/nota/nota_completa. asp?idCat=6358&idArt=2227944

[70] *Id.*; E. Velásquez, O. Iraheta & D. Marroquin, *Magistrada de CSJ cuestiona elección*, EL DIARIO DE HOY, Mar. 29, 2007; *Jueces critican el método de selección*, LA PRENSA GRÁFICA, Mar. 27, 2007, *available at* http://archive.laprensa.com.sv/20070327/nacion/745222.asp; Karen Molina & Oscar Iraheta, *Inconformidad Jueces Piden Mejor Salario*, EL DIARIO DE HOY, May 11, 2007, *available at* http://www.elsalvador.com/mwedh/nota/nota_completa. asp?idCat=6329&idArt=1367732 (reporting that judges in the ordinary justice system had delivered a sealed letter to the Supreme Court protesting salary disparities between specialized and ordinary judges, and in particular the recent raise of $500.00 that had been granted only to specialized judges).

[71] *Lecturas encontradas por juzgados especializados*, *supra* note 69.

[72] Interview with Ana Lucila Fuentes de Paz, Jueza Especializada de Instrucción de San Salvador [Judge in the First Instance, Specialized Instruction Tribunal, San Salvador], in San Salvador (Oct. 20, 2008).

process violates the requirement that judges should appear impartial.[73] The president of the Criminal Chamber of the Supreme Court, Ulises del Dios Guzmán, told the press that the Court should employ an ideological filter to select candidates to the specialized bench, to exclude "traditional" judges concerned with defendants' rights.[74] Although judicial candidates were required to take an entrance exam as part of the selection process, some of the selected judges failed the exam, and the majority received low marks.[75] Judge Juan Antonio Durán Ramírez, who brought this issue to the attention of the Inter-American Commission of Human Rights, explained "not just anybody, and least of all a judge that protects due process rights, can be a specialized judge. One of the appeals court judges failed the exam with a grade of 3.6 out of 10. So academic achievement and technical knowledge don't matter, all that matters is their ideological profile."[76] Judge Martín Rogel Zepeda similarly noted that although an impartial appointment process is formally in place, in practice, the decision regarding who would be appointed had been made before the exam.[77] At this stage,

---

[73] Seventh United Nations Congress on the Prevention of Crime and the Treatment of Offenders, Milan, Italy, Aug. 26-Sep. 6, 1985, *Basic Principles on the Independence of the Judiciary*, §2, *available at* http://www.unhchr.ch/html/menu3/b/h_comp50.htm.

[74] *See* Efren Lemus & Gabriel Labrador, *Nuevo filtro para jueces antimafia*, LA PRENSA GRÁFICA, Jan. 31, 2007, *available at* http://archive.laprensa.com.sv/20070131//nacion/705577. asp (quoting Ulises del Dios Guzmán who told the press that he will propose that judges be selected through a "juridico-ideológico" exam because "an essential element [in the selection process] is the kind of juridico-ideológico conception [of the law] held by the judge." He also criticized what he called the "traditional" conception of the law, expressed in the country's Criminal Code, as tending to favor delinquents and emphasized that the selection process should filter out candidates that adhere to this traditional view).

[75] *CNJ propone a seis reprobados para tribunales especiales. No superaron el exámen de conocimiento de leyes y obtuvieron puntuaciones desde 3.6 hasta 5.72*, LA PRENSA GRÁFICA, Mar. 24, 2007; *Comisión de CSJ analiza caso de jueces aplazados*, LA PRENSA GRÁFICA, Mar. 27, 2003; David Cabezas, *Hicimos una muy buena selección*, LA PRENSA GRÁFICA, Mar. 27, 2003; *Jueces darán garantías a las víctimas*, LA PRENSA GRÁFICA, Mar. 31, 2007; Karen Molina, *Jueces Defienden Trayectoria*, EL DIARIO DE HOY, Mar. 30, 2007.

[76] Interview with Juan Antonio Durán Ramírez, Juez de Sentencia de Chalatenango [Judge in the First Instance, Chalatenango Sentencing Tribunal], in San Salvador (Oct. 19, 2008).

[77] Interview with Rogel Zepeda, *supra* note 45.

in April 2009, after only two years of operation, the performance of specialized tribunals is still very much an open question. What appears clear, however, is that the selection process has been politicized and that judges have been exposed to pressure to convict defendants.

c)   Ordinary and Expert Witness Protection Measures

The use of witness protection measures during trial–such as voice distortion and faceless witnesses—has generated friction between the Office of the Prosecutor and the judiciary since the enactment of the first witness and expert witness protection regime in 2001.[78] The 2001 regime provided a thin measure of protection by allowing witness identity and personal characteristics to be kept secret and by providing for police protection during trial.[79] Because the regime did not include strong post-trial protection measures (such as relocation assistance), it did little to ensure witness safety in practice. Finding that the regime violated defendants' due process rights while failing to guarantee witness safety effectively, most judges refused to admit the testimony of faceless witnesses at trial.[80] Although the 2006 regime sought to provide more comprehensive protection, many judges considered it a minor improvement over the 2001 regime; after the changes, these judges

---

[78] The Salvadoran Congress has passed two laws to regulate witness and victim protection. The first, Protection Regime for Ordinary and Expert Witnesses, was enacted by Legislative Decree No. 281 and added Chapter VI-Bis to the Criminal Code (Arts. 210-A to 210-G). Decreto [Decree] No. 281/2001, Régimen de protección para testigos y peritos [Protection Regime for Ordinary and Expert Witnesses] [hereinafter Protection Regime for Ordinary and Expert Witnesses] (2001). The second, Special Victim and Witness Protection Law, was enacted by Legislative Decree No. 1029, replacing Decree No. 281 and aiming to provide more comprehensive protection. Decreto [Decree] No. 1029/2006, Ley Especial para la Protección de Víctimas y Testigos [Special Victim and Witness Protection Law] [hereinafter Special Victim and Witness Protection Law] (2006).

[79] *Id.*

[80] Karen Molina, *Jueces querían carear a víctimas con reos*, EL DIARIO DE HOY, Dec. 7, 2006; *Distorsionador de voz causa discordia en jueces y fiscales*, EL DIARIO DE HOY, Mar. 15, 2008, *available at* http://www.elsalvador.com/mwedh/nota/nota_completa. asp?idCat=6358&idArt=2182649; *Testigos vestidos de policías, otro elemento de pugna*. EL DIARIO DE HOY, Mar. 15, 2008, *available at* http://www.elsalvador.com/mwedh/nota/nota_ completa.asp?idCat=6342&idArt=2182641.

continued to believe that the new protection measures failed to ensure witness safety in practice.[81] As was the case when judges refused to apply LAM I and LAM II, the executive branch responded by publicly accusing judges of fostering impunity and warning them that they would be held responsible for the fate of those witnesses whose identities were not protected.[82]

In at least one case, the Office of the Prosecutor used its investigative powers to investigate members of the judiciary who refused to allow faceless witnesses. The prosecutor placed a three-judge panel under investigation for the murder of a witness who, at the request of the panel, testified at trial without identity-protection measures. According to two panel members, Judges Leonardo Ramírez Murcia and Juan Antonio Durán Ramírez, the Office of the Prosecutor refused to give them or their lawyers access to information about the case against them, alleging the investigation was ongoing. The prosecutor also requested access to their personnel files in what Murcia and Durán considered an inappropriate effort to influence the work of the judiciary.[83]

---

[81] Interview with Juan Antonio Durán Ramírez, Juez de Sentencia de Chalatenango [Judge in the First Instance, Chalatenango Sentencing Tribunal], in San Salvador (Mar. 26, 2008) ("In practice, protection is symbolic, because after witnesses give their testimony, they are sent back home. They continue living in the same environment and are rarely relocated.").

[82] *Emplazan a Jueces*, EL DIARIO DE HOY, June 17, 2006, *available at* http://www.elsalvador. com/noticias/2006/06/17/nacional/nac6.asp ("The government strongly criticized judges and urged that the judicial system be purged . . . A group of judges were cited due to their recent judicial decisions that released criminals and forced witnesses to show their faces at trial.").

[83] *Institutional threats to the independence of the Judiciary in El Salvador, supra* note 46. Decreto [Decree] No. 904/1996, Código Procesal Penal [Penal Process Code], art. 272 (1996) specifies that parties to an ongoing criminal investigation, as well as their legal representatives, shall have access to police and prosecutors' investigative files. The 2009 amendments to the Penal Process Code likewise provide parties and their legal representatives access to these investigative files. Decreto [Decree] 733/2009, Código Procesal Penal [Penal Process Code], art. 76.

> d) Proceedings to strip judges of immunity from criminal
> prosecution

The Office of the Prosecutor has attempted to use the crime of *prevaricato* (breach of judicial duty) to strip of immunity from criminal prosecution those judges whose judicial interpretation of the Code of Penal Procedure is not in line with executive-branch policies. Many Salvadoran judges agree that these charges are politically motivated and designed to coerce judges into interpreting the code so as to secure higher conviction rates for the Office of the Prosecutor.

On January 21, 2008, the Office of the Prosecutor asked the Supreme Court to allow three judges to be criminally prosecuted for having grossly misapplied the law.[84] Judges across the country were galvanized by what most considered to be a political maneuver to influence judicial decisions and to strongarm judges into interpreting the law in accordance with prosecutorial interests. Hundreds of judges marched to the Supreme Court to protest the Prosecutor's action and to request that the Supreme Court carry out an objective analysis of the three cases (see insert: The March of Judges).[85] San Salvador Judge Edward Sidney Blanco Reyes explained: "We did not want to call a conference or draft a press release. We wanted, for the first time, to make a public statement to stop the Office of the Prosecutor's action. Allowing this type of complaint to proceed would place judges in a permanent state of fear that they could be subject to criminal prosecution if the Prosecutor is not satisfied with the outcome of a particular case."[86]

In all three cases, the Supreme Court determined that the judges had issued reasoned decisions based on interpretations of the Code of Penal

---

[84] *Varios abogados en la mira de la FGR,* Diario Co Latino, Jan. 22, 2008; Edmee Velásquez, *Piden desafuero para cuatro jueces,* El Nuevo Diario, Jan. 21, 2008.

[85] Daniel Trujillo, *Centenares de jueces marchan contra procesos de antejuicio,* Diario Co Latino, Jan. 30, 2008; *Jueces marchan en El Salvador en protesta por conflicto fiscalía,* Reuters, Jan. 30, 2008; *Marchan jueces ante Corte Suprema de El Salvador,* Xinhua News Agency, Jan. 31, 2008, *available at* http://spanish.peopledaily.com.cn/31617/6348872.html.

[86] *Entrevista con el juez Sidney Blanco,* Diario Co Latino, Jan. 29, 2008, *available at* www.diariocolatino.com/attachment/000000345.pdf.

Procedure supported by precedent. The Supreme Court concluded that:

> [T]here is no evidence to support the charges of breach
> of judicial duty . . . We have verified that the judicial
> decisions at issue are based on reasoned interpretations
> of the Code of Penal Procedure. . . . [W]hat is at issue
> in this case is the use of different interpretive criteria.
> But different legal interpretations do not give rise to a
> breach of judicial duty. If this were the case, a breach
> of judicial duty would occur every time a decision is
> overturned by a higher Court, an unacceptable outcome
> in a democratic system that constitutionally guarantees
> judicial independence.[87]

Judge Astrid Torres, one of the three judges accused of *prevaricato* (breach of judicial duty), told our researchers that the Office of the Prosecutor harasses her frequently, including by accusing her of issuing political decisions to benefit the FMLN opposition party.[88] Another of the judges singled out for prosecution, Judge David Posada Vidaurreta, publicly accused members of the PNC and the Office of the Prosecutor of harassment. In particular, he complained that his family was under constant surveillance and accused two prosecutors of attempting to induce a detainee to testify falsely against him.[89] The Foundation for the Study of the Application of the Law (*Fundación de Estudios para la Aplicación del Derecho* or FESPAD), a research and advocacy group, filed a complaint with the Legislative Assembly to impeach the Director of Public Prosecutions Félix Safie (*Fiscal General de la República*) for abuse of power in trying to obtain a false confession against Posada

---

[87] Acuerdos de Corte Plena, Corte Suprema de Justicia de El Salvador, February 15, 2008, *available at* http://www.csj.gob.sv/Comunicaciones/febrero/2008/noticias_febrero_20.htm.

[88] Interview with Astrid Torres, Jueza de Vigilancia Penitenciaria y de Ejecución de la Pena [Judge for Penitentiary Oversight and Sentencing], in San Salvador (Oct. 22, 2008).

[89] Jaime López & Lissette Abrego, *Juez de Santa Tecla denuncia persecución*, EL DIARIO DE HOY, April 17, 2008.

Vidaurreta.[90]

Through legislative reforms that concentrate power in the hands of the Office of the Prosecutor and the National Police, through public statements that blame the judiciary for the failure of executive anti-gang policies, and through the use of disciplinary measures as a tool to influence judicial decisions, the executive and legislative branches have undermined the institutional legitimacy and credibility of the judicial branch.

---

[90] Suchit Chávez, *Fiscal Safie llama "corrupto" a juez Posada Vidaurreta*, EL DIARIO DE HOY, June 27, 2008, *available at* http://archive.laprensa.com.sv/20080627/nacion/1088688.asp.

The March of Judges

The mounting tension between the judicial and executive branches finally reached a breaking point in early 2008, when judges took their grievances to the streets. On January 30, 2008, as many as 500 judges and lawyers marched in downtown San Salvador to demand judicial independence.[1] While Giuseppe Verdi's *Nabucco* played in the background, judges and lawyers rallied together, hoisting signs against impunity and penal code reforms.[2] Their historic march ended with a demonstration at the Supreme Court building.[3]

Although the judicial complaints made public during the March of Judges were fueled by a long history of confrontation between the executive and judicial branches, the judges' rally was more directly inspired by two specific developments: a proposal to reform the code of penal procedure and the initiation of pre-trial proceedings against four judges. Judges voiced their opposition to the reform proposal,[4] arguing that the new code placed too much power in the hands of prosecutors.[5] Tensions also increased when on January 21, 2008, Director of Public Prosecutions Félix Garrid Safie initiated pre-trial proceedings in the country's Supreme Court, requesting that four Salvadoran judges be stripped of their immunity from criminal

[1] *Marchan jueces ante Corte Suprema de El Salvador*, Xinhua News Agency, Jan. 31, 2008.

[2] *Jueces marchan en El Salvador en protesta por conflicto fiscalía*, Reuters, Jan. 30, 2008.

[3] Daniel Trujillo, *Centenares de jueces marchan contra procesos de antejuicio*, Diario Co Latino, Jan. 30, 2008.

[4] *Jueces marchan en El Salvador en protesta por conflicto fiscalía*, Reuters, Jan. 30, 2008.

[5] *Id.*

prosecution.[6] The Director of Public Prosecutions alleged
that judges Astrid Torres, Luis Reyes Deras, David Posada, and
Roberto Antonio Ramírez were guilty of breach of judicial duty
and corruption.[7]

Though judges and lawyers alike underscored that they
did not oppose investigations into colorable claims of judicial
corruption, many considered that authorities initiated
prosecution against at least three of the four judges to discredit
the judiciary and strengthen the executive branch.[8] Many in
fact believed that those on trial had issued well-reasoned legal
decisions but had been prosecuted because their judgments had
not been favorable to the prosecution.[9] Sidney Blanco Reyes,
a well-known Salvadoran judge, noted that the Office of the
Prosecutor may have intended these proceedings as a message
to future judges, suggesting that those whose interpretation
of the law was not in line with executive policies could face
prosecution.[10]

Those involved in the March also submitted a letter to
the Supreme Court, asking for independence, objectivity, and
impartiality in the consideration of the charges against the four
judges.[11] These, they emphasized, are the rights of any citizen
accused of a crime.[12] - *Virginia Farmer*

---

[6] *Marchan jueces salvadoreños por el respeto a la Constitución*, NOTIMEX, Jan. 31, 2008.

[7] *Id.*

[8] *Entrevista con el juez Sidney Blanco*, DIARIO CO LATINO, Jan. 29, 2008.

[9] *Id.*

[10] *Id.*

[11] *Marchan jueces ante Corte Suprema de El Salvador*, XINHUA NEWS AGENCY, Jan. 31, 2008.

[12] *Id.*

B. *Failure to Build Effective Police Institutions in El Salvador*

The institutional weakness and politicization of the National Civil Police (*Policía Nacional Civil* or PNC) constitute central obstacles to ensuring human rights and establishing the rule of law in post-war El Salvador. According to El Salvador's Ombudsperson's Office, the PNC, more than any other institution in the country, has participated in human rights abuses associated with the recent crackdown on youth gangs.[91] For example, the Ombudsperson's Office identified the PNC as responsible for human rights abuses in twelve of the seventeen final resolutions concerning the rights of the child that office issued between January and September 2008. The Office of the Prosecutor and specialized tribunals were singled out in four and ordinary judges in two of these seventeen resolutions.[92] A similar pattern emerges from an examination of the initial resolutions issued by the Ombudsperson's Office.[93] The Ombudsperson's Office found the PNC responsible for human rights violations concerning the rights of the child in forty-eight of forty-nine initial resolutions, the Office of the Prosecutor responsible in eighteen, and specialized and ordinary tribunals responsible in two of these initial resolutions.[94] Luis Enrique Salazar Flores, the Adjunct Ombudsperson for Children and Youth (*Procurador Adjunto de la Niñez y la Juventud*), emphasized that because the Ombudsperson's Office relies on individual complaints to identify possible instances of abuse,

---

[91] Interview with Luis Enrique Salazar Flores, Procurador Adjunto de la Niñez y la Juventud (Adjunct Ombudsperson for Children and Youth), in San Salvador (Jan. 22, 2009).

[92] Departamento de Seguimiento [Monitoring Department], Procuraduría para la Defensa de los Derechos Humanos [Office of the National Human Rights Ombudsperson] (on file with authors).

[93] Initial resolutions are issued when there is strong indication that a human rights violation has been committed such that the case warrants further investigation. Each initial resolution can assign responsibility to more than one state entity. Following this preliminary finding of responsibility, the Office of the Prosecutor notifies the public institutions implicated in the human rights violations so that they can take measures to investigate and remedy the situation.

[94] *Supra* note 92.

these cases represent the "tip of the iceberg" of the universe of violations committed by the PNC, the majority of which are never reported to his office.[95] Still, the high proportion of cases with PNC involvement in this small sample strongly indicates a central PNC role in human rights violations, particularly of the rights of children and youth.

The PNC was established as part of the Peace Accords and resulted from careful deliberation by international negotiators.[96] Unfortunately, however, the PNC failed to develop into a transparent, professional, and competent public institution.[97] Domestic human rights organizations and international observers trace many of the PNC's current problems to its initial composition.[98] Under the terms of the Peace Accords, the PNC was to be composed primarily (60 percent) of civilians who had not participated in combat during the war. The rest of the force was to be evenly divided between former National Police (military) personnel and former FMLN combatants.[99] The post-war government did not abide by the terms of the Peace Accords, however, "plac[ing] former military personnel into the new force, including the wholesale incorporation of units slated to be disbanded."[100] According to a May 1994 report to the U.N. Security Council by the United Nations Observer Mission in El Salvador (ONUSAL), among the higher-ranking PNC officials, "[thirty] sub commissioners in the new police force belonged

---

[95] Interview with Salazar Flores, *supra* note 91.

[96] POPKIN, *supra* note 10, at 175.

[97] *Id.,* at 176.

[98] IDHUCA, *Los Derechos Humanos en el 2005 (II)*, PROCESO Jan. 11, 2006, at 12; *see also* POPKIN, *supra* note 10, at 176.

[99] Dominic Murray, *Post-Accord Police Reform*, *in* VIOLENCE AND RECONSTRUCTION 79 (John Darby ed., 2006).

[100] POPKIN, *supra* note 10, at 176; *see also* IDHUCA, *supra* note 98, at 12 (stating that certain existing patterns of police misconduct continued in the PNC from the time of its creation, undermining the integrity of the new force). *See generally* Jeannette Aguilar, *La Mano Dura y las 'políticas' de seguridad*, 667 ECA: ESTUDIOS CENTROAMERICANOS 439, 441-443 (2004) (describing the general structure of Salvadoran police forces).

to the old public security system, while only seven are from the FMLN and only seventeen are civilians."[101] The strong presence in the PNC of actors associated with the militarized public security institutions from the years of military rule has helped to foster a climate within the force antithetical to the protection of human rights and the rule of law in El Salvador. Seventeen years after the signing of the Peace Accords, combat affiliations may not be as visible or as expressly divisive as they were in the mid-1990s; however, the PNC is still seen as an institution that is frequently more responsive to powerful political and economic forces than to the exigencies of the rule of law.[102]

In addition, the Salvadoran government has increasingly relied on joint military-police patrols to combat gang-related crimes, despite clear language in the Peace Accords that emphasizes that safeguarding peace, order, and public security, both in urban and rural areas, lies under the civilian jurisdiction of the National Civil Police and outside the ordinary powers of the Armed forces.[103] The Salvadoran government created its first Joint Task Forces (*Grupos de Tarea Conjunta* or GTC) in 1994 under the Guardians Plan (*Plan Guardianes*) to combat crime in rural

---

[101] The Secretary General, *Report of the Secretary General on the United Nations Mission in El Salvador*, ¶ 36, *delivered to the Security Council*, U.N. Doc. S/1994/561 (May 11, 1994).

[102] Procuraduría para la Defensa de los Derechos Humanos, Informe de Labores de la Procuraduría para la Defensa de los Derechos Humanos Julio 2005-Junio 2006 [Office of the National Human Rights Ombudsperson, Report on the Work of the National Human Rights Ombudsperson hereinafter Informe de Labores de la Procuraduría 05-06] 15 (2006) (stating that the PNC has failed to improve in investigative capacity or professionalism and instead has demonstrated an increasingly authoritarian and repressive mentality); *see also* IDHUCA, *supra* note 98, at 12 (describing the PNC as a politicized institution).

[103] Chapultepec Peace Accords, *supra* note 42, at Chap. 1(1)(F) ("The maintenance of internal peace, tranquility, order and public security lies outside the normal functions of the armed forces as an institution responsible for national defence. The armed forces play a role in this sphere only in very exceptional circumstances, where the normal means have been exhausted, on the terms established in the constitutional reform approved in April 1991."); *id.* at Chap. 1(6)(A) ("[T]he safeguarding of peace, tranquility, order and public security in both urban and rural areas shall be the responsibility of the National Civil Police, which shall be under the control of civilian authorities.").

areas.[104] The UN Observer Mission in El Salvador strongly criticized the government's decision as violating "constitutional procedures"[105] that assigned to a professional civil police corps (the PNC), independent of the Armed Forces, exclusive authority to carry out public security functions.[106] The Salvadoran Constitution limits the Armed Forces' role to safeguarding territorial sovereignty but allows for performance of public security functions in extraordinary circumstances when "ordinary methods of maintaining public order and internal peace, tranquility and public security have been exhausted."[107] Arguing that violent crime constitutes a national emergency, Presidents Flores and Saca have continued the practice of employing joint military-police units and have expanded it to include joint anti-gang patrols (*Grupos de Tarea Anti-Pandilla* or GTA) that function in urban areas, as well as mobile joint patrol groups.[108] GTAs have included as few as a single

---

[104] Orlando J. Perez & Ricardo Córdova Macias, *El rol de las Fuerzas Armadas y su impacto sobre la democracia: Análisis de la situación en América Central*, at 6, http://www.resdal.org/producciones-miembros/redes-03-perez.pdf.

[105] United Nations Observer Mission in El Salvador (ONUSAL)—Background, http://www.un.org/Depts/dpko/dpko/co_mission/onusalbackgr2.html#four ("The decision in March 1994 to use military patrols to deter crime in rural areas was not in compliance with the constitutional procedures.").

[106] Constitución de la República de El Salvador [Constitution of the Republic of El Salvador] art. 159 ("National Defense and Public Security will be assigned to different Ministries. Public Security will be the responsibility of the National Civil Police, which will be a professional corps, independent of the Armed Forces and not involved in partisan activities. The National Civil Police will be responsible for ensuring the functioning of urban and rural police forces, which should guarantee order, security and public peace, as well as collaborate in criminal investigations, in accordance with the rule of law and with strict respect for Human Rights.").

[107] *Id.* at art. 168(2) ("Exceptionally, if ordinary means for the maintenance of internal peace, tranquility and security have been exhausted, the President of the Republic may deploy the Armed Forces to that end. The action of the Armed Forces will be of limited duration and only to the extent that is strictly necessary for the re-establishment of order, and will cease as soon as this goal is achieved.").

[108] Rosa Fuentes, *Militares ampliarán apoyo a la seguridad*, EL DIARIO DE HOY, Jan. 31, 2003, *available at* http://www.elsalvador.com/noticias/2003/1/31/elpais/elpais5.html; Alberto López, Douglas González, Jaime García, Jorge Beltrán & Abbey Alvarenga, *Detienen 144 mareros*, EL DIARIO DE HOY, July 25, 2003, *available at* http://www.elsalvador.com/

police officer and four soldiers and have been authorized to function "indefinitely" in high-crime areas in urban El Salvador.[109] Mobile joint patrol groups have been deployed to municipalities with high crime rates.[110] The government has also relied on a specialized anti-terrorist unit of the Army (*Comando Especial Antiterrorista*) to capture gang members it considered to be particularly dangerous during both LAM I and LAM II operations.[111]

Although technically serving a support role under the direction and control of police forces,[112] military officers have told the press that they are empowered to carry out arrests when they catch suspects in the act of committing a crime.[113] The Minister of Defense, Otto Romero,

---

noticias/2003/07/25/nacional/nacio13.html; Oscar Iraheta, *Operativos Combinados en Co-munidades*, EL DIARIO DE HOY, July 30, 2005, *available at* http://www.elsalvador.com/noti-cias/2003/07/25/nacional/nacio13.html; Beatriz Castillo, *Grupos de tarea antidelincuencial funcionarán en septiembre*, DIARIO CO LATINO, Aug. 25, 2005, *available at* http://www.dia-riocolatino.com/es/20050825/nacionales/nacionales_20050825_9035/?tpl=71; Agencia AFP, *Otros mil soldados patrullan calles de 20 municipios salvadoreños*, RADIO LA PRIMERÍSIMA, Oct. 11, 2006, *available at* http://www.radiolaprimerisima.com/noticias/4835; *Despliegan grupos conjuntos contra pandillas*, EL DIARIO DE HOY, Apr. 21, 2006, *available at* http://www. elsalvador.com/noticias/2006/04/21/nacional/suc4.asp#; Oscar Iraheta, *Ejército va a zonas acosadas por maras*, EL DIARIO DE HOY, Apr. 22, 2006, *available at* http://www.elsalvador. com/noticias/2006/04/22/nacional/nac9.asp#; K. Urquilla & S. Bernal, *Ejército, a la calle*, EL DIARIO DE HOY, Aug. 23, 2006, *available at* http://www.elsalvador.com/noticias/2006/08/23/ nacional/nac4.asp#; *Fuerzas especiales en municipios más violentos*, EL DIARIO DE HOY, May 14, 2008, *available at* http://www.elsalvador.com/mwedh/nota/nota_completa. asp?idCat=6358&idArt=2383303; David Marroquin, *Ejército refuerza con 500 soldados el plan "Caminante"*, EL DIARIO DE HOY, May 14, 2008, *available at* http://www.elsalvador. com/mwedh/nota/nota_completa.asp?idCat=6329&idArt=2382440.

[109] Iraheta, *supra* note 108.

[110] *Fuerzas especiales en municipios más violentos*, *supra* note 108.

[111] López et al., *supra* note 108.

[112] Press Release, Sr. Elias Antonio Saca, Presidente de la República, Posterior a la entrega de semilla de frijol mejorada 2006/2007 en San Juan Opico, La Libertad (Aug. 25, 2006), *available at* http://www.casapres.gob.sv/presidente/declaraciones/2006/08/dec2201.html ("One must distinguish military support to police forces, which is constitutionally valid, from militarization.").

[113] López et al., *supra* note 108 (Col. Ángel Román Sermeño told the press that while police carry out arrests pursuant to warrants, military personnel, much like any ordinary citizen,

noted that a military presence would "provide [police forces] with a new angle, teaching them how to be efficient with gang members" and how to achieve concrete results.[114] Given that military forces are trained in strategies to safeguard national security and territorial integrity, the import of military tactics into civilian patrols is problematic, first, because it blurs the line between civilian and military jurisdiction in violation of the Peace Accords, and second, because it imposes military culture and mindset on police forces. Reports of existing tensions between military and police personnel are a further cause for concern.[115]

In addition to the troubling, disproportionate presence of actors linked to the militarized national security forces of the pre-1992 era, a lack of resources and political will have impeded the professionalization of the PNC, generating serious deficiencies in its ability to investigate and prosecute criminal activity. International observers and members of the Truth Commission noted these deficiencies in the early 1990s.[116] Serious problems persist today.[117] A June 2007 study revealed that

---

can capture individuals caught in the act of breaking the law).

[114] Castillo, *supra* note 108.

[115] Orlando J. Pérez & Ricardo Córdova Macias, El rol de las Fuerzas Armadas y su impacto sobre la democracia: Análisis de la situación en América Central, at 6, http://www.resdal.org/producciones-miembros/redes-03-perez.pdf ("a series of interviews with members of the Salvadoran military and police forces reveal that there is tension between police and military officers that participate in joint task forces.").

[116] In 1993 the ONUSAL report to the United Nations noted an "inability to investigate crimes" that was "reflected in the failure of judges to show any initiative in taking the requisite legal steps in the early stages of the investigation; in the slow and delayed participation of the Office of the Attorney General; in the meager or invalid evidence gathered for the purpose of establishing criminal liability; and in lenience in investigating cases involving military personnel or agents of the security forces." The Secretary General, *Note by the Secretary General*, ¶ 77, *delivered to the Security Council and the General Assembly*, U.N. Doc. S/25521/Annex (Report of the Director of the Human Rights Division of the United Nations Observer Mission in El Salvador up to Jan. 31, 1993), A/47/912 (Apr. 5, 1993).

[117] Interview with Jaime Martínez Ventura, Coordinador, Oficina de Justicia Juvenil, Corte Suprema de El Salvador [Coordinator, Office of Juvenile Justice, Supreme Court], in San Salvador (Aug. 22, 2006); *see also* THE WORLD BANK ET AL., PREVENCIÓN Y CONTROL DEL CRIMEN Y LA VIOLENCIA EN EL SALVADOR: LINEAMIENTOS ESTRATEGICOS 10 (2004).

only 3.8 percent of all homicides registered by the Institute of Forensic Medicine (*Instituto de Medicina Legal* or IML) between January 1 and December 31, 2005, had resulted in a conviction by May 2007. Indeed, after periods ranging from 16 to 28 months, in only 14.21 percent of homicides registered by the IML, did the judicial processes even begin. Of those cases that were brought before a judge, only 26.89 percent led to a conviction. The study singles out the PNC and the Office of the Prosecutor as the two institutions most responsible for these low conviction rates. In particular, police forces were shown to have grave investigative deficiencies: in the vast majority of unsolved cases, the police failed to conduct a follow-up investigation after initial interviews at the crime scene and neglected to carry out basic inquiries (such as interviewing witnesses and victims) requested by the Office of the Prosecutor (see Figures 2a and 2b, pp. 42-43).[118]

---

[118] SIDNEY BLANCO REYES & FRANCISCO DÍAZ RODRÍGUEZ, DEFICIENCIAS POLICIALES, FISCALES O JUDICIALES EN LA INVESTIGACIÓN Y JUZGAMIENTO CAUSANTES DE IMPUNIDAD (2007), *available at* http://www.elfaro.net/secciones/Noticias/20070723/informe.pdf. The report highlights eight specific deficiencies in the homicide investigations of the Office of the Prosecutor and the PNC: (1) lack of ballistic analysis; (2) lack of blood tests; (3) failure to follow orders from the Office of the Prosecutor, failure to record results; (4) incomplete search, identification and interview of witnesses; (5) absent or incomplete inspections; (6) failure to collect fingerprints or carry out fingerprint analysis; (7) lack of autopsy report; (8) lack of measures to identify suspects. Only 3 percent of all cases showed no investigative deficiencies. In 24 percent of cases, no blood tests had been performed; in 19 percent, witnesses had not been identified and interviewed, and no ballistic analysis had been carried out.

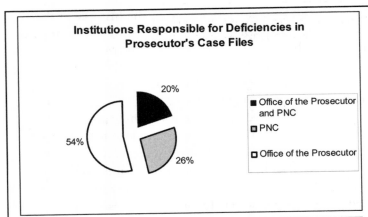

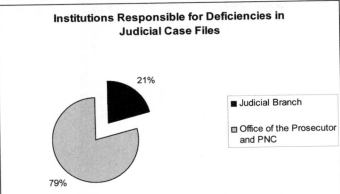

Figure 2a. Institutions Responsible for Deficiencies in Prosecutor's and Judicial Case Files
Source: SIDNEY BLANCO REYES & FRANCISCO DÍAZ RODRÍGUEZ, DEFICIENCIAS POLICIALES, FISCALES O JUDICIALES EN LA INVESTIGACIÓN Y JUZGAMIENTO CAUSANTES DE IMPUNIDAD (2007)

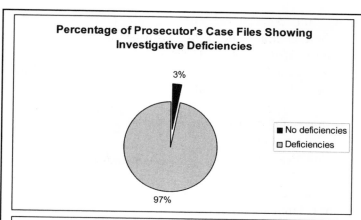

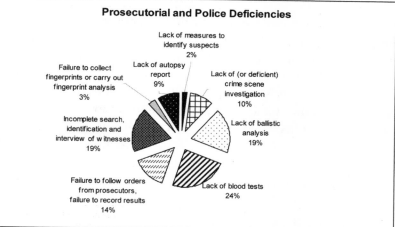

Figure 2b. Prosecutorial and Police Deficiencies in Prosecutor's Case Files
Source: SIDNEY BLANCO REYES & FRANCISCO DÍAZ RODRÍGUEZ, DEFICIENCIAS POLICIALES, FISCALES O JUDICIALES EN LA INVESTIGACIÓN Y JUZGAMIENTO CAUSANTES DE IMPUNIDAD (2007)

International and domestic activists and observers also point to the PNC's failure to comply with human rights standards, particularly concerning arbitrary arrests and physical violence,[119] as among the most fundamental institutional weaknesses of the Salvadoran police. These findings are discussed in greater detail in Chapter IV.

C. Failures of the Prison System

[Prison in El Salvador is] the waiting room to hell.

María Silvia Guillén, Executive Director, FESPAD, in San Salvador (March 26, 2008)

Like other criminal justice institutions, El Salvador's prisons in the post-war era, rife with rights abuses, have served to undermine both public security and the rule of law. These failures have as their origins the longstanding problems of the Salvadoran justice system as a whole, particularly with respect to the use of pre-trial detention.[120] In the years following the Peace Accords, poor conditions of detention, severe overcrowding, and prison violence became major national issues in El Salvador,[121] prompting ONUSAL to recommend in 1994 that

---

[119] *See, e.g.,* interview with Beatrice Alemmani de Carrillo, ex-Procuradora para la Defensa de los Derechos Humanos de El Salvador [National Human Rights Ombudsperson], in San Salvador (Mar. 27, 2006); interview with Luis Enrique Salazar Flores, *supra* note 91; interview with Ovidio González, Director, Tutela Legal del Arzobispado de San Salvador [hereinafter Tutela Legal], in San Salvador (Oct. 20, 2008); interview with José Roberto Lazos, Coordinador en el Área de Educación de Tutela Legal [Coordinator, Education Unit, Tutela Legal], in San Salvador (Oct. 20, 2008); interview with NGO staff member in Mejicanos (Oct. 21, 2008); interview with B.E., staff of a youth center, outside San Salvador (Jan. 21, 2009).

[120] In 1990, for example, a Salvadoran government law reform initiative funded by USAID estimated that approximately 90 percent of persons detained in Salvadoran prisons had not been sentenced. POPKIN, *supra* note 10, at 232 (citing CORELESAL, PROBLEMÁTICA DE LA ADMINISTRACIÓN DE JUSTICIA EN EL SALVADOR, 117-118 (1990)).

[121] *Id.* at 231-232; *see also El Salvador Prison Riot Kills 9*, N.Y. TIMES, Feb. 25, 1994, at A6 ("Hundreds of inmates rose up in a crowded prison in Santa Ana, 40 miles west of here, and killed nine fellow prisoners before talks today ended El Salvador's fourth prison mutiny since November.").

the Salvadoran government declare a state of emergency in the prison system and take systematic steps to address the crisis.[122]

After a period of relative calm, the prison crisis in El Salvador has intensified in recent years. The government's reliance on mass arrests to curb gang violence—one of several repressive strategies of the past several years—has contributed to overcrowding and deteriorating conditions within the prison system.[123] In conversations with our researchers, the Director of the Penitentiary System in El Salvador acknowledged that the physical infrastructure of the country's prison system is insufficient for the number of inmates it holds.[124] In 2008, 19,814 detainees inhabited a network of prisons with capacity for 8,227 inmates.[125] In addition to severe overcrowding and resultant poor conditions, the mass incarceration of gang members in a system without the resources or capacity to absorb them has generated a situation in which gangs wield vast power inside the prisons. This problem has intensified due to government efforts to segregate detainees into separate prisons by gang affiliation (or lack of gang affiliation).[126] Given the security limitations

---

[122] POPKIN, *supra* note 10, at 232.

[123] FESPAD & CEPES, INFORME ANUAL JUSTICIA JUVENIL 2004 35 (2004) [hereinafter INFORME ANUAL JUSTICIA JUVENIL 2004] (stating that large-scale arrests have exacerbated overcrowding and are responsible for worsening living conditions in centers of detention).

[124] Interview with Jaime Roberto Villanova, Director General, Centros Penales de El Salvador [Director General of Penal Centers], in San Salvador (Mar. 28, 2006).

[125] BUREAU OF DEMOCRACY, HUMAN RIGHTS, AND LABOR, 2008 HUMAN RIGHTS REPORT ON HUMAN RIGHTS PRACTICES: EL SALVADOR (2009), *available at* http://www.state.gov/g/drl/rls/hrrpt/2008/wha/119159.htm. More recent reports place the number of detainees at over 20,000. *See, e.g.*, Beatriz Castillo, *Familiares de reos marchan para exigir mejoras en el sistema carcelario*, DIARIO CO LATINO, Feb. 16, 2009, *available at* http://www.diariocolatino.com/es/20090216/nacionales/63838/. The number of people incarcerated in all correctional facilities within El Salvador in 2008 accounted for 0.3 percent of the overall population (5,744,113 inhabitants according to the 2007 census). DIRECCIÓN GENERAL DE ESTADÍSTICA Y CENSOS, VI CENSO DE POBLACIÓN Y V DE VIVIENDA 2007 [GENERAL BUREAU OF STATISTICS AND CENSUS, VI POPULATION AND V RESIDENCE CENSUS].

[126] Interview with Hugo Ramírez, Subcomisionado de la Policía Nacional Civil, Jefe de la División de Servicios Juveniles y Familia [PNC Subcommissioner, Head of Juvenile and Family Services Division], in San Salvador (Aug. 31, 2006) (observing that by segregating prisons by gang affiliation, the government has contributed to the gangs' level of organiza-

of the system, segregation appears to have been a necessary step to avoid violent inter-gang clashes (such as the notorious gang riots that took place in La Esperanza prison in 2004).[127] Still, these segregation measures have failed to prevent gang-related murders, including the January 2009 killings of four juvenile detainees under the care of the Salvadoran Institute for the Integral Development of Children and Adolescents (*Instituto Salvadoreño para el Desarrollo Integral de la Niñez y la Adolescencia* or ISNA)[128] In fact, the government's segregation policy has played a pivotal role in the structural transformation of the *Mara 18* (M-18) and *Mara Salvatrucha* (MS-13 or MS) gangs from loose organizations centered around local cells (*clikas*) to more hierarchical frameworks capable of operating nationally by concentrating power in fewer leaders and establishing defined roles for different rungs of the gang hierarchy. Segregation policies have facilitated this transition by bringing together gang leaders and members from across the country and enabling a single gang to exercise near-total control over the day-to-day operations of individual detention centers.[129]

---

tion); interview with Astrid Torres, Jueza de Vigilancia Penitenciaria y de Ejecución de la Pena [Judge for Penitentiary Oversight and Sentencing], Departamento La Libertad, in San Salvador (Aug. 21, 2006) (stating that the policy of placing members of the same gang together in the same prison strengthens the gang).

[127] *See* AMNESTY INTERNATIONAL REPORT 2005: THE STATE OF THE WORLD'S HUMAN RIGHTS 99 (2005), *available at* http://web.amnesty.org/report2005/slv-summary-eng (covering events in El Salvador from January-December 2004, describing the August 2004 deaths of thirty-one prisoners in the La Esperanza prison "allegedly as a result of disputes among prisoners, some of them members of *maras.*" Amnesty International reported that in October, "two prison guards and one prisoner were charged with offences including homicide, attempted homicide, illegal association and allowing forbidden materials . . . to be brought into the prison.").

[128] Press Release, Oscar Humberto Luna, Procurador de Derechos Humanos de El Salvador [Human Rights Ombudsman, El Salvador], Pronunciamiento ante muerte de 4 jóvenes en Centros de Internamiento (Jan. 12, 2009), *available at* http://www.pddh.gob.sv/modules.ph p?name=News&file=article&sid=167.

[129] Jeannette Aguilar, *Diagnóstico de El Salvador, in* WASHINGTON OFFICE ON LATIN AMERICA (WOLA), TRANSNATIONAL YOUTH GANGS IN CENTRAL AMERICA, MEXICO AND THE UNITED STATES 5-6 (2007), *available at* http://www.wola.org/media/Gangs/diagnostico_salvador(1).pdf (used with the author's permission).

In early 2009, poor prison conditions led to massive peaceful demonstrations in eleven detention centers, where inmates refused to participate in everyday prison activities or to enter their cells to call attention to their deplorable living conditions.[130] In addition to prison overcrowding and poor conditions, reports of physical and mental abuses by prison officials are widespread.[131] These problems appear to be systemic and institutional, extending to juvenile detention centers, where at least fifty-nine deaths of detainees have been reported in the past four years.[132] Human rights abuses in prisons and the role of the penitentiary system in the Salvadoran government's response to gangs are discussed in greater detail in Chapter IV.

---

[130] Castillo, *supra* note 125; Enrique Carranza & D.González, *Protesta pacífica*, El Diario de Hoy, Feb. 16, 2009, *available at* http://www.elsalvador.com/mwedh/nota/nota_completa.asp?idCat=6358&idArt=3357182.

[131] Informe de Labores de la Procuraduría 05-06, *supra* note 102, at 188-89 (stating that conditions in Salvadoran prisons are deplorable, that prison authorities frequently employ solitary confinement, and that mistreatment of prisoners and visitors continues to form part of the day-to-day pattern of denunciations received by the Ombudsperson's Office); Procuraduría para la Defensa de los Derechos Humanos, Informe de Labores de la Procuraduría para la Defensa de los Derechos Humanos Junio 2007-Mayo 2008 [Office of the National Human Rights Ombudsperson, Report on the Work of the National Human Rights Ombudsperson, hereinafter Informe de Labores de la Procuraduría 07-08] 181,191-193 (2008) (stating that conditions of detention in some Salvadoran prisons are inhumane, and that inmates are often kept in solitary confinement); *see also* interview with Torres, *supra* note 126.

[132] *See* Informe Anual Justicia Juvenil 2004, *supra* note 123, at 49-50 (describing two deaths in juvenile detention centers, alongside other deficiencies); FESPAD, Actualidad-Políticas Públicas: Continúan Asesinatos de Jóvenes en Centros de Internamiento (Jan. 2009), *available at* http://fespad.org.sv/wordpress/wp-content/uploads/2009/01/actualidad29.pdf.; Luna, *supra* note 128.

Chapter III:
The Gang Phenomenon
in El Salvador

"It's like being in a war and being the only one without a weapon."

- J.R., a 30-year-old former gang member, referring to daily life for non-gang members, in San Salvador (August 21, 2006)

Gang-related and youth violence in El Salvador must be understood as a feature of the country's legacy of deep socio-economic inequalities, pervasive violence, and weak democratic and legal institutions, all of which are discussed generally in the two preceding chapters. The rapid growth in the power and prevalence of Salvadoran street gangs, whose initial ascendance in El Salvador in the 1990s resulted in part from major shifts in U.S. immigration laws during that decade, is both a consequence and a cause of the failures of the post-war government to establish the rule of law and provide citizen security in El Salvador.

Because gangs are very secretive, complex, and dynamic in their organization and because they have become such a politicized topic in El Salvador and abroad in recent years,[133] objective and reliable information about how they function is difficult to obtain. In El Salvador, our researchers interviewed dozens of current and former gang members, staff of government, church, and NGO agencies that work with gang members on a daily basis, and academic experts at the José Simeón Cañas Central American University (*Universidad Centroamerica "José Simeón Cañas"* or UCA), and other research centers that study the gang phenomenon. We have also reviewed extensive secondary source material on the issue. This chapter provides an overview of the emergence and evolution of the gang phenomenon in El Salvador over the past fifteen years, based on information that we have been able to confirm through interviews, on-the-ground research, and reliable accounts from secondary sources.

A. *The Emergence of Youth Gangs*

El Salvador's gang history can be traced partly to the 1970s and 1980s, when civil strife forced many families to flee the country and resettle in

---

[133] A recent USAID report on Central American gangs noted that "[t]he [Salvadoran] media has tended to over-exaggerate the problem of the gangs while not focusing on other important social issues. While the media bombards the public with news accounts of gangs involved in criminal activity, there is little analysis of the origins and proliferation of the gang phenomenon. Instead, gangs are often the scapegoat for all social ills, which limits the public's deeper understanding of gangs and other issues affecting the country." CENTRAL AMERICA AND MEXICO GANG ASSESSMENT, *supra* note 6, at 48.

U.S. cites, such as Los Angeles, where youth street gangs were already an established feature of urban life.[134]   As newcomers in ethnically divided urban areas in the United States, many displaced Salvadoran youth sought to integrate into existing gangs or form their own gangs for self-protection.[135]   Salvadoran youth gravitated in particular toward two gangs that became increasingly organized in U.S. cities in the 1990s: the M-18, composed mainly of Mexican-American youth and named after 18th Street in Los Angeles, and the MS-13, a gang formed by Salvadoran youth.[136]   Over time, these Central American immigrants were absorbed into the broader U.S. street gang culture.   In the meantime, youth gangs also existed in Central American cities, but they tended to be smaller, more diverse and tied to particular neighborhoods, without the regional presence or organization that U.S. gangs had begun to attain.[137]

In 1996, changes to U.S. immigration laws dramatically expanded the crime-related deportability grounds for non-citizens, including lawful permanent residents.[138]   These legislative changes, along with

---

[134] Interview with Oscar Bonilla, Presidente, Consejo Nacional para Seguridad Pública [President, National Council for Public Security], in San Salvador (Mar. 27, 2006).

[135] *See generally* José Miguel Cruz, *Los Factores asociados a las pandillas juveniles en Centroamérica*, 685-86 ECA: ESTUDIOS CENTROAMERICANOS 1155, 1156 (2005) (tracing the current gang phenomenon to the migration of Central Americans to the United States and their integration into U.S. street gangs, such as the M-18, as well as their formation of new gangs based on shared ethnic identity).

[136] *Id*; COMUNIDAD CRISTIANA MESOAMERICANA [Mesoamerican Christian Community], UNA APROXIMACIÓN AL FENOMENO DE LAS MARAS Y PANDILLAS EN CENTROAMÉRICA 101, 104 (2006).

[137] Cruz, *supra* note 135, at 1156 (noting the existence of a wide range of small gangs in Central American cities).   Cruz et al. emphasize that youth gangs became a problem in El Salvador before they became a problem in other countries in the region; at the beginning of the 1990s, according to these researchers, gangs had been established in the San Salvador metropolitan area. José Miguel Cruz, Marlon Carranza & María Santacruz Giralt, *El Salvador: Espacios públicos, confianza interpersonal y pandillas*, *in* MARAS Y PANDILLAS EN CENTROAMÉRICA: PANDILLAS Y CAPITAL SOCIAL Vol. II 81 (UCA eds., 2004).

[138] The changes to immigration laws were included in two major pieces of legislation passed in 1996: The Illegal Immigration Reform and Immigrant Responsibility Act, Pub. L. No. 104-208, 110 Stat. 3009-546 (1996) (codified in sections of 8 and 18 U.S.C.) and the Antiterrorism and Effective Death Penalty Act, Pub. L. No. 104-132, 110 Stat. 1214 (1996) (codified

others that restricted access to lawful status for non-citizens who had been in the United States unlawfully and restricted avenues for discretionary relief from removal,[139] resulted in the deportation of thousands of Salvadorans who had lived in the United States for many years (see Figure 3).[140] Some of those thousands were gang members, and their arrival in El Salvador served as a catalyst for the development of a U.S.-style gang culture there.[141]

The deported Salvadorans brought with them not only distinctive fashions and behaviors, but also the "process of violence" that they had been living in the United States—particularly the practice of staking out territory to defend against encroachment by rival gangs.[142] There is some evidence that the experience of having lived in the United States and having been associated with U.S. gangs gave deported gang members a certain stature among Salvadoran youth that permitted them to wield

---

in sections of 8, 18, 22, 28, 40, and 42 U.S.C.)). The provisions of these bills that most affected long-term Salvadoran residents of the United States were sections that expanded the scope of crime-related grounds that render lawful permanent residents removable (deportable).

[139] *See generally* Nancy Morawetz, *Understanding the Impact of the 1996 Deportation Laws and the Limited Scope of Proposed Reforms*, 113 Harv. L. Rev. 1936 (2000) (describing the "virtual elimination" of the ability of adjudicators under pre-1996 laws to conduct an assessment of the appropriateness of deportation).

[140] More than 74,000 Salvadorans were deported from the United States between 1998 and 2007. The number of deportees remained relatively stable between 1998 and 2003 (with a high of 5,561 deportees in 2003 and a low of 3,928 deportees in 2001), increased steadily between 2003 and 2006, escalating from 5,561 deportees in 2003 to 11,050 in 2006, and skyrocketed in 2007 when the U.S. government deported 20,045 individuals. Department of Homeland Security, Yearbook of Immigration Statistics 2007 Tbl. 37 Aliens Removed by Criminal Status and Country of Nationality Fiscal Years 1998-2007 (2008), *available at* http://www.dhs.gov/xlibrary/assets/statistics/yearbook/2007/ois_2007_yearbook.pdf.

[141] World Health Organization, World Report on Violence and Health 38 (2002) (linking these gang member deportations with the emergence of U.S.-modeled groups and rising youth violence in El Salvador); Central America and Mexico Gang Assessment, *supra* note 6, at 34.

[142] L. Santacruz Giralt & Alberto Concha-Eastman, Barrio Adentro: La Solidaridad Violenta de las Pandillas 13 (2001); Comunidad Cristiana Mesoamericana, *supra* note 136, at 104.

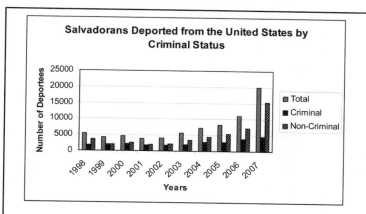

Figure 3. Salvadorans Deported from the United States by Criminal Status
Source: DEPARTMENT OF HOMELAND SECURITY, YEARBOOK OF IMMIGRATION STATISTICS 2007 Tbl. 37
Aliens Removed by Criminal Status and Country of Nationality Fiscal Years 1998-2007 (2008), *available at* http://www.dhs.gov/xlibrary/assets/statistics/yearbook/2007/ois_2007_yearbook.pdf.

particular influence and replicate U.S. gang structures in Salvadoran neighborhoods.[143]   At the very least, the deportation of gang members from the United States in the late 1990s helped trigger the rapid development of organized gang activity in El Salvador. Further, the U.S. government's continued deportation of Salvadoran gang members has served to strengthen the transnational presence of these gangs.[144]

Academic and non-governmental experts note, however, that the gang phenomenon is not simply a foreign problem imported by deportees from the United States, but rather has evolved and grown in

---

[143] Interview with Bonilla, *supra* note 134 (describing how deportees returning immediately after the war commanded a great deal of respect among Salvadoran youth in their neighborhoods, leading the local Salvadoran youth to adopt styles of clothing, music, and behavior that deportees had brought back from cities such as Los Angeles); interview with C.A., former gang member, in San Salvador (Mar. 30, 2006) (observing that Salvadoran youth give greater weight to the experience of deported gang members).

[144] *See* Robert J. Lopez, Rich Connell & Chris Kraul, *Gang Uses Deportation to Its Advantage to Flourish in U.S.*, LOS ANGELES TIMES, Nov. 1, 2005 (". . . a deportation policy aimed in part at breaking up a Los Angeles street gang has backfired and helped spread it across Central America and back into other parts of the United States.").

response to domestic factors and conditions.[145] The failure of the post-war Salvadoran government to address the structural causes of the civil war, to build effective democratic institutions, and to invest in social services meant that conditions on the ground in El Salvador were ripe for the spread of gang culture, especially in marginalized communities. In particular, relatively limited government expenditures on social services throughout the 1990s served to limit severely opportunities for youth to pursue decent and dignified lives in El Salvador.[146] Further, the Salvadoran government has pursued policies aimed at transforming its traditional dependence on the agricultural sector and promoting foreign investment and labor-intensive exports. These policies have led thousands to migrate to urban areas. Growth in the export sectors, however, has not kept pace with the displacement of rural populations who depended on agriculture for their survival. As a result, the Salvadoran economy has come to depend increasingly on remittances from abroad.[147] The World Bank estimates that approximately 17 percent of El Salvador's Gross Domestic Product (GDP) comes from remittances to family members by migrants working abroad. The flow of remittances to El Salvador has been negatively affected by the 2007 slowdown of the U.S. economy.[148] Global economic shocks in late 2008

---

[145] *See, e.g.,* interview with José Miguel Cruz, then Director of the Instituto Universitario de Opinión Pública [University Institute for the Study of Public Opinion, hereinafter IUDOP], in San Salvador (Mar. 31, 2006).

[146] CENTRAL AMERICA AND MEXICO GANG ASSESSMENT, *supra* note 6, at 44 ("The challenges facing youths in El Salvador are numerous and further exacerbated by a high level of income inequality . . . the majority of youths aged 14-25 years old face social exclusion characterized by the lack of basic services . . . that could improve their lives.").

[147] UNITED NATIONS DEVELOPMENT PROGRAM, HUMAN DEVELOPMENT REPORT: EL SALVADOR, A LOOK AT THE NEW 'U.S.': THE IMPACT OF MIGRATION, Part I: Overview at 20 (2005) [hereinafter UNDP Report 2005], *available at* http://www.desarrollohumano.org.sv/migraciones/idhes2005pdf/IDHES2005Overview.pdf ("For the past 15 years El Salvador has fostered a growth model aiming to overcome the country's high dependence on traditional agricultural exports, and turn the country into a platform for investment and labor-intensive exports. However, the country has become a service economy that grows at a slow pace and depends more and more on remittances to fund the growing level of imports.").

[148] THE WORLD BANK, REMITTANCES AND DEVELOPMENT: LESSONS FROM LATIN AMERICA 4 (Pablo Fajnzylber & J. Humberto López eds., 2008), *available at* http://siteresources.

and early 2009 seemed likely to intensify this negative trend.

A range of sources concur in assessing the situation facing impoverished teenagers and young adults in El Salvador as bleak.[149] This decline in remittance flow, coupled with a dearth in employment opportunities for urban youth, and limited access to social services leave poor, marginalized youth in post-war El Salvador with few options for the pursuit of a dignified life. Many international and domestic observers note that this lack of opportunities for young people has fueled the rise of the gang phenomenon.[150]

worldbank.org/INTLAC/Resources/Remittances_and_Development_Report.pdf. Report authors point out that the 2007 slowdown of the U.S. economy has had disastrous consequences for the flow of remittances to Latin America, which in 2007 grew only at an average rate of 6 percent, thirteen points lower than the annual average rate of 19 percent recorded between 2000 and 2006. Press Release, World Bank, U.S. Slowdown Affects Remittances in LAC. Washington, DC (April 8, 2008), *available at* http://web.worldbank.org/WBSITE/EX-TERNAL/COUNTRIES/LACEXT/0,,contentMDK:21719310~pagePK:146736~piPK:14683 0~theSitePK:258554,00.html. In a press release, the World Bank called upon policy makers in both donor and recipient countries to institute policies to facilitate remittance transfers. Failure to do so "could potentially impact the ability of poor recipient households to deal with negative economic shocks, such as the recent increases in food prices." Press Release, World Bank, WB Urges Governments, Private Sector to Facilitate Remittances (Apr. 8, 2008), *available at* http://web.worldbank.org/WBSITE/EXTERNAL/NEWS/0,,contentMDK: 21720688~pagePK:64257043~piPK:437376~theSitePK:4607,00.html.

[149] *See, e.g.,* THE LATIN AMERICAN AND CARIBBEAN DEMOGRAPHIC CENTRE (CELADE), YOUTH, POPULATION AND DEVELOPMENT IN LATIN AMERICA AND THE CARIBBEAN 5 (2000), *available at* http://www.eclac.org/publicaciones/xml/1/4771/lcg2084i.pdf ("Today, working-class urban youth suffer an unprecedented risk of social exclusion. From the market to the State and society, a confluence of forces tends to concentrate poverty among the young and to distance them from the 'central course' of the social system.").

[150] Interview with Mirna Antonieta Perla Jiménez, Magistrada de la Sala de lo Civil de la Corte Suprema de Justicia, Corte Suprema de Justicia de El Salvador [Justice of the Civil Chamber, Supreme Court of Justice of El Salvador], in San Salvador (Aug. 25, 2006) (describing a lack of opportunity for youth, among other social and political factors, as contributing to the growth of gangs in El Salvador); *see also* JOSÉ MIGUEL CRUZ, STREET GANGS IN CENTRAL AMERICA 26 (2007) ("[Y]oung people who join gangs, in general, are those whose families must struggle to survive and whose possibilities for a dignified life are limited by the level of education and type of job of their parents or primary caregivers"); RIBADO, *supra* note 5, at 2-3 (noting that extreme poverty, social inequality, "growing youth populations," and "high unemployment rates" are all frequently cited as factors contributing to the growth of gangs in Central America); *Gangs and Crime in Latin America: Hearing Before the Subcommittee on the Western Hemisphere of the Committee on International Relations,* 109th

In addition, generalized levels of violence in post-war Salvadoran society have remained extraordinarily high.[151]   Observers often cite a "culture of violence" in El Salvador as a central factor that has facilitated the rapid development of gangs in the country over the past decade.[152] The weaknesses of post-war criminal justice institutions, described in detail in Chapter II, have also contributed to the expansion of the gang phenomenon by failing to establish the rule of law or provide for citizen security in the country. The following chapter turns to the ways in which El Salvador's major gangs have evolved from small units under the control of local leaders to more complex and sophisticated national networks.

B.   *How Gangs Function Today: From Small, Independent* Clikas *to Sophisticated National Structures*

Current estimates of the total number of gang members in El Salvador vary widely, from approximately 10,500 (a PNC estimate) to 39,000 (a 2006 National Council for Public Security estimate).[153]   The two major gangs in El Salvador, the M-18 and the MS-13, engage in

---

Cong. 44 (2005) (statement of Stephen C. Johnson, Senior Policy Analyst for Latin America, The Kathryn and Shelby Cullom Davis Institute for International Studies).

[151] Interview with Jeanne Rikkers, Program Director, Christians for Peace in El Salvador [hereinafter CRISPAZ], in San Salvador (Aug. 21, 2006).

[152] Cruz, *supra* note 135, at 1165.

[153] Central America and Mexico Gang Assessment, *supra* note 6, at 45. These estimates may be inaccurate, however. The police raids following the passage of LAM I arrested 19,275 individuals, almost twice the number of the estimated 10,000 gang members in El Salvador. *Aplicación de la ley Combate a las pandillas: una Mano Dura y otra suave*, El Diario de Hoy, Sept. 28, 2005, *available at* http://www.elsalvador.com/noticias/2005/09/28/ nacional/nac21.asp. As the United Nations Office on Drugs and Crime points out, "it is unlikely the entire gang population of the country was arrested twice in that period." Even though the police likely arrested many who were not gang members, such a large discrepancy between estimated numbers of gang members and numbers of arrests suggests the actual gang population in El Salvador may be much larger. United Nations Office on Drugs and Crime (UNODC), Crime and Development in Central America (2007), *available at* http://www.unodc.org/pdf/Central%20America%20Study.pdf.

violent conflict in neighborhoods throughout the country. As noted above, both have U.S. roots[154] and were among several groups whose members—including top leaders—were deported to El Salvador in the 1990s.[155]

In the mid to late 1990s, there were a number of small, local gangs in El Salvador. In the past decade, however, the M-18 and the MS-13 have consolidated their power and established themselves as the two dominant gangs.[156] Both are characterized by their fluid, dynamic organization and complex, clandestine hierarchies, which makes it virtually impossible to present a complete picture of their structures and functioning. However, several fundamental features of the two gangs have become increasingly pronounced in recent years. Each of these features will be explored in greater depth below.

1. *Sophisticated Organizational Structure*

Once organic and territorially-bound, El Salvador's gangs have been developing more complex vertical structures, defined member roles, and consolidated chains of command.[157] The organizational structures of both the MS-13 and the M-18 involve local sub-groups within the gangs, or *clikas*, whose members typically include young people from a common neighborhood or sub-neighborhood. A 2002 police study

---

[154] Comunidad Cristiana Mesoamericana, *supra* note 136, at 104.

[155] Interview with Bonilla, *supra* note 134; interview with Rodrigo Ávila, Director, PNC, in San Salvador (Mar. 31, 2006).

[156] Interview with J.R., former gang member, in San Salvador (Aug. 21, 2006); interview with Alan Edward Hernández Portillo, Jefe Unidad Elite Anti-Extorsiones, Fiscalía General de la República [Chief of the Elite Anti-Extortion Unit, General Office of the Prosecutor], in San Salvador (Jan. 20, 2009).

[157] Interview with Jeannette Aguilar, Director, IUDOP, in San Salvador (Aug. 24, 2006); Jeannette Aguilar & Lissette Miranda, *Entre la articulación y la competencia: las respuestas de la sociedad civil organizada a las pandillas en El Salvador, in* Vol. IV Maras y Pandillas en Centroamérica: Las Respuestas de la Sociedad Civil Organizada 42 (José Miguel Cruz ed., 2006) (noting that the scale of gang operations now transcends individual streets and neighborhoods).

indicated that approximately 300 *clikas* were operating in El Salvador.[158] Until recently, local *clikas* worked relatively independently from each other to maintain territorial control over their neighborhood. Gang members were local residents whose sphere of influence did not extend past their geographically limited home turf. In the past several years, however, these *clikas* have become increasingly organized and effective at communicating and coordinating with one another. For example, former *clika* leader B.R. told our researchers that the four leaders of his fifty-member *clika* were in communication with leaders from other neighborhoods, and often held meetings with them. B.R. also explained that his *clika* held regular membership meetings in which gang members would discuss strategies for the defense of their neighborhood from rival gangs, collect any proceeds from extortion operations, and arrange for the purchase of weapons. According to B.R., these meetings also served to ensure that gang members paid a required membership fee. [159]

Expert Jeannette Aguilar explained to our researchers that the leadership roles within the hierarchy of each gang have become specific and defined, and that each gang increasingly operates according to internal rules and values.[160] In addition, each hierarchical position in current gang structures is assigned very specific tasks. Lower rungs in the hierarchy ("*soldados*," soldiers) patrol and defend the territory, while intermediate rungs ("*misioneros*," missionaries) are tasked with carrying out more important operations. Upper echelons include the so-called *palabreros* or *primera palabra* (heralds), and *segunderos* (second-in-command), who relay orders from gang leaders and ensure they are carried to completion. Above these are the gang leaders themselves (often called *ranfleros*). According to government sources and

---

[158] Aguilar & Miranda, *supra* note 157, at 48.

[159] Interview with B.R., in San Salvador (Oct. 22, 2008).

[160] Interview with Aguilar, *supra* note 157 (stating that gang organization has become more complex, coordinated, and vertically structured, with well-defined roles, clear internal hierarchies extending to the national level, and increasingly rigid systems of norms and values); Aguilar, *supra* note 129, at 5-6.

independent experts, gang members who were deported from the United States (*veteranos*, veterans) enjoy special status within the gang hierarchy. Because deportee gang members are often familiar with the more sophisticated investigative techniques employed by U.S. police, they are considered key consultants in the planning of gang operations, such as missions or the collection of extortion payments (*renta*).[161] A 2007 study of Central American gangs corroborates this vertical specialization within Salvadoran gang structures. The authors of the study found that, in local Salvadoran *clikas*, more than 40 percent of all gang members interviewed considered themselves "someone who obeys orders," 25 percent considered themselves "someone who both obeys and gives orders," and only 10 percent thought of themselves as "someone who gives orders."[162] This division of labor has increased gangs' ability to act in a coordinated manner, for example, enabling their members to carry out more complicated extortion operations.[163] Hierarchies permeate gang life. Thus, for example, B.R., a former *clika* leader, told our reserachers that they often used soldiers to stand guard outside residences where gang leaders drank alcohol and consumed drugs.[164]

Governmental staff interviewed for this report agreed that the MS-13 and M-18 have developed increasingly organized and hierarchical structures. The Office of the Prosecutor separates the development of Salvadoran gangs into four stages. In their initial stage, corresponding roughly to the years 1992-94, MS-13 and M-18 established themselves as the two dominant national gangs, organized loosely as individual *clikas* with control over discrete local territories and opportunistic engagement in criminal behavior. During the second or predatory stage, MS-13 and M-18 consolidated their national dominance by employing

---

[161] Interview with Hernández Portillo, *supra* note 156; DEMOSCOPÍA, S.A., MARAS, PANDILLAS, COMUNIDAD Y POLICÍA EN CENTROAMÉRICA 17, *available at* http://www.undp.org.gt/data/publicacion/Maras%20y%20pandillas,%20comunidad%20y%20polic%C3%ADa%20en%20centro%20am%C3%A9rica.pdf; Aguilar, *supra* note 129, at 5-6.

[162] DEMOSCOPÍA, S.A, *supra* note 161, at 18.

[163] Aguilar, *supra* note 129, at 5.

[164] Interview with B.R., *supra* note 159.

increasingly violent methods to control local territories—actively eliminating rival gang members, creating local extortion operations—and displaying higher levels of hierarchical organization. Gang activities, however, were still organized around maintaining control over local neighborhoods. This second stage, according to the Office of the Prosecutor, describes the organization of MS-13 and M-18 between the years 1995 and 2002. In the third or parasitic stage, MS-13 and M-18 increased their level of hierarchical organization, which allowed them to expand their operations to a broader geographic area. Gang activities were no longer organized around local neighborhood control. Rather, gangs developed strategic agendas to carry out illicit businesses, including drug-peddling and extortion. At this stage, the analysis continues, gangs began to interact with political actors to shield their operations from police scrutiny. According to Alan Edward Hernández Portillo, Chief Prosecutor for the Special Extortion Unit, the MS-13 and M-18 gangs entered stage three in the year 2003: "They now have a hierarchical structure with the ability to assign specific responsibilities to those members best positioned to carry them out. Distinct groups of individuals are tasked with intimidating others, with murder, with conducting drug sales."[165]

The Office of the Prosecutor and some international observers believe that Salvadoran gangs—and in particular the MS-13 gang—are now entering a fourth phase in which their organization resembles that of transnational crime syndicates, with deepening links to established structures of organized crime.[166] Although evidence of increased

---

[165] Interview with Hernández Portillo, *supra* note 156; *see also* John P. Sullivan, *Third Generation Street Gangs: Turf, Cartels and Net Warriors*, 13 CRIME & JUST. INT'L (1997). (Sullivan describes a similar framework for analyzing the gang phenomenon based on a three-generation concept. First generation gangs are street gangs whose activities center around defending their home turf; second generation gangs "assume a market rather than a turf orientation;" third generation gangs are sophisticated, "mercenary-type group[s].")

[166] Interview with Hernández Portillo, *supra* note 156; Gary I. Wilson & John P. Sullivan, On Gangs, Crime, and Terrorism, Special to Defense and the National Interest (Feb. 28, 2007), http://www.d-n i.net/fcs/pdf/wilson_sullivan_gangs_terrorism.pdf ("*Maras* as typified by MS-13 are a transnational gang phenomena that meet the third generation gang criteria of politicization, internationalization, and sophistication."); Ana Arana, *How the Street Gangs Took Central America*, FOREIGN AFF., May-June 2005, *available at* http://www. foreignaffairs.org/20050501faessay84310/ana-arana/how-the-street-gangs-took-central-

transnational activity does exist,[167] academics and NGOs interviewed for this report have questioned whether Salvadoran gangs have reached the level of sophistication required to orchestrate and coordinate large-scale criminal operations across borders on a systematic basis.[168] In

---

america.html ("Ultraviolent youth gangs, spawned in the ghettos of Los Angeles and other U.S. cities, have slowly migrated south to Central America, where they have transformed themselves into powerful, cross-border crime networks."); CELINDA FRANCO, CONGRESSIONAL RESEARCH SERVICE, CRS REPORT FOR CONGRESS, THE MS-13 AND 18TH STREET GANGS: EMERGING TRANSNATIONAL GANG THREATS? 5 (2008), *available at* http://fas.org/sgp/crs/row/RL34233.pdf (noting that some U.S. commentators consider MS-13 to have evolved into a highly sophisticated mercenary type organization "with goals of power or financial acquisition and a set of fully evolved political aims."). *But cf.* UNODC, *supra* note 153, at 65 (emphasizing that the characterization by U.S. commentators of youth gangs as "the new urban insurgency" is "dangerous . . . in a region known for brutal repression of insurgents, in a world where the lines between organised crime and terrorism is [sic] becoming increasingly blurred.").

[167] *See, e.g.,* Press Release, Department of Justice, MS-13 Leader Sentenced to Life in Prison (Sept. 24, 2007), *available at* http://www.usdoj.gov/criminal/gangunit/press/2007/sep/09-24-07ovasqez-sent.pdf (Evidence introduced at the trial of MS-13 *clika* leader Henry Zelaya showed that he had issued orders regarding gang operation from prison, including instructing an MS-13 member to contact another member in El Salvador. Witnesses also testified that co-defendant Omar Vásquez had been sent from El Salvador to operate all of the Maryland, Washington D.C., and Northern Virginia *clikas*.); Samuel Logan & Ashley Morse, *The Mara Salvatrucha Organization and the U.S. Response*, POWER & INT. NEWSREP., Jan. 31, 2007, *available at* http://www.pinr.com/report.php?ac=view_report&report_id=610&language_id=1 (describing several instances of direct communication between Central American and U.S. gang leaders).

[168] *See, e.g.,* UNODC, *supra* note 153, at 64 ("The maras are often referred to as 'transnational' in their character, as groups exist with the same name in different countries. Since some mareros are former deportees, it would be odd if there were not some communication between these groups. But the spectre of 'mega gangs', responding to a single command structure and involved in sophisticated trafficking operations, does not, at present, seem to have been realised, at least insofar as drug trafficking is concerned."); FRANCO, *supra* note 166, at 17 ("Whether the MS-13 and M-18 gangs pose a threat to the domestic security of the United States is not definitively known. Moreover, with the exception of established MS-13 and M-18 cliques in Central America and Mexico, it is not altogether clear whether these two gangs pose a transnational threat. It is noteworthy, however, that despite the transnational aspects of the MS-13 and M-18 gangs—they are criminally active in more than one country—in many respects, they are no different that other domestic street gangs."); interview with Jaime Martínez Ventura, Coordinador, Oficina de Justicia Juvenil, Corte Suprema de El Salvador [Coordinator, Office of Juvenile Justice, Supreme Court], in San Salvador (Oct. 23, 2008).

particular, experts emphasize the dearth of rigorous studies assessing the international reach of Salvadoran *clikas*,[169] and point out that both the police and the Office of the Prosecutor have a vested interest in portraying gangs as "the worst of the worst."[170] Indeed, crime statistics quoted by the government and the media often inflate the magnitude of gang-related violence.[171] For example, Salvadoran government authorities have consistently overemphasized the role of gangs in the country's rising homicide rates (often attributing up to 80 percent of all murders to gang activity),[172] even though reports from various other reliable sources question this disproportionate gang role in murders in El Salvador.[173] Similarly, though the link between gangs and international

---

[169] *See, e.g.*, interview with Salazar Flores, *supra* note 91 (noting that he does not know of any serious study in the past five years designed to understand the current features of the gang phenomenon and their social determinants); *see also*, UNODC, *supra* note 153, at 62 (noting that "[t]here is also reason to question the extent of the involvement of the maras in other forms of criminal activity [such as drug trafficking] for which they are frequently blamed." Study authors highlight two reasons why such links with organized crime are unlikely: "all indicators suggest that drug markets in the region are small, insufficient to be a major source of income to organised criminals," and "the importance of Central American trafficking networks to the United States market appears to be limited.").

[170] Interview with Jaime Martínez Ventura, *supra,* note 168; *see also* UNODC, *supra* note 153, at 64 ("young gang members may have become a convenient scapegoat on which to blame the country's rising crime rates, when they may be minor players in countries with much endemic violence and sophisticated organised crime operations that operate with impunity due to law enforcement corruption.").

[171] *See, e.g.*, Raúl Gutiérrez, *Gangs Are 'Perfect Scapegoats', Say Experts*, INTER PRESS SERV. NEWS AGENCY, Apr. 25, 2008, *available at* http://ipsnews.net/print.asp?idnews=42129 (citing opinion of expert Jeannette Aguilar who told the press that the Salvadoran government had turned gangs into "their 'perfect scapegoats' by identifying them as the main culprits and overlooking the activities of organized crime and drug traffickers."); *see also* interview with Aguilar, *supra* note 157 (according to Aguilar, government statistics were inflated and the percentage of crimes attributable to *maras* in 2006 was no higher than 30 percent).

[172] Interview with Ávila, *supra* note 155 ("More than 80 percent of all murders in El Salvador are linked to gang violence."); *see also El Salvador Unites Law Effort with U.S. Police*, ORG. CRIME DIG., Oct. 14, 2004, *available at* http://findarticles.com/p/articles/mi_qa4441/is_200410/ai_n16065846 (Police Chief Ricardo Menesses-Orellana told the press that "police have linked gangs to about 80 percent of the murders in El Salvador.").

[173] UNODC, *supra* note 153 , at 45 ("While youth gangs do represent a source of criminality, they do not appear to be responsible for a particularly disproportionate share of the mur-

drug trafficking is tenuous,[174] Salvadoran state authorities may well be interested in emphasizing the transnational nature of the gangs, as well as their connection to organized crime, as a means of obtaining international support for their criminal justice initiatives. In fact, the Salvadoran government has frequently emphasized that gangs are a transnational problem posing a regional security threat and has called for a regional alliance to address the problem.[175] The U.S. government has supported El Salvador's call for regional cooperation by establishing the Mérida Initiative—an anti-crime and counter-drug aid package for Mexico and Central America which in 2008 earmarked $13 million for direct anti-gang efforts in the region.[176]

A research initiative that investigated whether gangs operate as a transnational network indicated that communications between

---

ders in the countries where they predominate."). Data provided by the Director of Research of the National Institute of Forensic Medicine, Dr. Fabio Molina Vaquerano, reveal that, in 2006, the Institute of Forensic Medicine attributed only 15 percent of homicides in the country to gangs. Interview with Fabio Molina Vaquerano, Jefe de la Unidad de Estadísticas Forenses, Instituto de Medicina Legal [Research Director of the National Institute of Forensic Medicine], in San Salvador (Aug. 29, 2006); Tutela Legal annual reports attributed 24.46 percent of all homicides investigated in 2006 and 28.4 percent of all homicides investigated in 2007 to gang violence. Tutela Legal, Informe Anual de Tutela Legal del Arzobispado de San Salvador: La Situación de los Derechos Humanos en El Salvador 2007 18 (2007) [hereinafter La Situación de los Derechos Humanos en El Salvador 2007]; Tutela Legal, Informe Anual de Tutela Legal del Arzobispado de San Salvador: La Situación de los Derechos Humanos en El Salvador 2006 16 (2006) [hereinafter La Situación de los Derechos Humanos en El Salvador 2006].

[174] *See, e.g.,* UNODC, *supra* note 153, at 62.

[175] For example, at a 2005 meeting on transnational gangs convened by the Organization of American States, President Saca urged U.S., Mexican, and Central American authorities to forge a regional alliance to fight gang-related crime, emphasizing that "maras have become a regional problem." *Diez gobiernos se unen contra las maras transnacinales,* La Nación, June 28, 2005, *available at* http://www.conace.gov.cl/inicio/noticias2.php?id=1564&noticias=1&sec=1. Similarly, at the 2008 Fourth International Anti-Gang Conference, which brought together government officials from Central America, Puerto Rico, Mexico and the United States, Director of the PNC, Francisco Rovira, emphasized that "the gangs have brought sorrow and mourning and have forged ties with organized crime." Gutiérrez, *supra* note 171.

[176] Ribado, *supra* note 5, at 1.

Salvadoran gang members and their counterparts outside El Salvador take place in an informal, unsystematic fashion. The authors concluded that: "though we have documented several instances of cooperation, there is no evidence of an institutional and systematic relationship among gang structures that operate in different countries, and even less so of an international network that conducts regional operations throughout the Meso-American corridor." [177]   Even so, the report's authors warn that gangs' increased organizational sophistication and international presence may lay the groundwork for alliances with established international mafias and organized crime syndicates in the near future. The relationship between gangs and organized crime is explored in more detail in Chapter V.

Although horizontal coordination among Salvadoran *clikas* and vertical coordination with *clikas* operating abroad may be fragmented and informal, our researchers have uncovered reliable evidence that international contacts can be deployed when cooperation is needed for specific tasks, such as seeking revenge against particular individuals or eliminating members who have betrayed the gang and fled the country. For example, Henry Fino, a human rights expert at the Human Rights Institute of "José Simeón Cañas" Central American University (*Instituto de los Derechos Humanos de la Universidad Centroaméricana "José Simeón Cañas"* or IDHUCA) told our researchers that gang members were able to target a schoolbus driver who had fled to Honduras. IDHUCA had helped these gang members file a case against the bus driver, who had sexually abused them as children. The bus driver was found guilty, but the sentencing court did not impose a prison term. Although IDHUCA staff who followed the case were unable to obtain information regarding the driver's whereabouts upon his release from custody, they received an anonymous phone call letting them know that the bus driver had been murdered in Honduras. Fino believes it is extremely likely that *clikas* in El Salvador in coordination with their counterparts in Honduras were able to track down and murder the sex offender to avenge the abuse against their members. [178]   Similarly,

---

[177] Aguilar, *supra* note 129, at 30.

[178] Interview with Henry Fino, Abogado, IDHUCA [IDHUCA staff attorney], in San Salva-

Assistant Police Inspector José Arturo Amaya Márquez, who works in crime prevention in the city of Santa Tecla, told our researchers: "The MS-13 gang has the ability to track down those individuals who attempt to leave the gang both in El Salvador and abroad. The *clikas* control their territory and are also in communication with the *clikas* in the United States."[179] Gangs' ability to target people in other countries is a function of several factors, including the degree of cooperation between and among Salvadoran and foreign *clikas* and the capacity of law enforcement personnel in those countries. Thus, it is far more likely that gangs will be able to target and kill individuals with impunity in Honduras and other Central American states than they will in countries with much greater law enforcement capacity, such as the United States and Canada.

In spite of their strengthened leadership and organizational structure, gangs have still proven to be flexible and dynamic. According to researchers Jeannette Aguilar and Lissette Miranda of the Institute for Public Opinion Research (*Instituto Universitario de Opinión Pública* or IUDOP), the arrest of *clika* leaders has actually resulted in a broadening and diversifying of their leadership, as new leaders quickly assume the responsibilities of those taken into custody.[180]   In fact, most experts attribute the organizational evolution and consolidation of the two major gangs largely to the Salvadoran government's law enforcement crackdowns of the past several years.[181]   Specifically, the *Mano Dura* and

---

dor (Oct. 23, 2008).

[179] Interview with José Arturo Amaya Márquez, Subinspector, Área de Prevención, Departamento de La Libertad [Assistant Police Inspector, Crime Prevention Unit, La Libertad Department], in Santa Tecla (Oct. 22, 2008).

[180] Aguilar & Miranda, *supra* note 157, at 43. Jeannette Aguilar has participated in several large-scale studies of the gang phenomenon, including a recent longitudinal study involving hundreds of interviews with gang members, as well as research (conducted jointly with Miranda) drawing upon interviews with a wide range of NGO and government officials who work with gang members. The latter study has led to the publication of four volumes of analysis.

[181] Aguilar & Miranda, *supra* note 157, at 42, 44 (citing these programs' particular effect of concentrating gang leaders together in prisons, from which they transmit orders to *clika* leaders in various communities); see further discussion of the *Mano Dura* measures in

Súper Mano Dura (Super Firm Hand) anti-gang policies (discussed in Chapter IV) have catalyzed the development of more sophisticated organizational structures within Salvadoran gangs. These policies, for instance, have led to the arrest and detention of high-level gang leaders (as well as many other gang members) and to efforts to segregate the resultant high number of prisoners by gang affiliation. In practice, they have resulted in the extended concentration of gang leaders in single locations, providing them the opportunity to strengthen their organizations.[182] Special prosecutor Alan Edward Hernández Portillo told our researchers that leaders direct much of their gangs' day-to-day operations from detention centers:

> [R]anfleros give instructions to the *palabreros* who in turn relay them to *clika* leaders so that they can give their soldiers precise instructions regarding the collection of extortion money. Moreover, inside every detention center there is a gang member who is in charge of the "money box." This individual is in direct contact with those who execute the extortions, be it via cell phone, or through those who visit the detention center, or through *willas*—which are documents that contain written instructions signed by gang leaders.[183]

Police crackdowns have also led to the adoption of more clandestine practices within the two major gangs. Until recently, gang members communicated their gang association through visual images—a particular style of clothing and hair, tattoos, etc.—and through strong

---

Chapter IV.

[182] Aguilar & Miranda, *supra* note 157, at 44. Even while the senior members of the gang hierarchy become increasingly sophisticated, however, our researchers were told that the "foot soldiers" of gangs—youth in marginalized neighborhoods who have been recruited or coerced into some form of gang association—continue to face poverty and risk in their neighborhoods, without access to the wealth generated by the upper echelon's illicit activities. Interview with Aguilar, *supra* note 157.

[183] Interview with Hernández Portillo, *supra* note 156.

territorial associations. However, in response to the *Mano Dura* plan and subsequent anti-gang crackdowns that rely on police profiling based, for instance, on tattoos, gangs have shifted tactics, seeking to avoid visibility and gang identification. Behaviors such as walking together in groups and remaining tied to a particular area have changed significantly, as individual gang members and *clikas* have become increasingly mobile and capable of uprooting and reinserting themselves within El Salvador or even in Mexico or the United States.[184] Gang experts similarly point to mandated alterations in gang members' appearance, a strategy adopted to conceal members' once easily-discernible identity from law enforcement officials, as a tactical response to the government's anti-gang efforts. For example, many gang members no longer keep their hair in the once-characteristic, short-trimmed *rapado* style.[185] Likewise, many now wear ordinary clothing—"like any normal kid."[186] Researchers and NGO workers in El Salvador told us that gangs no longer encourage new members to mark themselves with tattoos, and that in some cases they may even forbid the practice.[187] Far from being weakened by the campaigns against them, El Salvador's gangs "[e]very day become more specialized, more organized,"[188] and more adept at "going unnoticed."[189]

---

[184] Interview with Aguilar, *supra* note 157; interview with B.F., staff of a youth center, outside San Salvador (Aug. 22, 2006); *see also* Aguilar & Miranda, *supra* note 157, at 49 (reporting that gangs have increased in mobility in response to state anti-gang initiatives, an adaptation that includes the emigration of some gang members to Mexico and the United States).

[185] Aguilar & Miranda, *supra* note 157, at 43.

[186] Interview with B.F., *supra* note 184; interview with Jeannette Aguilar, *supra* note 157.

[187] Interview with Aguilar, *supra* note 157; interview with Martínez Ventura, *supra* note 117. Our researchers also interviewed several younger active gang members—ages 16-17—who did not have tattoos, in marked contrast to their older counterparts.

[188] Interview with B.F., *supra* note 184.

[189] Aguilar & Miranda, *supra* note 157, at 43.

2. *Power*

In the 1990s, both of the major Salvadoran gangs concentrated on consolidating their territorial presence and power, allowing them in effect, to eliminate smaller rival gangs.   In the past six to seven years, however, the aims of gangs have been transformed.[190]   Whereas Salvadoran gangs once primarily constituted a space for young people to socialize and engage in local-level delinquency, they have become more sophisticated organizations seeking wealth and power at, and perhaps beyond, the national level. According to a 2006 research report by the UCA:[191]

> The motives for joining and staying active in the gang, as reported by young members, are no longer primarily symbolic ones, such as solidarity, friendship, or feelings of belonging and group identity that in the past appeared as the principal attractions for joining those groups. Now, the principal motivations are the benefits that they can obtain, like access to . . . economic resources, [and] to power.[192]

One illustration of this new dynamic is the increasingly widespread practice of extorting businesses and individuals, commonly referred to as "collecting *renta*."[193] While gangs have engaged in asking for money

---

[190] *See* Cruz, *supra* note 137, at 1157 (stating that since roughly the year 2000, the main goal of the gangs has evolved away from solidarity and mutual support for members, and toward greater involvement in drug trafficking and violent activities).

[191] COMUNIDAD CRISTIANA MESOAMERICANA, *supra* note 136, at 103; SANTACRUZ GIRALT & CONCHA-EASTMAN, *supra* note 142, at 26.

[192] Aguilar & Miranda, *supra* note 157, at 41; *see also* SANTACRUZ GIRALT & CONCHA-EAST-MAN, *supra* note 142, at 112-113 (noting that the reasons why individuals join gangs have changed from seeking emotional support and camaraderie to seeking financial gain, access to drugs and power).

[193] FLASCO-UNICEF, *Una Agenda por la Niñez, la Adolescencia y la Juventud*, 22 (Feb. 26, 2004) (prepared by Carlos Ramos and Antonieta Beltrán).

on the streets for years, the phenomenon of organized extortion is relatively new and has become a notable problem only during the last seven years.[194] Such extortion has been a particular problem in the transportation sector.[195] One former gang member told our researchers, for example, about one such system of charging bus operators a daily fee of $1 per vehicle: "We would charge the owners or the drivers."[196] His gang also exacted *renta* from others in its territory: "We would charge stores and taxi drivers a dollar a day. Every day."[197] Other sources, including bus owners, their associations, and attorneys, corroborate this practice, which appears structured, mandated, and overseen by gang leadership.[198] A female gang member told us that her gang targeted area stores in particular for collecting *renta*.[199] Our researchers in El Salvador also spoke to residents of various neighborhoods who told us that their families were charged *renta* simply because they happened to live in a sub-neighborhood controlled by a particular *clika*.[200]

---

[194] Interview with Martínez Ventura, *supra* note 117; Aguilar & Miranda, *supra* note 157, at 50-51 ("Demanding attention over recent years have been crimes of extortion that the *clikas* in various sectors are committing against vehicles transporting merchandise, small businesses, prostitutes, and transportation providers.").

[195] *See* Francisco Mejía, *Extorsión en San Miguel, Soyapango y San Salvador*, EL DIARIO DE HOY, Oct. 2, 2006 (describing extortions as an increasingly common phenomenon in El Salvador, particularly in the transportation sector. The article also quoted police sources as saying that in less than one month, the police had received 987 complaints of extortions nationwide though a police sub-director estimated that only about 5 percent of extortions are reported to police because victims are so afraid of retaliation).

[196] Interview with D.M., former gang member, in San Salvador (Aug. 21, 2006).

[197] *Id.*

[198] Interview with Aguilar, *supra* note 157 ("Gang members must pay daily or weekly dues to the gang. Greater structure of the gangs has facilitated this. Some are charged with gathering funds, and those that do not pay their part 'get the bill' (they are threatened and even killed). There is control over the members.").

[199] Interview with A.V., gang member, in Ilobasco (Aug. 23, 2006).

[200] Interview with F.R., outside San Salvador (Aug. 31, 2006); interview with T.C., in Ilobasco (Aug. 25, 2006).

To escape police detection, gangs have relied increasingly on members of the community to collect extortion money. For example, Carlos Manuel Quintanilla, a defense attorney, told our researchers that he had tried several cases in which gangs had pressured community members to collect their rent money. In one such case, a 69-year-old bus dispatcher had been forced to collect extortion money under threat of retaliation against his family. Quintanilla emphasized: "[The] dispatcher's mother and sons heard gang leaders tell the dispatcher over the phone that if he did not want to collaborate with the gang they would kill his mother, his children, his entire family. Gang leaders know where the dispatcher lives, where he works, where his children go to school, the places they visit on their days off. They can exert enormous psychological pressure on their victims."[201] Father Domingo Solís Rodríguez told us a similar story: a woman in his congregation had come to him for advice because her son had been receiving phone calls from a detention center asking him and three others to collect extortion money on behalf of the gang. The callers had threatened to kill the woman's son if he refused to comply with their demands.[202]

One of the most frightening features of the gangs' recent extortion practices is their enhanced capacity to fulfill their death threats against those who do not comply with their demands. In 2005, for example, more than two thousand non-public transportation operators reported being subjected to extortion, and over one hundred were killed that year.[203] Community members who refuse to collect extortion money have also been targeted. For example, Aída Luz Santos de Escobar, a judge in the juvenile courts in San Salvador, told our researchers that she had dealt with many cases in which gangs had murdered non-gang members who had refused to continue collecting money on behalf of

---

[201] Interview with Carlos Manuel Quintanilla, abogado penalista y criminólogo [criminal defense attorney], in San Salvador (Oct. 23, 2008).

[202] Interview with Domingo Solís Rodríguez, Párroco de la Parroquia Reina de La Paz en San Bartolo [Parish Priest in the Reina de La Paz Parish in San Bartolo], in San Bartolo (Oct. 21, 2008).

[203] IDHUCA, Balance de los Derechos Humanos del 2005 8 (2006).

the gang. In one case, fourteen youths had been accused of extortion. The sentencing judge found that five of them were gang leaders who had coerced the remaining nine non-gang members to collect extortion money. Only these five gang leaders were mandated to serve time in prison. The remaining nine were released, but remained under the court's supervision. Unfortunately, gang members continued to coerce Balmore Agustín Paz Castillo—one of the nine who had been released—to collect extortion money. According to Aída Luz Santos de Escobar, the judge in charge of supervising Paz Castillo's compliance with the court's terms of release, "when he refused, they invited him to play a soccer game, ambushed him, cut off his tongue, gouged out his eyes, and killed him."[204] Paz Castillo died on September 7, 2008, of multiple gunshot wounds to the head and limbs.[205]

In short, gangs' systematic and sophisticated efforts to increase their wealth and power have become not only increasingly common in the past several years, but also increasingly aggressive.

3. *Violence*

As the gangs' animating values have shifted, and their leadership structures have become more consolidated, several defining aspects of gang activity have taken on a markedly more violent character. As discussed below, many sources with whom our researchers spoke in El Salvador report that in recent years, the violence associated with entry into gang membership, day-to-day gang life, efforts to leave that life behind, and failure to comply with the group's demands, has grown much more severe.[206] Further, female gang members and women loosely

---

[204] Interview with Aída Luz Santos de Escobar, Jueza Primera de Ejecución de Medidas al Menor de San Salvador [San Salvador Juvenile Sentencing Judge], in San Salvador (Oct. 22, 2008).

[205] Death certificate No. 54016, Libro [Book] No. 1, Folio [Folder] No. 324, September 19, 2008, Balmore Agustín Paz Castillo, issued by the Family Registry of the Republic of El Salvador, Municipality of Ciudad Delgado (on file with authors).

[206] While there has undoubtedly been an intensification in the violence employed by gangs in El Salvador in recent years, resulting in a concomitant rise in homicides in which gang members are either victims or perpetrators, reliable statistics regarding the percentage of

associated with gangs have been subject to physical abuse by male gang members with alarming frequency.

a) *Entry into the Gang*

Young people in certain regions of El Salvador increasingly find themselves coerced into some form of association with a gang. Indeed, resisting such association often means being targeted for physical abuse or death.[207]   Our researchers heard this assessment from young people themselves, as well as from staff of organizations that work with at-risk youth. Matthew Eisen, a Catholic community worker who had worked in an urban area on the outskirts of San Salvador for more than a decade, told our researchers: "Many [young people] do not want to be involved at all [in gangs], but have to in order to survive. There are youth in this country who simply have no choice . . . This is something that the police, churches, NGOs have found nothing to do about. It happens at 9 p.m., when [these other institutions] are not there."[208]   An NGO coordinator who works with youth in a different marginalized community on the outskirts of San Salvador likewise told our research team: "People join gangs because they are forced to. In the past, youth had the luxury of joining voluntarily."[209]   Judge Aída Luz de Escobar added, "A youth who refuses to join a gang will likely be killed. This is what I have observed in most of the cases I have dealt with. Gang members are increasingly

---

total violence in El Salvador that is gang-related are difficult to obtain. Aguilar & Miranda, *supra* note 157, note discrepancies in police estimates of the percentage of homicides for which gang members are responsible, stating in particular that available statistics do not support the PNC's assertion at the time that 60 percent of El Salvador's intentional deaths were gang killings. Similarly, a 2007 report by the U.N. Office on Drugs and Crime remarks that there is no clear evidence to support the government's assertion that 60 percent of all murders are carried out by *maras*. UNODC, *supra* note 153, at 61.

[207] Interview with T.C., *supra* note 200; interview with D.M., *supra* note 196.

[208] Interview with Matthew Eisen, human rights activist and former youth organizer, in San Salvador (Mar. 30, 2006).

[209] Interview with Tim McConville, Coordinator of Equipo Nahual [Team Nahual Coordinator], in Ilopango (Aug. 24, 2006).

resorting to aggressive recruitment tactics, because imprisonment or death have thinned their ranks. And when gangs recruit new members, joining their *clika* is not voluntary."[210] Former 22-year-old gang member J.T. confirmed that recruitment efforts have intensified as a response to increased incarceration rates: "When there are only a few gang members left in a *clika*, the gang's own internal code of conduct mandates that whoever is left has to go out and recruit new members."[211]

Even when resisting recruitment efforts does not involve physical abuse or death, the confluence of extreme poverty, lack of a family support structure, targeting by rival gangs (who will often impute membership to a rival *clika* to any youth who resides in the territory under that *clika*'s control), and targeting by police forces often leave youth with little option but to join the gang. For example, José Miguel Cruz, former Director of the Institute for Public Opinion Research, emphasized that youth who live in an area dominated by a gang "may be harassed, or physically assaulted. They are left with no other option but to join the gang."[212] Howard Augusto Cotto Castaneda, Police Commissioner in the La Paz District, explained: "I am convinced that youth are coerced to join gangs. Pressure to join gangs is also dictated by less-visible factors: what can we expect from youth living in conditions of extreme poverty and marginalization, with little or no access to education and recreation? What can we expect when youth are faced with a gang that will be hostile to them if they don't join, but will grant them access to resources to support their family, and to power, if they do join it? Gangs are a survival strategy."[213]

Frequently the initial association between young people and a local gang occurs informally and does not rise to the level of full "membership." Gang members ask—often with an express or implicit threat of

---

[210] Interview with Santos de Escobar, *supra* note 204.

[211] Interview with J.T., former gang member, in Mejicanos (Jan. 21, 2009).

[212] Interview with Cruz, *supra* note 145.

[213] Interview with Howard Augusto Cotto Castaneda, Jefe de la Delegación de La Paz, PNC [Chief of the La Paz Police Unit], in Santa Tecla (Oct. 22, 2008).

violence—that neighborhood children and youth do "favors" for them, such as giving them small amounts of money[214] or running errands.[215] Gangs may initially convince individuals targeted for recruitment to "hang out" with them by offering cell phones or expensive sports shoes. According to former gang member J.T., these youths who are informally connected to the gang but have not yet undergone initiation rites are already considered part of the gang structure. And there can be grave repercussions for those who decide to sever these ties: "When you start hanging out with a gang member, the gang already considers you part of their structure, you are like their brother, initiation rites serve only to consolidate that bond."[216] Soon after such informal links are established, new recruits are often asked to collect extortion money or to attack or kill specific individuals. It is also increasingly common for gangs to charge *renta* to their own members, including those still not initiated, as a form of membership fee. Uninitiated members who refuse to carry out these tasks, who do not pay the *renta,* or who decide to leave the gang may be beaten or killed.

Experts and community workers also told our researchers that gangs were approaching increasingly younger children.[217] Researcher and IUDOP Director Jeannette Aguilar told our team that her research had uncovered evidence that gangs were targeting children as young as eight or nine years-old for recruitment.[218] Further, a longitudinal study revealed that a much larger percentage of gang members expressed their desire to remain active in the gang in 2001 than in 1996 (57.2 and 14 percent, respectively). The authors of the study concluded: "A preliminary assessment suggests that young males are less likely to abandon the most violent practices of the gang lifestyle."[219]

---

[214] Interview with E.R.M., in Ilobasco (Aug. 25, 2006).

[215] Interview with Aguilar, *supra* note 157.

[216] Interview with J.T., *supra* note 211.

[217] Interview with Rikkers, *supra* note 151.

[218] Interview with Aguilar, *supra* note 157.

[219] Santacruz Giralt & Concha-Eastman, *supra,* note 142, at 71-72.

If this is the case, the recruitment of increasingly young members may increase the intensity and frequency of violent gang practices. Likewise, the coming of age of an entire generation of children of gang members—who grew up with gang members as role models—is likely both to perpetuate and exacerbate levels of gang violence. For example, Lisette Miranda, the National Director of the Pro-Youth Program (*Proyecto Pro-Jóvenes*), told our research team that the young children with whom she works aspire to be gang members just like their parents. They can often be seen, she told our research team, making gang hand gestures similar to those used by gang members.[220] Similarly, Police Commissioner Howard Augusto Cotto Castaneda emphasized that by 2010, a large group of children of gang members will have the necessary physical maturity to become active gang members. "We will have to deal with a new phenomenon in which new members will unquestioningly accept the gang lifestyle because their parents were gang members."[221] Cotto Castaneda added that teachers have often told him about the high levels of violence that children of gang members display in school, that includes beating and threatening their classmates with death. Nevertheless, schoolteachers feel powerless to address this issue, as their own lives have been threatened by gang members whose children they have attempted to discipline.[222]

Consistent with the trend toward increased levels of violence within gang culture generally, the initiation rites associated with becoming a full-fledged member of one of the two major gangs have become much more extreme in recent years.[223] Until recently, the typical methods of welcoming new members into the gang involved gang sexual exploitation of female recruits (sometimes alternatives were offered), and beatings

---

[220] Gang members use hand gestures to communicate membership to a particular gang, and thus to a particular territory or neighborhood, in a practice called *rifar el barrio*, or auctioning the neighborhood. Interview with Lissette Miranda, Directora Nacional del Proyecto Pro-Jóvenes [National Director of the Pro-Youth Program], in San Salvador (Jan. 20, 2009).

[221] Interview with Cotto Castaneda, *supra* note 213.

[222] *Id.*

[223] Interview with Aguilar, *supra* note 157.

within certain set parameters for males. Our team's on-site research—in particular, extensive conversations with those who have witnessed or themselves undergone these rites—revealed the prevalence and violence of such events.[224] Our team also documented a recent shift toward still more violent entrance requirements that involve sending new recruits on "missions" (*misiones*) to kill rival gang members or others. For example, K.T., a 19-year-old gang member detained in a juvenile detention center when we spoke with her in August 2006, told our researchers that when she joined the gang, she went with several other members on a mission to kill a taxi driver who was supposedly a member of the rival gang.[225] Likewise, J.T. told our research team in 2009 that one of the options available to recruits who decided to join his *clika* was to kill three rival gang members.[226]

Rosa Anaya Perla, a Salvadoran human rights activist who has worked with youth in prisons for years, told our researchers that while myths about violent gang initiation were exaggerated for many years by the media, reports of brutal entrance rites are increasingly true today. In particular, she confirmed that beatings lasting either thirteen seconds (for MS-13 recruits) or eighteen seconds (for M-18 recruits) had become a standard feature of gang initiation by 2006 and even earlier.[227] Other sources who work with young people involved in gangs

---

[224] Interview with A.V., *supra* note 199 ("My initiation was four gang members beating me for eighteen seconds. They beat me hard, mostly on my back and my legs, but I wasn't severely injured. I wasn't given any other option for initiation."); interview with L.A., female gang member, in Ilobasco (Aug. 23, 2006). A.V. and L.A.'s accounts are consistent with the description that sociologist Lorena Cuerno Clavel gave our team of the differences between the M-18's and the MS-13's entrance requirements. Specifically, Clavel reported that initiation into the M-18 involved beatings lasting 18 seconds (regardless of gender) and that the MS-13 allowed female recruits to choose between being beaten and having sexual relations with members of the gang. Interview with Lorena Cuerno Clavel, Social Anthropologist, in San Salvador (Mar. 29, 2006).

[225] Interview with A.V., *supra* note 199.

[226] Interview with J.T., *supra* note 211.

[227] Interview with Rosa Anaya Perla, human rights activist and former youth organizer, in San Salvador (Mar. 29, 2006); *see also* SANTACRUZ GIRALT & CONCHA-EASTMAN, *supra* note 142, at 37 (stating that many aspects of gang initiation that formerly were exaggerated in popular accounts are true today, and that "[a]ny male that wants to be part of a gang

told our researchers that the notorious practice of the "train" ("*tren*"), in which female recruits are forced to have sex successively with several gang members as a means of initiation, had also become a routine part of a young woman's transition to full-fledged gang membership.[228] C.A., once a member of MS-13, explained that "when a girl wanted to be part of the gang, she would have sex with all the members of the *clika*. She had one other option: either she would be forced to have sex with them or she would be beaten by the other girls."[229] The "train" can be a physically devastating ritual. Olga Isabel Morales, a nurse with the Goodbye Tattoos (*Adiós Tatuajes*) program in Mejicanos, El Salvador, recounted an incident described to her by two young female gang members: "[T]here was one gang rape as a rite of initiation in which the victim had been left bloody and nearly unconscious. She was taken to the hospital but it was hard to get any help."[230] While in El Salvador, our team spoke with several gang members who confirmed from their personal experience the veracity of these accounts of gang initiation practices.

b) *Gang Life and Barriers to Leaving the Gang*

Just as the practices associated with entrance into a gang have become more violent in recent years, so too have the lives of young people currently active in gangs as well as those seeking to leave gang life (or "calm down").[231] Numerous sources with whom we spoke in El

---

must submit himself to a 'ceremony,' involving a beating that lasts either 13 or 18 seconds, depending on the rule of the gang he is entering.").

[228] Interview with Anaya, *supra* note 227; *see also* interview with Eisen, *supra* note 208 ("[Males] get beaten severely, [while] girls have the option of getting beaten or sleeping with various gang members.").

[229] Interview with C.A., *supra* note 143.

[230] Interview with Olga Isabel Morales, Administradora, Programa Adiós Tatuajes, Clínica Octavio Ortíz [Administrator, Goodbye Tattoos Program, Octavio Ortiz Health Clinic], in San Salvador (Aug. 25, 2006).

[231] Many of the current and former gang members interviewed by our researchers used the term *calmarse* (literally, "to calm down") to refer to the process of withdrawing from active

Salvador referred to the conflict between the MS-13 and the M-18 as a war in which members of each side were obligated by internal codes to kill anyone thought to belong to the enemy.[232]   Once a young person is considered to be affiliated with a gang—regardless of whether or not he has actually become a member—he is "marked" by the other gang as a target for life.[233]   Indeed, our researchers spoke with young people who were not members of any gang, but whose simple residence in a neighborhood controlled by one gang rendered them targets for violence by the opposing gang.[234]   In practice, this war mentality and the accompanying intense fighting mean that inter-gang violence and killings are a daily part of gang life.[235]   The ongoing conflict between the M-18 and the MS-13 also involves the use of increasingly sophisticated weapons.[236]

Intra-gang violence and purges also occur with growing frequency.[237] One priest who works with active and non-active gang members in a community outside San Salvador told our researchers in 2006 that gang leaders have "intensified the system of internal obedience. . . . There's greater control from the top. Punishments can be death."[238] Gang members seeking to withdraw from active gang life face the same threat of fatal retribution from their fellow members.   In this regard,

---

gang membership.

[232] Interview with Cruz, *supra* note 145.

[233] Interview with L.F.G., gang member, in Cabañas (Aug. 25, 2006) (reporting that even if he left his gang, he would always be marked as a member in the eyes of the rival gang).

[234] Interview with T.C., *supra* note 200.

[235] Interview with D.M., *supra* note 196; interview with C.A., *supra* note 143 (reporting that members of the rival gang killed six or seven members of his *clika* alone).

[236] Interview with Aguilar, *supra* note 157 ("Hand-made weapons are no longer used. Now commercially produced arms, and sometimes those of the armed forces, are used.").

[237] *Id.* (noting the increasing prevalence of intra-gang killings, sometimes relating to drug or extortion activities).

[238] Interview with B.F., *supra* note 184.

a number of gang members and employees of organizations that work with gangs told our researchers that whereas in the past it was difficult, but feasible,[239] for a gang member to disassociate safely from a gang, in recent years it has become virtually impossible to do so.[240] Lorena Cuerno Clavel, a social anthropologist who has worked with gangs for over ten years, explained that in practice, a gang member never ceases being part of a gang but may, in certain rare circumstances, become inactive. She also suggested in 2006 that there were three ways of becoming inactive in a gang: embracing evangelical Christianity, forming a family, and migrating.[241] But migration is not always effective: Gilma Pérez, Director of the Migrants Program at IDHUCA, explained to our researchers that those gang members who leave the gang and migrate to the United States face very serious threats to their safety if they are deported back to El Salvador.[242] Likewise, for those who remain in El Salvador, joining an evangelical sect may not suffice to allow them to leave gang life: one ex-gang member reported, "Right now the only way to leave a gang is to die. They tell you that if you find God you can leave, but even then they still kill you."[243]

Our research team spoke with several active and former gang members who emphasized that it was nearly impossible to leave the gang. For example, we interviewed one young man who had been trying to leave the MS-13 gang for the past six years following several years of active membership. He told our researchers that his former *clika* had repeatedly threatened him and his family. He reported that recently the

---

[239] Several sources told us that conversions to evangelical Christianity and becoming a parent used to serve, at least nominally, as accepted reasons for leaving a gang. Interview with E.C.C., in Chalatenango (Mar. 28, 2006); interview with Cuerno Clavel, *supra* note 224.

[240] Interview with D.M., *supra* note 196; interview with L.F.G., *supra* note 233; interview with Tim McConville, *supra* note 209.

[241] Interview with Cuerno Clavel, *supra* note 224.

[242] Interview with Gilma Pérez, Director of the Migration Program of the IDHUCA, in San Salvador (Mar. 27, 2006).

[243] Interview with J.R., *supra* note 156.

targeting had intensified, with members of the *clika* coming to his house to charge him *renta* and to tell him they would kill him. Following an incident in which members of the MS-13 shot at him and killed one of his friends, he told us that he sought police protection, but received none.[244] Likewise, former gang member J.T. told our team that when he decided to leave the gang he was forced to pay a weekly fee of twenty-five dollars, under threat of death. He attributes having been able to leave the gang to the fact that several other *clika* members, who were also his childhood friends, interceded on his behalf. He underscores, however, that most other gang members are not as lucky. According to J.T., gangs consider membership to be for life and remain in constant contact with those members whom they have allowed to "calm down." For example, gangs will often rely on inactive gang members to "build up the *clika*" ("*levantar la clika*") when active gang members have been incarcerated and to carry out operations in the territory of rival gangs when active gang members would be too conspicuous.[245] Police Commissioner Cotto Castaneda and Assistant Police Inspector Amaya Márquez remarked that they have investigated countless cases in which gangs marked for death those who attempted to leave or who testified against the gang—a practice called "giving the green light" (*darle la luz verde*) to kill specific targets.[246]

Young people with gang tattoos are particularly at risk when they attempt to leave behind gang life. A staff person of a health clinic outside San Salvador, which offered a tattoo removal program sought by many former gang members, told our researchers that she has received threats. She also told us that she had heard that current gang members kept watch on the clinic, presumably to threaten those who seek help there.[247] Similarly, gang members who return to El Salvador will be

---

[244] Interview with D.M., *supra* note 196.

[245] Interview with J.T., *supra* note 211.

[246] Interview with Cotto Castaneda, *supra* note 213; interview with Amaya Márquez, *supra* note 179.

[247] Interview with Morales, *supra* note 230.

considered traitors if they do not rejoin the gang.[248] Lissette Miranda added that, as gang membership has become a lifestyle, rather than a stage in young people's lives, tattooed youth who attempt to leave the gang are increasingly vulnerable to violence by their former gang members, rival gangs, and police forces.[249]

c) *Women and Gang Violence*

Female gang members represent, on average, approximately 20 percent of the total gang population, although the number of women per *clika* varies—with some *clikas* having no female members and others having as many as twenty. [250] With very few exceptions, women have a subordinate status to men in the gang hierarchy. Their roles in day-to-day gang operations, as well as their relationships with male gang members, reflect attitudes toward women in Salvadoran society at large. According to Mauricio Figueroa, an expert who has worked extensively with female gang members in the prison system, "the status of women in gangs is exactly the same as that of women in society at large. Gangs reproduce patterns of social exclusion and violence, as well as the traditional roles assigned to women in society. Female gang members provide sexual favors to male members, take care of their children, cook, clean, iron, and run errands."[251] Likewise, María L. Santacruz Giralt and Alberto Concha-Eastman, researchers with IUDOP, emphasize: "Gangs employ the same mechanisms of marginalization and abuse against

---

[248] *See* IDHUCA, Programa de Migrantes [Migrants' Program], Registro de Casa, V.M.E. (May 27, 2005) (on file with authors); *see also* interview with W.M., in San Salvador (Aug. 30, 2006) (W.M. described the killing of a deportee from Los Angeles who attempted to leave gang life behind: "What I heard is that they took him down a [street] and asked if he was with them [e.g. would join the gang] and he said 'I'm not with anyone.' They said, 'If you're not with us, you're against us,' and they shot him.").

[249] Interview with Miranda, *supra* note 220.

[250] Santacruz Giralt & Concha-Eastman, *supra*, note 142, at 66.

[251] Interview with Mauricio Figueroa, ex-Director de la Fundación Ideas y Acciones para la Paz, Quetzalcoatl (Former Director, Ideas and Actions for Peace, Quetzalcoatl Foundation), in San Salvador (Jan. 22 and Jan. 23, 2009).

women present in civil society: machismo, violence, abuse, sexual objectification."[252] Indeed, a recent survey of Latin American attitudes vis-à-vis women confirms that El Salvador remains a particularly patriarchal society. The survey singled out El Salvador, together with Honduras, Guatemala, Nicaragua, and the Dominican Republic, as the only countries in the region in which more than half of those polled believed women should concentrate on the home while men should concentrate on work.[253]

Salvadoran society's patriarchal view of the appropriate role of women in society, combined with the culture of violence and the search for power that characterize gang structures, create an environment in which women are constant and easy targets of abuse not only by rival gangs, but also by male members of their own *clika*. A 2001 study showed that a much smaller proportion of female than male gang members were responsible for violent crimes (for example, 11.1 percent of female gang members had killed in the prior year, versus 88.9 percent of male gang members). By contrast, female gang members were the targets of higher levels of violence than their male counterparts, as measured by a "Victimization Index" developed by IUDOP researchers.[254] While a higher percentage of male gang members had been injured with firearms, women were much more likely to have been raped and robbed: in fact, close to 50 percent of all female gang members interviewed for the study had been raped at least once during the previous year (versus 2.1 percent of male gang members), and 41.6 percent of them had been robbed (versus 24.2 percent of male gang members) (see figure 4).[255]

---

[252] SANTACRUZ GIRALT & CONCHA-EASTMAN, *supra* note 142, at 152 (calling for increased attention to the issue of female gang members as victims of gang violence).

[253] LATINOBARÓMETRO, INFORME LATINOBARÓMETRO 2004 56 (2005).

[254] Researchers determined a "victimization index" by assigning particular weights to different types of crimes (for example, homicide weighed more heavily than robbery) and then generating a weighted average that took into account both the gravity of the offense and its frequency. SANTACRUZ GIRALT & CONCHA-EASTMAN, *supra* note 142, at 49-50.

[255] *Id.* at 87-89. The study also indicated that women carry out proportionately fewer acts of violence than men.

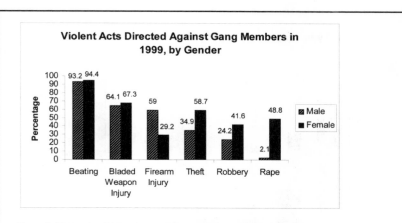

Figure 4. Violent Acts Directed Against Gang Members in 1999, by Gender
Source: L. SANTACRUZ GIRALT & ALBERTO CONCHA-EASTMAN, BARRIO ADENTRO: LA SOLIDARIDAD VIOLENTA DE LAS PANDILLAS 13 (2001).

Study authors emphasized that, because male gang members were much more likely to carry firearms than women, male victims of firearm violence were also likely to have been actively involved in violent gang activities. This correlation between active gang involvement and levels of victimization was absent in the case of women. The high incidence of robbery and rape among women gang members indicated that they were more likely than men to have been passive recipients of gang violence.[256] In addition, same-gang violence represents a larger proportion of the total amount of aggression experienced by women than it does for aggression experienced by men (see figure 5).[257]

Although, as a general rule, women are subordinate to men within the gang structure, not all female gang members occupy the same place in the gang hierarchy. Women may be ranked in one of two groups

---

[256] *Id.* at. 86.

[257] *Id.* at 95.

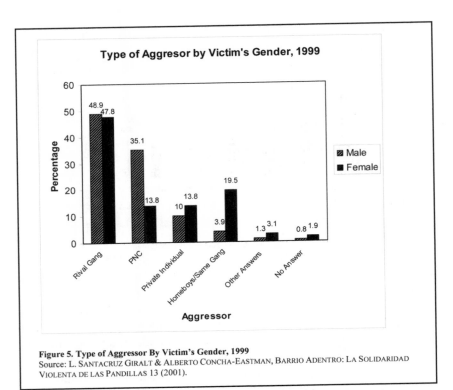

Figure 5. Type of Aggressor By Victim's Gender, 1999
Source: L. SANTACRUZ GIRALT & ALBERTO CONCHA-EASTMAN, BARRIO ADENTRO: LA SOLIDARIDAD
VIOLENTA DE LAS PANDILLAS 13 (2001).

based on the method of their initiation into the gang. The women who withstood a beating are assigned a higher status: their ability to endure and recover from a beating is taken to be sign of strength. The women who had sex with gang members, on the other hand, are assigned a lower status.[258] In fact, demonstrating high levels of endurance, as well as the capacity to perpetrate violent acts, is one of the few ways in which female gang members can occupy positions of power within the gang, a feat that takes place very infrequently. For example, Mauricio Figueroa told our researchers that in his ten years working with women in prison he knew of only one woman who became a *clika* leader because "she wasn't afraid of anything."[259] Similarly, Tránsito Ruano, the Director

---

[258] Interview with Figueroa, *supra* note 251.

[259] *Id.*

of an NGO that works with both male and female gang members, remarked that "only a female gang member who is very violent, who has a lot of leadership ability, can have a degree of influence over male gang members."[260] Female partners of male gang leaders can often ascend to positions of power—but their power is tied to these male gang leaders and dependent on the male partner's maintaining a leadership position.[261]

The role of women in gangs has changed in response to governmental anti-gang initiatives. Before the implementation of LAM I, female gang members were active participants in gang operations, often carrying out tasks similar to those entrusted to male gang members. Since then, according to one analyst, female gang members have been ordered to "calm down," and fewer females have been initiated to full gang membership. These changes arose in part as a response to the increased number of male gang members serving prison time. In this context, women were needed to look after detainees and relay messages to and from prison, rather than engage in violent activities that might expose them to police detection.[262] The drop in full female membership may also be attributed to male gang leaders' belief that women are a debilitating influence on the gang. Increasingly, as larger numbers of female gang members have become mothers, women have been considered less likely to carry initiation missions to completion, and more likely to have different priorities—such as emphasizing home life and child-rearing over gang-related activities.[263]

Even before the enactment of LAM I, however, a significant number of women associated informally with gang members without undergoing gang initiation rites to become full-fledged gang members themselves. This network of women, which includes mothers, sisters, and girlfriends,

---

[260] Interview with Tránsito Ruano, Director, Proceso de Atención a Situaciones de Sufrimiento Social (PASSOS) [Director, Care and Support for Situations of Social Suffering], in San Salvador (Jan. 22, 2009).

[261] Interview with Figueroa, *supra* note 251.

[262] *Id*; interview with Miranda, *supra* note 220.

[263] DEMOSCOPÍA, S.A., *supra* note 161, at 37-39.

has expanded with the increased number of incarcerated gang members and higher barriers to female gang membership. Gang leaders often deploy this network of women to run errands back and forth from prison, to carry messages, and to provide other services. Thus, gang leaders' zone of influence often extends beyond gang members themselves to include their families and girlfriends. According to Mauricio Figueroa, "gangs expect the same level of commitment and loyalty to the gang from gang members as from their family. This is a tacit, de facto agreement."[264]

Several of those interviewed for this book told our team of frequent instances in which gang members exercised near total control over their girlfriends, other females, or even women not tied to the gang. For example, Tránsito Ruano told our team of one situation in which the girlfriend of an imprisoned gang member would not leave her house or speak with her mother under orders relayed by her boyfriend from prison. In another case, gang members refused to let the teenage girlfriend of a murdered gang member leave his wake to go back to her family, emphasizing that her foremost responsibility was to the gang and to her murdered partner.[265] Likewise, Police Commissioner Cotto Castaneda told our researchers of a case in which a gang member coerced a woman to date him under threat of killing her boyfriend, who was not a gang member.[266]

Women who are considered to have been disloyal to the gang face dire consequences. For example, Police Commissioner Cotto Castaneda told our team of an imprisoned gang member who had ordered the killing of his girlfriend for having dated someone else. He had given specific directions that she be killed in front of their 5-year-old son, so that the child would learn the consequences of betraying his father.[267] Eighteen-year-old A.P. told our researchers of her brutal plight, and that of her friend, L.R., by two gang members. The gang members had

---

[264] Interview with Figueroa, *supra* note 251.

[265] Interview with Ruano, *supra* note 260.

[266] Interview with Cotto Castaneda, *supra* note 213.

[267] *Id.*

apparently mistaken A.P. and L.R. for two female friends of a rival gang member who had crossed them:

> L.R. and I left school and went to see my mom to ask her for money [for a chore] . . . . Then we went to [a wooded area to talk]. . . . A man approached us. . . . Later a second man joined him. The second one spoke on the phone and said "we've got them." He was smoking. He was twenty-four or twenty-five years old. He wore a long-sleeved shirt and loose pants. We told them we were leaving, but this second guy told us that if we tried to run away we would leave our brains splattered on [the ground]. So we stayed. . . . They took us to a [more deserted area]. There, one of the men grabbed my friend and took her inside. The first one dragged me by the hand and tied my hands behind me with a tie [from my school uniform]. He forced me to have sex with him. . . . The second man tied up my friend and threw her to the ground. He started to strangle her. . . . Then, the second man said to the other "she is yours, it's your turn to kill her." . . . He started strangling me and kicking me on the neck and back while forcing something down my throat. I still have a scar. Then, I fainted. When I came to the police were there. My face was covered in blood. . . . I tried to speak with L.R. I felt she was warm and I yelled to the police to help me. But she was already dead.[268]

In sum, female gang members, as well as those women who have informal relationships with the gang structure (such as gang members' extended family or girlfriends), are an extremely vulnerable group. Nevertheless, government officials have not prioritized the design and implementation of intervention strategies that target this particularly vulnerable segment of the population.

---

[268] Interview with A.P., in San Salvador (Oct. 23, 2008).

C. Targets of Gang Violence

The group most vulnerable to gang violence is comprised of those who have a degree of regular contact with gang members: those who oppose gangs (for example, by deciding to leave gang life behind), who live in gang-dominated neighborhoods, who are intimately involved with gang members, or whose relatives are gang members.

This part contains testimonies from some of the interviews our researchers conducted with victims and witnesses of gang violence in El Salvador. These testimonies are not intended to provide a complete picture of the situation of human rights in El Salvador, nor are they analytical in focus. Instead, we hope that these excerpts of victim and witness narratives will help the reader to understand the gravity and human dimension of gang violence in El Salvador.

1. *Those Who Oppose Gangs*

Salvadorans who oppose gangs, whether by refusing to join, leaving a gang, not complying with gangs' demands, or "betraying" the gang (for example, by collaborating with the police or by using the name of the gang to extort for personal gain) may face violent retribution. Those who attempt to resist coercive recruitment into gangs risk harassment, extortion, and even death.[269] Those who were once part of gang life and seek to change their life paths face severe consequences; gangs generally consider abandoning the gang as a betrayal that justifies death.[270] Moreover, the transformation of gangs and their tactics has extended gang aggression to include anyone who interacts with gangs and those from whom gangs extort lucrative tolls.[271] As the cases below illustrate, the state has failed to provide protection to these victims of gang violence.

---

[269] *See* testimonies in Part a), *infra.*

[270] *See* testimonies in Part b), *infra.*

[271] *See* testimonies in Part c), *infra.*

a) *Those Who Refuse to Join Gangs*

Several former gang members interviewed for this book told our researchers that they had initially joined gangs because they lived troubled lives at home and faced a violent environment in the streets.[272] They had hoped that gangs would provide them with the support, protection, and financial resources they lacked.[273] For example, B.R. told our researchers that through the gang, youth were trying to find the support and affection they did not get at home. "If you don't have shoes, gang members tell you they will find shoes for you, clothes, anything you need."[274] Many of the interviews conducted by our researchers, however, also revealed that gang recruitment increasingly involves pressure, threats, and intimidation. Gang members harass potential members through direct physical abuse, bothering their families, extorting regular payments from them, theft, and direct acts of violence, even murder.[275] This leaves many who oppose recruitment by gangs in a difficult situation: they face intimidation, threats, and physical harm from the gang recruiting them, while their residence in a certain neighborhood signals gang affiliation to outsiders and leaves them vulnerable to police violence and to violence from other gangs.[276] Youths with whom our

---

[272] Interview with M.P., in San Salvador (Mar. 30, 2006) (explaining that in the gang he found the support that his family was not providing him); interview with J.R.T., in San Salvador (Mar. 28, 2006) (explaining that he joined a gang after his father did not accept him at home following several days of being absent because of problems he had with his father); interview with R.E., in San Salvador (Mar. 28, 2006) (explaining that he left his home to join the gang to contradict his mother and that his friends in the gangs fed him, gave him clothes, and even cut his hair); interview with J.R., *supra* note 156 (explaining that as he was growing up during the Civil War there was so much violence and so many conflicts that a group banded together for protection).

[273] *Id.*

[274] Interview with B.R., *supra* note 159.

[275] Interview with L.A., *supra* note 224.

[276] Interview with Cruz, *supra* note 145; interview with T.C., *supra* note 200.

researchers spoke, for example, reported an incident in which gang members attacked and killed a man who lived in gang territory but had failed to join the gang,[277] as well as many incidents in which gang members murdered youths who had rejected the members' explicit invitations to join them.[278] These deadly recruitment practices create an environment of pervasive fear that leads to a sense of inevitability among the youths. The thought of being harassed, abused, or even killed makes them feel that they have to join gangs to survive, even when they have not received a direct threat from gang members.[279]

> 1. *We would tell. . . . young people to join. . . . We recruited four or five at a time. We killed several [people in the neighborhood] for not wanting to join us. . . . Ever since I was eleven, I was always with them. We killed about six guys around thirteen or fourteen years old. . . . It wasn't my job to do that, kill those who did not want to join.* [280] -25-year-old former gang member who left his gang seven years ago and was facing death threats by former fellow members, in San Salvador (August 21, 2006)

> 2. One young man told our researchers of the constant pressure to join a gang, including physical violence that eventually led to a deadly confrontation:

> *The ones from Mara 18 were always harrassing me [for not joining the gang]. They wanted to rob things from me and my family. This was happening for like two years before I killed that guy Tiny. Tiny did this to a lot of people in our area. Whenever a kid was twelve or thirteen years old, he'd want that kid to do what he said. The ones in 18 would always bother me in the streets. If they saw*

---

[277] Interview with A.Y., in San Salvador (Aug. 30, 2006).

[278] Interview with A.Z., in Ilobasco (Sept. 1, 2006).

[279] Interview with Cruz, *supra* note 145.

[280] Interview with D.M., *supra* note 196.

that I had money, they'd take it away from me. If I rode a bike, they'd take that away from me. They had a strong presence in my neighborhood. And I couldn't go to another neighborhood, because that neighborhood was MS, and they thought that I was in the 18, just because of my neighborhood. They said that I hung out with the 18 and they threatened me. I didn't want to get involved with any gang, because I didn't like how they are. The gang members are always in the streets harrassing people. . . . They started to bother my family when we didn't do what they said.[281] - 17-year-old, in Ilobasco (August 25, 2006)

3. *Gangs have lost all rationality. They are recruiting increasingly younger kids, including 12-year-olds, at schools. They force them to join. They threaten them, tell them they will kill their parents if they don't join.*[282] - B.F., Director, "Father Rafael Palacios" Guidance and Training Center, in Mejicanos (October 22, 2007)

4. *We pretty much forced one of my neighbors to join the gang. He had money, and we would send people to threaten [him and his family if he didn't join]. This type of thing happened often. Many times, we threatened both guys and girls with beatings if they didn't join the gang. We would extort money from the majority of those who refused to join; we would also beat them up, grab them, take away their money.*[283] - Former *clika* leader, in San Salvador (October 22, 2008)

5. *There are several neighborhoods here [in El Salvador] where you have no option other than being a gang member. That's it. There's no other choice. I've listened to testimonies from kids*

---

[281] Interview with T.C., *supra* note 200.

[282] Interview with B.F., Director del Centro de Formación y Orientación "Padre Rafael Palacios" [Director of the Guidance and Training Center "Father Rafael Palacios" Center], in Mejicanos (Oct. 22, 2007).

[283] Interview with B.R., *supra* note 159.

*in those neighborhoods who tell you: I have to join the gang or
leave my neighborhood.*[284] - Luis Enrique Salazar Flores, Adjunct
Ombudsperson for Children, in San Salvador (January 22, 2009)

b) *Those Who Try to Leave a Gang*

There was consensus among those we interviewed that joining a
gang is a life commitment.[285] While there are success stories about those
who have left the gangs, these are rare exceptions. Occasionally, gangs
have allowed members to become inactive when they have become
parents or have undergone a religious conversion.[286]   Nevertheless,
interviews with current and former gang members reveal that gangs no
longer consider having a family or experiencing a religious conversion
a sufficient reason for leaving gang life behind. In fact, several former
gang members interviewed by our team were able to leave their gang
only because the vast majority of the members of their *clika* had been
killed.[287]

The following excerpts from our interviews further demonstrate
that the threat of being killed after leaving a gang is not just a reason for
members of gangs to fear leaving, but is further considered an inevitable
element of gang life. For example, one former gang member told us
that killing people who left the gang was part of the initiation for new
gang members.[288] Moreover, as the testimonies below show, members
know that if they leave a gang they have to think not only about possible
threats to their lives by fellow members but also from members of other
gangs, as they will forever be associated with the gang to which they
once belonged.

---

[284] Interview with Salazar Flores, *supra* note 91.

[285] Interview with E.C.C., *supra* note 239; interview with C.A., *supra* note 143; interview
with Cuerno Clavel, *supra* note 224; interview with J.T., *supra* note 211.

[286] Interview with J.R., *supra* note 156; interview with L.A., *supra* note 224.

[287] Interview with B.R., *supra* note 159; interview with B.E., in San Salvador (Mar. 30, 2006)
("I had spent two years with my *clika* when I got out. I was lucky. Some *clika* members had
left for the U.S., others were killed. My *clika* no longer exists.")

[288] Interview with L.A., *supra* note 224.

1. *[Whether a gang member can leave his gang] depends also on the gang. The MS-13 is more vicious and strict. It is still possible to leave the Mara 18 if you get married or if you adopt a religious faith, but these are the only two options. The gang will always monitor those gang members who leave the gang due to marriage or religious conversion: if the former gang member breaks the rules he gets the "green light" [in effect, a death sentence, to be carried out by other gang members]. The MS-13 does not allow their members to leave. If they try, they get the "green light," which follows them throughout the country. If they leave the country, "green light." The* clikas *control the national territory and are in communication with* clikas *in the U.S. I have taken testimonies of Mara-18 gang members who have calmed down. But there are no calmed-down gang members in the MS-13. They may do it, but it's not sanctioned by the gang.*[289] - Assistant Police Inspector José Arturo Amaya Márquez, in Santa Tecla (October 22, 2008)

2. *I could leave the gang but I would always have* mi color *(my affiliation).*[290] *I could always get killed by those in the other gang. . . . There are many cases in which [gang members] have left the gang and they have been killed.*[291] - 18-year-old gang member, in Cabañas (August 25, 2006)

3. *If people tried to leave the gang, we would kill them. This happened maybe six times during my time, always guys. This was a "mission" for new gang members.*[292] - 18-year-old former gang member, in Ilobasco (August 23, 2006)

---

[289] Interview with Amaya Márquez, *supra* note 179.

[290] *Mi color* is a slang term used in El Salvador to refer to affiliation in a group; it is a common way for gang members to refer to their affiliation with a gang.

[291] Interview with L.F.G., *supra* note 233.

[292] Interview with L.A., *supra* note 224.

4. *Once I get out of here [detention] . . . I'm going to go [elsewhere]*
to live with my aunt. If they knew where I was they'd kill me.
Either my gang or the other gang.[293] - 19-year-old former gang
member, in Ilobasco (August 23, 2006)

5. *I told them I wanted to get out because my wife was pregnant.*
They told me that if they found me smoking or with alcohol they
would kill me. . . . About five months ago they surrounded me.
There were about four of them. They said, what's up? Why aren't
you paying renta? *This was with a gun in my stomach. . . . My*
son and daughter hugged me and cried and said "not my daddy."
My children saved my life. . . . They later sent someone to tell me
that they would kill me. . . . About eight or nine months ago I was
with [someone] who left the [Mara Salvatrucha]. . . . They killed
him with five shots in the head. . . . They wanted to kill me but
killed someone else."[294] -25-year-old former gang member who
faced persecution and death threats, in San Salvador (August
21, 2006)

The day after we interviewed him, he and his family were forced
to move in the middle of the night to escape this persecution.

6. *My mom cried when she came to visit me. She would ask me to*
go back to the neighborhood to live with her, but I would tell her
that I couldn't, that if I went back the gang would kill me [because
I had left the gang]. Now, when I go to school I'm afraid I may
bump into someone who used to know me [when I was a gang
member]. Once I bumped into another gang member. He just
stared at me, it was like who's going to kill who first. . . . I'm still
afraid. The leader of a rival clika *escaped several times from jail.*
I'm afraid of taking the bus because I may bump into people who
knew me then. That's why I don't live with my daughters in my old

---

[293] Interview with A.V., *supra* note 199.

[294] Interview with D.M., *supra* note 196.

neighborhood. [I'm still alive because] most of the gang members in my old neighborhood are dead.[295] - Former *clika* leader, in San Salvador (October 22, 2008)

7. *I know one thing for certain: once a recruit is initiated into the gang, he is a member for life, even if he wants to calm down. His family and people outside the gang may think he is no longer a gang member, but not other gang members. If they need his help, they will call on him to help the gang. And if he tries to erase his tattoo he'll be killed.*[296] - 22-year-old former gang member, in San Salvador (January 21, 2009)

8. *Gang members are forbidden from erasing tattoos that identify the gang they belong to, and "R.I.P." tattoos. A gang member who attempts to erase these tattoos gets the "green light." This means other gang members have the duty to kill him. The green light follows you in all of El Salvador. . . . We've seen many killings. In 2002-2003 a clika killed the brother of a gang member who wanted to leave the gang. Then they killed the gang member himself. All because he wanted to leave.*[297] - Israel Figueroa, educator focusing on incarcerated youth, in Santa Ana (October 20, 2007)

9. *I believe in preventive work as the only way to address the gang problem. I've been working on this issue for many years and have seen youth who were interested in changing their lifestyle but their environment would not let them do so. A youth who leaves a gang is as vulnerable as one who is about to enter a gang: he can be targeted by his own gang, a rival gang or the police. . . . I know of only one person who was able to leave the gang after spending*

---

[295] Interview with B.R., *supra* note 159.

[296] Interview with J.T., *supra* note 211.

[297] Interview with Israel Figueroa, Educador del Equipo Multidiciplinario del Juzgado de Ejecución de Medidas al Menor, Santa Ana [Educator, Multidisciplinary Team, Juvenile Tribunal for Penitentiary Oversight of Santa Ana], in Santa Ana (Oct. 20, 2007).

some time in a state-sponsored rehabilitation program. She had to move, sever all relationships, and isolate herself from anyone that knew her when she was a gang member. She is the only one of a group of eleven women who entered that rehabilitation program that I know is alive. We've lost track of the rest. Two or three of them have died at the hands of gang members, or because they started peddling drugs.[298] - Lissette Miranda, National Director, Pro-Youth Program, in San Salvador (January 20, 2009)

10. *Parolees who have left the gang tell us that they will be killed if they leave their homes. They often cannot even attend our support groups. In fact, a parolee gang member who had told us of his plans to leave the gang was killed on his way to one of these support groups, apparently for attempting to leave the gang. So we no longer ask former gang members to join us at our parolee support groups. Individuals who have too many tattoos get house visits.*[299] - Miguel Ernesto Anaya Perla, Coordinator, Information Technology Services of the Department of Probation and Parole, in San Salvador (January 19, 2009)

c) *Other People Targeted for Living in the Same Territory as Gangs or Refusing To Comply with Gang Demands*

Our interviews revealed that gangs increasingly target people outside their own territory, including neighborhood residents who happen to be in the wrong place at the wrong time,[300] local businesses, or those who do not comply with gangs' demands for *renta*. Gang violence has greatly limited the freedom of movement for ordinary people, who often live

---

[298] Interview with Lissette Miranda, *supra* note 220.

[299] Interview with Miguel Ernesto Anaya Perla, Coordinador, Centro de Informática del Departamento de Prueba y Libertad Asistida (DEPLA) [Coordinator, Information Technology Services of the Department of Probation and Parole], in San Salvador (Jan. 19, 2009).

[300] *See* excerpt from interview with D.L, *infra* note 305.

in fear of moving around or outside their neighborhoods and who face violence because of their residence in gang-controlled areas. Former gang members and community residents interviewed by our researchers reported that residents of areas controlled by gangs are constantly subjected to extortion and threats of violence by gang members. Former gang members explained to us that it is common to extort the owners of local stores and supermarkets in the neighborhood.[301] Other common targets for extortion are buses and taxis, with gangs charging either the operators or the drivers.[302]

These people who live under constant threats or in fear of being threatened with *renta* collections have legitimate reason to be concerned. As María Julia Hernández, Director of the Human Rights Office of the Archbishop of San Salvador (*Tutela Legal del Arzobispado de San Salvador* or *Tutela Legal*) explained, "those who don't pay *renta* run the risk of being executed, among other things."[303]

> *1. My son's grandfather told me that his family had begun receiving telephone calls from people threatening to hurt our family if he did not give them money. They knew about different members of the family and threatened them, saying they would come for my son's father first. They asked him, "where are your detectives now?" They told him they could kill him if they wanted, that they were in front of his house and that he could come out and see. He looked and they were outside. . . . We have not received any form of protection since we filed the complaint. We know a lot of people who have been extorted."*[304] -Young mother who was packing to flee El Salvador as we spoke because of repeated threats of extortion that made her fear for her son's life, in San Salvador (August 26, 2006)

---

[301] Interview with A.V., *supra* note 199; interview with L.A., *supra* note 224.

[302] Interview with D.M., *supra* note 196; *see also* Chapter III, Part C.1.c).

[303] Interview with María Julia Hernández, then Director, Tutela Legal, in San Salvador (Aug. 25, 2006).

[304] Interview with K.H.D., in San Salvador (Aug. 26, 2006).

2. *At first we thought that the violence was only between [the gangs]. But now we know that is not the case. My sister-in-law, her husband, and his brother were killed. They were between eighteen and twenty-three years old. None of them was involved in gangs. . . . [They] were taking water [to a communal house] at 10 p.m., and they ran into a group of gang members. It was a fight between the two gangs. And the police were following the gangs. [My sister-in-law, her husband, and his brother] were with another woman and two kids. The woman said that the gang members said "raise your shirts" and they did and then they just shot them. And they killed them. The woman survived. The gang members were armed with heavy weapons. There were only three police there. The gang members were well armed. . . . [There is] a theory that someone had killed one from the [Mara Salvatrucha] and so they were looking for vengeance, [and were] ready to kill whomever. There is delimitation of territory. There is no freedom to move. People from here cannot pass to the other side.*[305] - Woman living in a marginalized community of San Salvador (August 31, 2006)

3. *They send you on a mission. . . . [The victims were] from the other gang or competition in the drug business. And those who weren't paying. We charged each bus $1 daily. We charged the owners or those who drove. We charged $1 daily to stores and taxi drivers. Every day. Today it is in dollars. Before it was in colones, ten colones per day.*[306] - 25-year-old former gang member, in San Salvador (August 21, 2006)

4. *There are several gang members in this area, and the community is afraid of them. They collect* renta *from bus drivers. They have already killed a bus driver and a passenger.*[307] - César Gómez, Director, New Dawn, in San Salvador (October 21, 2008)

---

[305] Interview with D.L., in San Salvador (Aug. 31, 2006).

[306] Interview with D.M., *supra* note 196.

[307] Interview with César Gómez, Director, Nuevo Amanecer [New Dawn], in San Salvador (Oct. 21, 2008).

The following summarized narrative of the case of a deportee, who was represented by the IDHUCA, further evidences how victims and witnesses feel unprotected by the government and thus may choose not to denounce or testify against gang members:

> *V.M.E. was deported to El Salvador from the United States in late 2003. Upon his arrival he was detained by the National Police in the context of the Anti-Gang Law, because he had formerly belonged to a gang and had tattoos. He was not convicted of any charges and was released after trial. However, he started receiving death threats from his former fellow gang members who had learned about his return. One of them beat his wife and his two children, who are four and two years old. He and his wife went to the police to report the case, and he was scheduled for an appointment to identify that person, but he decided not to attend for fear of being captured by gang members when he came out of the police station. Instead, he tried to apply for political asylum.[308]*

2. *Killings of Suspected Gang Members by Rival Gangs*

As discussed earlier in this Chapter, one of the fundamental characteristics of gang life is the constant warfare between the two main, opposing gangs, with inter-gang killings taking place both as required initiation rites and as routine occurrences. The following testimonies demonstrate that the threat of murder by members of a "rival" gang is not only a source of legitimate fear for gang members themselves, but also for those stereotyped as gang members due to appearance, having acquaintances in a gang, or simply living in the wrong area.

> 1. *They killed one of my brothers one year and eight months ago. He was coming from his girlfriend's house and they killed him. He was twenty-two years old. The place where his girlfriend lived, there were MS there. . . . They killed my other brother this year.*

---

[308] IDHUCA, *supra* note 248.

He was about to turn 18. It was members of the MS who killed him. My brothers lived in the area of the Mara 18 and everyone thought they were from the Mara 18. . . . It is assumed that people who come and go in this area are members of the Mara 18.[309] - Resident of a marginalized community of San Salvador (August 31, 2006)

2. *I've had problems with the other gang because I have friends in the gang from this area, the MS, and the members of the other gang think that if you walk around with people in a certain gang then you are one of them. And they also think that everyone who lives in a certain gang's territory is a member of that gang.*[310] - 24-year-old resident of San Salvador, not a member of any gang, in San Salvador (August 27, 2006)

3. *One kid [from an area where CRISPAZ works], a 9-year-old . . . he was killed by the MS—for having family in the Mara 18—while playing sports. . . . Someone can't just relocate within El Salvador [to avoid the gangs]; the gangs are everywhere and they move quickly, so they can find you. People are identified, so nobody feels safe just by going to another part of the country. The communication between gangs (or different groups within gangs) is rapid and efficient. One can't be sure if one is on the list of people to be killed, but one can be sure that if one is on that list, one will be found and killed.*[311] - Jeanne Rikkers, Coordinator of CRISPAZ, in San Salvador (August 21, 2006)

4. *I decided to leave the gang because I was full of problems. The members of the other gang were looking for me to kill me. . . . I had to hide myself because of that. . . . Now the level of violence has begun to rise again. . . . There are killings in broad daylight. Fifteen days ago one of my friends was shot; he half-belonged to a*

---

[309] Interview with F.R., *supra* note 200.

[310] Interview with A.F., in Mejicanos (Aug. 27, 2006).

[311] Interview with Rikkers, *supra* note 151.

gang but never made up his mind. He went around with members of one, then the other, which is why he was in danger.[312]- 27-year-old former gang member, in Ilobasco (September 1, 2006)

5. *In my mom's neighborhood they recently killed two kids. They found them buried by the river. I think they mistook them for members of the Mara-18. I've had problems coming to the center [a center that sponsors activities for youth] because it's close to Mara-18 territory, and I have to go through MS-13 territory to get here, so they think you're an MS-13. Even if they know you're not, they think you are giving them information. That's what I think happened with those two kids.*"[313] -20-year-old, not a member of any gang, in Mejicanos (January 21, 2009)

6. *I could file a report [of the threats against my life] but why? It won't do any good and I don't want to put my children in danger. Even when walking in the park with my daughters I have been approached by people [threatening me]. I've been followed while going on the bus route. I've been told my throat would be cut.*[314] - 25-year-old former gang member, in San Salvador (August 31, 2006)

In early 2007, the authors received word that this same woman was in the hospital, having been shot just weeks after the above interview took place.

7. *I went to a school that was controlled by a rival gang to the gang in my neighborhood. I started hanging out with my school gang [the Mara 18], but I never really tried to become a member. If I had, the gang members in my neighborhood—who belonged*

---

[312] Interview with E.D.R., in Ilobasco (Sep. 1, 2006).

[313] Interview with S.T., in Mejicanos (Jan. 21, 2009).

[314] Interview with X.D.H., in San Salvador (Aug. 31, 2006).

to the MS—would have killed me.[315] - Former *clika* leader, in San Salvador (October 22, 2008)

8. *We have a problem [in our community exchange program] because youth who are not gang members feel safe inside their homes, and they don't want to leave their house to participate in our program. But the goal of the program is to encourage intercommunity exchanges to break the barriers imposed by gang violence. There are kids who don't know what's going on one kilometer away from their homes because they are scared of going out.* [316] - Lissette Miranda, Director, Pro-Youth Program, in San Salvador (January 20, 2009)

9. *There are parolees who try to leave the gang, but as a consequence many of them can no longer leave their house. They tell us that they can't leave their house for fear of being killed.*[317] - Miguel Ernesto Anaya Perla, Coordinator, Information Technology Services of the Department of Probation and Parole, in San Salvador (January 19, 2009)

---

[315] Interview with B.R., *supra* note 159.

[316] Interview with Miranda, *supra* note 220.

[317] Interview with Anaya Perla, *supra* note 299.

SUSPECTS IN CUSTODY await transfer to a police station in San Salvador. *Photograph and caption by Juan Carlos.*

A POSTER WITH THE IMAGES and names of suspects wanted by authorities is displayed at a local police station in San Salvador. *Photograph and caption by Juan Carlos.*

A TEENAGE BOY shot in the head on his way to school, a victim of gang violence. *Photograph and caption by Juan Carlos.*

POLICE IN EL SALVADOR conducting a bus search. *Photograph and caption by Juan Carlos.*

A WOMAN CRIES over the body of a relative, a 21-year-old man shot in the head by a group of young adults. *Photograph and caption by Juan Carlos.*

BENCH on which a victim of gang violence was shot earlier in the day in a San Salvador park. *Photograph and caption by Juan Carlos.*

"I TOLD YOU NOT TO GO OUT," repeats a woman, referring to the words she spoke to her boyfriend before he left home and was shot to death on a street corner in San Salvador. *Photograph and caption by Juan Carlos.*

FUNERAL of 17-year-old Erick Mauricio Ancheta Rodríguez, shot more than a dozen times by gang members while waiting for a bus. *Photograph and caption by Juan Carlos.*

Chapter IV:
State Responses to Crime/Gang Phenomenon

"Institutions have closed their doors to youth. We have not created the necessary conditions for them to leave gangs and re-enter society."

- Lissette Miranda, National Director,
Pro-Youth Program, in San Salvador (Jan. 20, 2009)

This chapter describes and analyzes the Salvadoran state's responses to the gang phenomenon and violence in the country more generally. Part A of this chapter provides an overview of direct state responses, including an examination of the various legislative and law enforcement initiatives the government has launched since 2003 as well as a discussion of the impacts of these initiatives. Part B of this chapter analyzes the lack of adequate state responses to the phenomenon, considering the ways in which the Salvadoran government has failed to act to protect its citizenry from gang-related and other forms of violence. Finally, part C of the chapter discusses the relationship between and among the deep political polarization of the Salvadoran state, its responses to the gang phenomenon, and violence in the country more generally.

A. Direct State Responses to Violence

> *Crime prevention strategies are centered on state repression which, in turn, generates more violence. New laws are constantly being formulated, as if laws were a magic wand that will solve the country's problems.*
>
> - Doris Luz Rivas Galindo, Presiding Justice of the Juvenile Court of San Salvador, in San Salvador (Jan. 22, 2009)

In 2003, the Salvadoran government launched a major military-law enforcement initiative (*Mano Dura* or Iron Fist or Firm Hand) aimed at cracking down on gangs in the country. Through early 2009 at least, the punitive strategies embodied in the *Mano Dura* plan continued to be the primary focus of the government's anti-gang efforts, though court rulings and unabated violence have forced modifications in the legislative framework and rhetoric associated with government crackdowns.

1. Legislative Background

In July 2003, President Flores, of El Salvador's conservative ARENA party, announced the launching of a major military-police operation

(*Mano Dura*) to capture gang members in urban and rural areas throughout the country.[318] Flores invoked urgent and harsh rhetoric to describe the criminality and gang violence occurring in the country and to justify granting broad powers to the PNC and Armed Forces to combat gang violence and detain alleged gang members.[319] He called upon the Salvadoran legislature to pass anti-gang legislation to legalize his planned crackdown, but emphasized that he would be willing to use exceptional measures (*medidas excepcionales*) to suspend constitutional guarantees in zones with a heavy gang presence if that legislation did not pass.[320] In the end, the Salvadoran legislature did pass LAM I, President Flores' proposed version of the Anti-Gangs Act, without modifications, as a temporary (six-month) measure in October 2003.[321] International and domestic rights groups noted that President Flores' announcement and the passage of LAM I coincided with the intensification of electoral campaigning for the March 2004 presidential elections, suggesting that the legislation and military-police operations were aimed at garnering political support for President Flores' successor, Antonio Saca, rather than at implementing effective anti-crime policies.[322] (See Table 3 for a

---

[318] Julio Calderón, *El estado de excepción es la última alternativa*, EL DIARIO DE HOY, July 24, 2004, *available at* http://www.elsalvador.com/noticias/2003/07/24/nacional/nacio13.html; ESTADO DE LA SEGURIDAD PÚBLICA Y LA JUSTICIA PENAL EN EL SALVADOR 2004, *supra* note 52, at 13.

[319] In response to questions about whether the Salvadoran detention system could absorb the numbers of people that could be swept up in this operation, Flores was quoted in the Salvadoran daily *El Diario de Hoy* as saying, "What matters to me is the Salvadoran citizenry. I am not concerned about the well-being of criminals." Calderón, *supra* note 318.

[320] *Id.*

[321] LAM I, *supra* note 51, at art. 49; Alexandra Bonilla & Lauri García, *Ley Antimaras Aprobada*, EL DIARIO DE HOY, Oct. 10, 2003, *available at* http://www.elsalvador.com/noticias/2003/10/10/nacional/nacio18.html.

[322] *See* AMNESTY INT'L, EL SALVADOR: OPEN LETTER ON THE ANTI-MARAS ACT 6 (2003), *available at* www.amnesty.org/en/library/info/AMR29/009/2003/en ("Amnesty International believes that this situation would not have arisen if this controversial legislation—if deemed necessary—had been properly formulated and subject to careful scrutiny, bearing in mind the obligations to respect the Constitution and relevant international treaties. Everything indicates that this was not the case, which may give support to a growing body of opinion that the main reason behind promulgation of the LAM, and the introduction

summary of relevant legislation.)

Law	DecreeNo./ Vol. Diario Oficial	Issuance Date	Presi- dent	Comments
Reformas al Código Procesal Penal (Amendments to the Code of Penal Procedure)	281/350	February 13, 2001	Flores	Chapter VI-BIS enacts a protection regime for witnesses and expert witnesses.
Ley Anti Maras (Anti-Gangs Act) (LAM I)	158/361	October 10, 2003	Flores	A component of the *Mano Dura* Plan. Amended by Decree 189.
Reformas al Código Penal (Amendments to the Penal Code)	121	October 13, 2003	Flores	Amends Art. 345 which defines the crime of illicit associations. Classifies *maras* as illicit associations. Amended by Decree 393.
Reformas a la Ley Anti Maras (Amendments to LAM I)	189/361	November 18, 2003	Flores	A component of the *Mano Dura* Plan. Found unconstitutional by the Supreme Court on April 1, 2004.
Ley para el Combate de las Actividades Delincuenciales de Grupos o Asociaciones Ilícitas Especiales (Act to Combat Delinquent Activities of Certain Illicit Groups or Associations) (LAM II)	305/363	April 2, 2004	Flores	A component of the *Mano Dura* Plan. Considered unconstitutional by several judges, who refused to apply it during its ninety-day validity period.
Reformas al Código Penal (Amendments to the Penal Code)	393/ 364	July 30, 2004	Saca	Amends Art. 345, which defines the crime of illicit associations.
Ley Especial para la Protección de Víctimas y Testigos (Special Victim and Witness Protection Law)	1029/371	May 11, 2006	Saca	Creates an Executive-Technical Unit to administer a victim and witness protection program.
Reformas al Código Penal (Amendments to the Penal Code)	1031/371	May 11, 2006	Saca	Criminalizes revealing personal data or the likeness of those persons protected under the Special Witness and Victim Protection Law with a four to eight-year prison sentence
Ley Especial contra el Terrorismo (Special Anti-Terrorism Law)	108/373	October 11, 2006	Saca	Defines act of terrorism and terrorist organizations. Sets forth precautionary measures and criminal penalties.
Ley Contra el Crimen Organizado y Delitos de Realización Compleja (Organized and Complex Crimes Law)	190/374	January 22, 2007	Saca	Establishes a specialized procedure—which includes the creation of specialized tribunals—to prosecute organized and complex crimes.
Creation of Specialized Tribunals	246/374	March 5, 2007	Saca	
Reglamento de la Ley Especial para la Protección de Víctimas y Testigos (Regulation to the Special Victim and Witness Protection Law)	89/377	October 2, 2007	Saca	
Código ProcesalPenal (Code of Penal Procedure)	733/382	January 16, 2009	Saca	

Table 3. Gang-Related Legislation

a) *The Anti-Gangs Act and the April 2004 Supreme Court Ruling*

LAM I was enacted with the stated goal of "establishing a special and temporary legal regime to combat those groups known as *maras* or *pandillas*."[323] Article 1 criminalized membership in gangs, defined as a group of people that "disrupts the public order and offends decorum or good customs."[324] The Act further enumerated specific criteria that established gang membership, including holding habitual meetings,

---

of the so-called Get Tough Initiative, Plan *Mano Dura*, was political and, particularly, for election's purposes."); *see also* INFORME ANUAL JUSTICIA JUVENIL 2004, *supra* note 123, at 21 (observing that while the *Mano Dura* plan was presented as an innovative measure during the electoral campaign, large-scale arrests of gang members were in fact "nothing new.").

[323] LAM I, *supra* note 51, at art. 1

[324] *Id.*

using signs or symbols as a means of identification, and having tattoos.[325] LAM I also contained provisions that allowed the trial of juveniles as adults[326] and that granted the PNC authority to initiate judicial proceedings against suspected gang members, enabling it to sidestep the Office of the Prosecutor.[327] The Act provided for the imposition of fines against any person "found wandering about without an identity document in . . . any settlement, without justified cause or who is not known by the inhabitants."[328] Domestic and international organizations argued that they violated El Salvador's Constitution, several international treaties and norms, and basic principles of criminal law.[329]

Just ten days before LAM I was set to expire in April 2004, and

---

[325] *Id.*

[326] *Id.* at art. 2, para. 3 (allowing for youth from twelve to eighteen years of age to be prosecuted as adults if a Juvenile Court judge and the prosecutor believe that the defendant in question is capable of understanding the illicit nature of his or her conduct as an adult would).

[327] *Id.* at art. 30 (In Spanish: *"Serán titulares de la acción para entablar la acusación ante el juez competente la Policía Nacional Civil, por medio de sus agentes de autoridad o apoderados del Señor Director General y la Fiscalía General de la República, por medio de los agentes auxiliares del Señor Fiscal General."*)

[328] *Id.* at art. 29 (translation in AMNESTY INT'L, *supra* note 322).

[329] *See, e.g.,* IDHUCA, ANÁLISIS DEL IDHUCA SOBRE LA "LEY ANTI MARAS" Y PROPUESTA DE REFORMAS, SAN SALVADOR, EL SALVADOR [IDHUCA ANALYSIS ON THE "ANTI-GANG LAW" AND PROPOSED REFORMS], 6 (2003), *available at* http://www.uca.edu.sv/publica/ idhuca/leymaras.pdf (asserting that the Anti-Gangs Act violated Constitutional principles such as that of proportionality, that it impermissibly granted to the PNC prosecutorial powers which Article 193 of the Salvadoran Constitution vested exclusively in the Office of the Prosecutor, and that there was no legal basis for special legislation for gangs when appropriate judicial instruments already existed in the Penal Code); AMNESTY INT'L, *supra* note 322 (asserting that the Anti-Gangs Act contravened international instruments and treaties to which El Salvador is a party, including the Convention on the Rights of the Child and the American Convention on Human Rights); *see also* Office of the High Commissioner for Human Rights, Committee on the Rights of the Child, *Concluding Observations: El Salvador,* ¶¶ 67-68, U.N. Doc. CRC/C/15/Add.232 (June 30, 2004) [hereinafter *Concluding Observations: El Salvador*] (expressing concern that the law allowed for the possibility of prosecuting a child as young as twelve as an adult and that it undermined the already existing Juvenile Offenders Act by introducing a dual system of juvenile justice).

after the March 2004 presidential election, El Salvador's Supreme Court of Justice declared the law unconstitutional.[330] The Court held that Articles 1 and 3 of LAM I, which established a special regime to combat gangs, violated the constitutional right to equality before the law by allowing an arbitrary differentiation for crimes committed by gangs.[331] The Court also found Article 1 unconstitutional for violating the Salvadoran principle of injury (*lesividad*), under which criminal law may only penalize acts that actually put someone at risk or cause him or her injury.[332] Other articles found unconstitutional under the same principle were those that penalized those who identified themselves with gangs through tattoos or signs,[333] gang members who gathered in abandoned or deserted property[334] or in cemeteries at night without justification,[335] and those found wandering without documentation in residential areas.[336] The Supreme Court also found that provisions that authorized punishment based solely on physical appearance or membership in a gang were unconstitutional because they penalized personal characteristics and lifestyles and did not respect the presumption of innocence.[337] An example of such a provision was

---

[330] Sala de lo Constitucional de la Corte Suprema de Justicia [Constitutional Chamber of the Supreme Court of Justice] (Dec. 52-2003/56-2003/57-2003) at Falla 16; IV, 3, B (Apr. 1, 2004), *available at* http://www.jurisprudencia.gob.sv/exploiis/indice.asp?nBD=1&nDoc=31904&nItem=32534&nModo=1.

[331] *Id; see also* LAM I, *supra* note 51, at Arts. 1, 3; Constitución de la República de El Salvador [Constitution of the Republic of El Salvador], art. 3.

[332] Sala de lo Constitucional de la Corte Suprema de Justicia, *supra* note 330, at IV, 3, B.

[333] LAM I, *supra* note 51, art. 18.

[334] *Id.* at art. 19.

[335] *Id.* at art. 22.

[336] *Id.* at art. 29, para. 1.

[337] Sala de lo Constitucional de la Corte Suprema de Justicia, *supra* note 330, at V, 1, c.; *see also* Juan J. Fogelbach, Comment, *Mara Salvatrucha (MS-13) and Ley Anti Mara: El Salvador's Struggle to Reclaim Social Order*, 7 SAN DIEGO INT'L L.J. 223 (2005).

Article 29, which established that a deportee entering the country whose history, appearance, or conduct indicated that he/she belonged to a gang would be detained and presented before a judge.[338] Finally, the Supreme Court held that LAM I violated the Constitution and the Convention on the Rights of the Child because, in effect, it did not exempt children of any age from its application.[339] The ruling stressed that LAM I was not only inappropriate but also unnecessary because the Penal Code already provided the legal instruments necessary to respond to gang crimes.[340]

The same day the Supreme Court of Justice declared the Anti-Gang Law unconstitutional, President Flores submitted a new temporary law to the Congress, the Act to Combat Delinquent Activities of Certain Illicit Groups or Associations (*Ley para el Combate de las Actividades Delincuenciales de Grupos o Asociaciones Ilícitas Especiales* or LAM II).[341] President Flores and the bill's supporters in Congress argued that this new law overcame the legal deficiencies of the original LAM I. However, judges and civil society organizations argued that many of its provisions were essentially the same as those found unconstitutional in the first law.[342] Like LAM I, the modified version established a special regime to combat gangs; the principal difference between the two versions was that LAM II added a provision stating that the law would combat gangs' "delinquent activities"[343] and not just gangs in general. LAM II still criminalized membership in or association with a gang, modifying

---

[338] LAM I, *supra* note 51, art. 29, para. 2.

[339] LAM I gave judges discretion to determine whether a child between twelve and eighteen should be tried as an adult and whether a child under twelve should be tried subject to certain modifications for minors. *Id.* at art. 2, paras. 3, 5 and at art. 45; *see also* Constitución de la República de El Salvador [Constitution of the Republic of El Salvador], art. 144.

[340] Sala de lo Constitucional de la Corte Suprema de Justicia, *supra* note 330.

[341] LAM II, *supra* note 62; Alexandra Bonilla & Lauri Garcia, *FMLN dice que la aprobación no pasó por proceso normal*, EL DIARIO DE HOY, Apr. 2, 2004, *available at* http://www.elsal-vador.com/noticias/2004/04/02/nacional/nac21.asp.

[342] INFORME ANUAL JUSTICIA JUVENIL 2004, *supra* note 123; Salamanca, *supra* note 63.

[343] LAM II, *supra* note 62, art. 1.

LAM I by adding that gangs were groups of people who "through their actions" affect the public order, decorum, good customs, etc.[344] Although LAM II did not contain any specific provision penalizing the use of signs or tattoos to identify individuals with gangs,[345] it still provided that membership in a gang may be determined by tattoos or usage of gang signs.[346] Membership or association with a gang was made punishable by three to six years in prison.[347] Notably, LAM II eliminated the provision allowing for the detention of Salvadoran deportees on the basis of appearance, though many deportees have reported that police routinely engaged in this sort of profiling well after LAM II entered into force.[348] Finally, regarding treatment of minors, while LAM II set twelve years as the minimum age for the application of its provisions, it still allowed a judge to determine whether a minor between twelve and eighteen years should be tried as an adult.[349] In its June 2004 session, the U.N. Committee on the Rights of the Child expressed concern that LAM II, like LAM I, violated the Convention on the Rights of the Child and recommended that El Salvador "immediately abrogate" it and apply only the Juvenile Offenders Act in the area of juvenile justice.[350] Despite the fact that LAM II was never declared unconstitutional, many judges refused to apply it throughout the ninety-day period in mid-2004 during which it was in effect.[351]

---

[344] LAM II, *supra* note 62, art. 3, para. 2.

[345] LAM I did penalize the use of certain signs and tattoos. LAM I, *supra* note 51, at art. 18.

[346] LAM II, *supra* note 62, at art. 3, para. 4.

[347] *Id.* at art. 4.

[348] *See* Chapter IV, Part D. 1. c), *infra.*

[349] LAM II, *supra* note 62, at art. 3, para. 1.

[350] *Concluding Observations: El Salvador, supra* note 329.

[351] Salamanca, *supra* note 63.

b) *Súper Mano Dura*

In March 2004, the ARENA party presidential candidate, Antonio Saca, defeated FMLN candidate Schafik Handal. As discussed *infra*, criminality in El Salvador and *Mano Dura* plans played prominent roles in the 2004 presidential campaign, and Saca came to power promising to maintain the "iron fist" policies of his predecessor.[352] In August 2004, President Saca announced the *Súper Mano Dura* plan, another anti-gang initiative, this time proposing permanent penal code reforms in addition to the continuance of joint military-police anti-gang operations.[353] Saca insisted that *Súper Mano Dura* constituted a more effective plan than the previous ones and that it would not be legally challenged.[354] Unlike the *Mano Dura* initiatives of the Flores administration, *Súper Mano Dura* purported to embrace a comprehensive approach to gang violence prevention by establishing civil society-government "working groups" to address issues of reintegration of ex-gang members and prevention of gang violence.[355] Rights groups argued, however, that the emphasis and major focus of the initiative remained on police repression and increased military-police operations and that the plan failed to address fundamental problems, such as the need for effective criminal investigations.[356] Further, while civil society organizations applauded the government's acknowledgment that an effective anti-gang strategy

---

[352] Lauri García Dueñas, *René Figueroa, Nuevo ministro de Gobernación*, EL DIARIO DE HOY, Apr. 3, 2004, *available at* http://www.elsalvador.com/noticias/2004/04/03/nacional/nac9. asp (quoting René Figueroa, Saca's *Ministro de Gobernación* (Minister of the Interior), as promising to continue the work initiated by the Flores' Administration in citizen security and to redouble its efforts with the *Súper Mano Dura* Plan).

[353] INFORME ANUAL JUSTICIA JUVENIL 2004, *supra* note 123, at 29; *see also Se Inicia la Súper Mano Dura*, EL DIARIO DE HOY, Aug. 31, 2004, *available at* http://www.elsalvador.com/noticias/2004/08/31/nacional/nac18.asp.

[354] *Se Inicia la Súper Mano Dura*, *supra* note 353.

[355] *Id.*

[356] INFORME ANUAL JUSTICIA JUVENIL 2004, *supra* note 123, at 29.

must include social components,[357] they have reported that the state-sponsored youth prevention and rehabilitation plans *Mano Amiga* (Friendly Hand) and *Mano Extendida* (Extended Hand) have been relatively underfunded and ineffective.[358]

Súper Mano Dura included permanent reforms to the Penal Code, the Code of Penal Procedure, and the Juvenile Offenders Act. The 2004 Penal Code reforms made membership in an illicit association an aggravating circumstance in a crime.[359] The law amended Article 345 of the penal code, which governs illicit associations, to increase the punishment for membership in such an association from three to five years in prison, and for leadership in such an association from six to nine years in prison.[360] Under the pre-existing Article 345, only committing or planning to commit crimes was punished.[361] The definition of illicit

---

[357] FESPAD & CEPES, Violencia Juvenil en Centroamérica, Respuestas desde la Sociedad Civil: Informe Nacional El Salvador 51 (2005); *see also* Aguilar & Miranda, *supra* note 157, at 68-69 (praising the government's recognition of prevention and social reinsertion as necessary components of its anti-gang strategy).

[358] Interview with Miranda, *supra* note 220. ("Our Project is financed by international cooperation. Fifty percent of the government's budget in this area went to the police; only two or three million were directed to prevention programs, and even then that money went to political institutions, not to projects like ours which are independent from the executive branch and which employ technical criteria to develop policies."); *see also* Aguilar & Miranda, *supra* note 157, at 51 (emphasizing that the propaganda associated with these programs far outweighs their actual results); *id.* at 68-69 (stating that these programs are too limited in their scope and resources to address the gang phenomenon). USAID also gave a lukewarm assessment of these programs in its Central America and Mexico Gang Assessment. *See* Central America and Mexico Gang Assessment, *supra* note 6, at 54 ("The prevention and intervention policies of Mano Extendida and Mano Amiga are fairly new, and the impact is difficult to measure to date. However, the percentage allocated to prevention and intervention approaches to gangs makes up only 20 percent of the available government funding, while a larger percentage goes toward law enforcement (*Súper Mano Dura*)").

[359] Decreto [Decree] No. 393/2004, Reformas al Código Penal [Penal Code Reforms], art. 1; *see also* Decreto No. 1030/1997, Código Penal [Penal Code], art. 30.

[360] Decreto No. 393/2004, *supra* note 359, at art. 6; Decreto No. 1030/1997, *supra* note 359, at art. 345, para. 1.

[361] Decreto No. 393/2004, *supra* note 359, at art. 6; Decreto No. 1030/1997, *supra* note 359, at art. 345, para. 1.

associations was amended to include any group that carries out violent acts or that uses violent means in the initiation, retention, or exit of its members.[362]

In the years following the implementation of the *Súper Mano Dura* Plan, homicide rates continued to rise sharply, from 33.0 per 100,000 inhabitants in 2003 to 40.9 and 55.5 per 100,000 inhabitants in 2004 and 2005, respectively.[363] Nevertheless, the Saca administration continued to defend the *Mano Dura* strategies in the face of growing skepticism regarding their efficacy and continued to rely on punitive legal reforms to address the country's growing crime rates.[364] Following the 2004 reforms to the Penal Code and Juvenile Offenders Act, President Saca introduced four other major legal initiatives, each of which facilitated or expanded the hard-line law enforcement policies of the *Súper Mano Dura* plan: the Special Victim and Witness Protection Law; the Anti-Terrorism Law; the Organized and Complex Crimes Law; and the reform of the Code of Penal Procedure.

c) *Victim and Witness Protection Law*

The 2006 Victim and Witness Protection Law replaced an older regime (the Protection Regime for Ordinary and Expert Witnesses) and

[362] Decreto No. 393/2004, *supra* note 359, at art. 2, para. 2. (In Spanish: *"Serán considera-das ilícitas las agrupaciones, asociaciones u organizaciones temporales o permanentes, de dos o más personas que posean algún grado de organización, cuyo objetivo o uno de ellos sea la comisión de delitos, así como aquellas que realicen actos o utilicen medios violentos para el ingreso de sus miembros, permanencia o salida de los mismos."*)

[363] Forensic Statistics Unit, *Reconocimiento de Defunciones por Homicidios Realizados por los (las) Médicos(as) del Instituto de Medicina Legal de El Salvador Año 2004* [hereinafter *Reconocimiento de Defunciones por Homicidio 2004*]; Forensic Statistics Unit, 2 BOLETÍN SO-BRE HOMICIDIOS [HOMICIDES BULLETIN], Jan. 2006, [hereinafter BOLETÍN SOBRE HOMICI-DIOS 2005]. Homicide rates continued to rise in 2006 and 2007. According to the Forensic Statistics Unit, the homicide rate in El Salvador was 56.2 per 100,000 in 2006 and 60.9 per 100,000 in 2007. Forensic Statistics Unit, 3 BOLETÍN SOBRE HOMICIDIOS [HOMICIDES BULLETIN], Jan. 2007 [hereinafter BOLETÍN SOBRE HOMICIDIOS 2006]; BOLETÍN SOBRE HOMICIDIOS 2007, *supra* note 3.

[364] *See, e.g.*, Mirna Jiménez, *Saca defiende Plan Súper Mano Dura*, DIARIO CO LATINO, Jan. 27, 2005, *available at* http://www.diariocolatino.com/nacionales/detalles.asp?NewsID=6818.

sought to provide a more comprehensive protection framework.[365] The new law created an executive technical unit (*Unidad Técnica Ejecutiva* or UTE) charged with administration of the program, which included the selection of those who qualified for protection.[366] A Coordinating Commission was entrusted with the general supervision of the program.[367] The law authorizes the Office of the Prosecutor, the PNC, and the judiciary to adopt temporary protection measures in urgent circumstances, subject to revision by the UTE.[368] The UTE's decision to grant or deny specific protection measures can be administratively appealed to the UTE itself and the Coordinating Commission.[369] Article

---

[365] The Special Victim and Witness Protection Law, *supra* note 78, replaced the Protection Regime for Ordinary and Expert Witnesses, *supra*, note 78.

[366] Special Victim and Witness Protection Law, *supra* note 78, at art. 6 (In Spanish: "*La Unidad Técnica Ejecutiva del Sector de Justicia . . . además de las funciones y atribuciones que le señala su Ley Orgánica, será el organismo administrador del Programa de Protección de Víctimas y Testigos.*"); at art. 8 (In Spanish: "*La Unidad Técnica, en el marco de la presente Ley, tendrá las atribuciones siguientes: . . . c) Identificar, autorizar, implementar, modificar y suprimir las medidas de protección y atención destinadas a las personas que califiquen para recibir beneficios del Programa.*").

[367] *Id.* at art 5 (In Spanish: "*La Comisión Coordinadora del Sector de Justicia (Justice Sector Coordinating Commission). . . además de las funciones y atribuciones que le señala su Ley Orgánica, será el ente rector del Programa de Protección de Víctimas y Testigos.*"). The Justice Sector Coordinating Commission was established in 1996 by Legislative Decree 639/1996. It has five members: the President of the Judicial Branch (*Presidente del Órgano Judicial*); the General Ombudsperson (*Procurador General de la República*); the Director of Public Prosecutions (*Fiscal General de la República*); the Public Security and Justice Minister (*Ministro de Seguridad Pública y Justicia*); the President of the National Judicial Council (*Presidente del Consejo Nacional de la Judicatura*). Decreto [Decree] 639/1996, Ley Orgánica de la Comisión Coordinadora del Sector de Justicia y de la Unidad Técnica Ejecutiva, [Organic Law of the Justice Sector Coordinating Commission and the Technical Executive Unit] (1996).

[368] Special Victim and Witness Protection Law, *supra* note 78, at art.17. (In Spanish: "*Los jueces y tribunales, la Fiscalía General de la República, la Procuraduría General de la República, la Policía Nacional Civil y la Unidad Técnica Ejecutiva, deberán adoptar una o varias medidas de protección urgentes . . . en su caso, se informará inmediatamente a la Unidad Técnica. La Unidad Técnica, dentro del plazo de diez días . . . confirmará, modificará o suprimirá las medidas de protección urgentes que se hubieren adoptado, notificándolo a la persona interesada y a las autoridades correspondientes.*")

[369] Special Victim and Witness Protection Law, *supra* note 78, at arts. 26-27. (In Spanish: "*El*

28 of the law permits judges to reveal protected witnesses' identities to the parties only under exceptional circumstances.[370] A concurrent amendment to the criminal code, however, criminalizes revealing personal data or the likeness of individuals protected under the new law with up to eight years in prison. Public authorities are subject to increased penalties.[371]

As emphasized in Chapter II, judges have criticized the Witness and Victim Protection Law as encroaching upon defendants' due process rights while failing to provide adequate protection to vulnerable witnesses.[372] Judges have also expressed concern that the amendment to the Penal Code, imposing grave penalties on those who reveal information about protected witnesses, will further undermine judicial independence. More specifically, several judges have emphasized that the amendment is likely to create an environment in which judges will be reluctant to invoke either Article 28 provisions or constitutional due process guarantees to reveal any personal information about witnesses to the parties, for fear of criminal prosecution.[373] According to Salvadoran

---

recurso deberá ser interpuesto . . . mediante escrito dirigido a la Unidad Técnica en el plazo de tres días, contados a partir del siguiente al de la notificación respectiva." (art. 26). "*Denegada la revocatoria, sólo será admisible el recurso de revisión para ante la Comisión* [sic] *. . . El recurso deberá ser resuelto en el plazo de ocho días. Dicha resolución no admitirá otro recurso en sede administrativa.*" (art. 27).)

[370] Special Victim and Witness Protection Law, *supra* note 78, at art. 28. (In Spanish: "*El juez podrá, excepcionalmente, dar a conocer a las partes la identidad de la persona protegida, previa petición debidamente razonada, sólo para efectos del interrogatorio y en circunstancias que no sea observado por el imputado.*")

[371] Decreto [Decree] No. 1031/2006, Divulgación de la Imagen o Revelación de Datos de Personas Protegidas [Revealing the Likeness or Personal Data of Protected Persons], art 147-F (2006).

[372] *See, e.g.,* interviews with Juan Antonio Durán Ramírez, Juez de Sentencia de Chalatenango (Judge in the First Instance, Chalatenango Sentencing Tribunal), in San Salvador (Mar. 26, 2008 and Oct. 19, 2008); *see also,* interview with Rogel Zepeda, *supra* note 45.

[373] Interview with Durán Ramírez, *supra* note 76; *Institutional threats to the independence of the Judiciary in El Salvador,* Hearing Before the Inter-American Commission for Human Rights (2007) (statement of Juan Antonio Durán Ramírez), *available at* http://www.cidh.oas.org/Audiencias/select.aspx (follow "128 Period of Sessions (July 16-27, 2007)" hyperlink; then select "Friday, July 20, 2007" from "Select a date" dropdown menu) ("Those judges

judges, such a result would amount to an effective abdication of the judicial responsibility to guarantee defendants' due process rights to the UTE.[374]

In fact, the new witness protection regime has allowed both prosecutors and police officers to rely disproportionately on protected witnesses to secure convictions—often at the expense of carrying out a thorough investigation.[375] For example, Judge Martín Rogel Zepeda told our research team of cases in which a single witness had been used as key evidence to convict up to a hundred gang members.[376] Likewise, both Specialized Appeals Judge Sandra Luz Chicas Rivas and Appeals Judge Doris Luz Rivas Galindo told our researchers of their mounting concern over prosecution efforts to secure convictions based primarily on the testimony of a single anonymous witness.[377] They also indicated that the Office of the Prosecutor has increasingly relied on *testigos criteriados*— witnesses who themselves played a part in the crime and who are offered special benefits in exchange for their testimony against co-defendants. Specialized Appeals Judge Sandra Luz Chicas Rivas emphasized that this is a particular problem in the specialized court system (created by the Organized and Complex Crimes Law discussed *infra*): *testigos criteriados* had been used in the overwhelming majority of the 350 cases

---

who seek to guarantee defendants' due process rights and apply the Salvadoran Constitution and International Treaties [may] violate the law [under article 147-F of 1031/2006].").

[374] Interview with Durán Ramírez, *supra* note 81 ("There is no longer judicial control over protection measures, [they are under the purview of the] UTE, which is an administrative unit."); Efren Lemus, *Jueces señalan peligro de testigos anónimos,* LA PRENSA GRÁFICA, May 25, 2005, *available at* http://archive.laprensa.com.sv/20050525/nacion/211404.asp (Carlos Sánchez, *Juez Tercero del Tribunal de Sentencia de San Salvador* (Judge in the Third Sentencing Tribunal of San Salvador), told the press that it is the purview of the judiciary to determine whether a witness should be given protection measures or not.).

[375] *See, e.g,* interview with Rogel Zepeda, *supra* note 45; interview with Sandra Luz Chicas Rivas, Presidenta de la Cámara Especializada [President of the Specialized Appeals Court], in San Salvador (Oct. 21, 2008); interview with Rivas Galindo, *supra* note 68.

[376] Interview with Rogel Zepeda, *supra* note 45.

[377] Interview with Chicas Rivas, *supra* note 375; interview with Rivas Galindo, *supra* note 68.

that had reached the country's two specialized appeals courts since June 2007, when the specialized court system heard its first case. [378]

In contrast, the Director of the UTE, Mauricio Rodríguez, told our researchers that he considered the program "a success" because it had led to the conviction of over two thousand defendants in 2007. He also remarked that prosecutors and police officers were using the program with increased frequency, in particular to provide protection to gang members who had agreed to testify against other gang members.[379] According to Rodríguez, as of January 2009, gang members comprised the majority of those receiving witness protection. Nevertheless, Rodríguez admitted he remains "worried about investing in someone who may give false testimony" and noted that "protection regimes sometimes act as palliatives for shortcomings in the area of technical crime scene investigation."[380] He added that there has been little investment in the technical equipment necessary, for example, to conduct ballistic tests. "We should put more emphasis on fingerprint banks, on ballistic analysis. We should pay attention to crime scene investigation techniques: dealing with a case should have a more technical focus than relying on protected witnesses," he concluded.[381] Numerous other sources, including members of the judiciary, independent experts, and rights groups, emphasized that the police and the Office of the Prosecutor often fail to conduct thorough criminal investigations because it is easier to rely on witness testimony. For example, Judge Martín Rogel Zepeda told our researchers that "prosecutors consider their work is done when they find a witness" and rarely introduce other evidence to confirm the testimony of their protected witnesses, even though the majority of these

---

[378] Interview with Chicas Rivas, *supra* note 375; *see also,* Edith Portillo, *Tribunales Especializados con 109 casos en tres meses,* EL FARO, July 2, 2007, http://www.elfaro.net/secciones/Noticias/20070702/noticias9_20070702.asp.

[379] Interview with Mauricio Rodríguez, Director del Programa de Protección de Víctimas y Testigos [Director, Victim and Witness Protection Program], in San Salvador (Jan. 22, 2009).

[380] *Id.*

[381] *Id.*

witnesses are co-defendants who likely have a vested interest in helping the prosecution secure a conviction.[382] Likewise, Ovidio González, the Director of *Tutela Legal*, remarked that investigators regularly neglect to conduct adequate crime scene investigations, an oversight which he considered "a grave denial of justice." He emphasized that most investigators failed to do even basic, routine tests, which in his opinion strongly suggested that "evidence is never gathered because it is easier to look for witnesses."[383] This widely held perception of those deeply involved in the system is corroborated by the 2007 report on the Salvadoran criminal justice system authored by Sidney Blanco Reyes and Francisco Díaz Rodríguez, discussed in Chapter II.[384]

Of particular concern are reports that the Office of the Prosecutor has employed false witnesses, often using the same individual at different trials, under different code names. Newspaper sources have reported at least seven cases involving false witnesses in 2007 and 2008.[385] Our own research has uncovered at least one instance of police and prosecutorial misconduct: the former Director of Ideas and Actions for Peace, Quetzalcoatl Foundation (*Fundación Quetzalcoatl, Ideas y Acciones para la Paz*), Mauricio Figueroa, told our research team that a prosecutor and several police officers had asked him to give false testimony against several youth accused of committing a murder nearby his office.

---

[382] Interview with Rogel Zepeda, *supra* note 45. Judge Zepeda also told us of a case in which a gang member was brought in as a protected witness to introduce evidence against thirty other gang members. "He [the protected witness] started linking specific individuals with particular criminal acts, and giving us details. But this protected witness had a much more extensive criminal record than that of his co-defendants. Once we carefully combed through his testimony, it became evident that it had discrepancies; for example, he was in Mexico when he was supposed to have witnessed some of the crimes. And he was the prosecution's star witness."

[383] Interview with González, *supra* note 119.

[384] BLANCO REYES & DÍAZ RODRÍGUEZ, *supra* note 118.

[385] Daniel Valencia, *Los Testigos Falsos de la Fiscalía,* EL FARO, July 28, 2008, http://www.elfaro.net/secciones/Noticias/20080728/noticias1_20080728.asp; Daniel Valencia, *Paulina y Vicente, Arcángel, Perla y José María,* EL FARO, July 28, 2008, http://www.elfaro.net/secciones/Noticias/20080728/noticias2_20080728.asp; *Fiscalia Usa Testigos Falsos,* DIARIO CO LATINO, April 28, 2008.

Figueroa had told the police he had not witnessed the murder:

> Both the prosecutor and the investigators came to
> my office three times to ask me to testify at trial that
> I had seen [the youth], as this would guarantee the
> situation would not repeat itself. . . . They offered me
> all guarantees at trial: voice distortion, changing my
> appearance, dressing like a policeman. . . . And when
> I refused to collaborate, they asked me whether I knew
> anyone else that would be willing to testify in my
> place.[386]

This over-reliance on witness testimonies at trial may, paradoxically, also be responsible for increased attempts on the lives of witnesses (or potential witnesses). According to Judge Juan Antonio Durán: "Attacks against witnesses are a relatively recent phenomenon, which began taking place in 2003 when the government launched its Firm Hand initiative. In a way, [by relying almost exclusively on protected witnesses], the government has sent a message to gang members that if they can get rid of witnesses, the case against them will disappear."[387] Similarly, criminal defense attorney Carlos Manuel Quintanilla told our researchers that, in his experience, gang members actively seek to kill potential witnesses who could testify against them because they know this will likely ensure their impunity.[388] In fact, newspaper sources contain innumerable narratives of witnesses who have been targeted by gang members. Likewise, our researchers spoke with witnesses of gang-related violence who had reason to fear for their lives but were not provided adequate protection. These victim narratives, including their experiences with the victim and witness protection program, are explored in detail below.

---

[386] Interview with Figueroa, *supra* note 251.

[387] Interview with Durán Ramírez, *supra* note 76.

[388] Interview with Quintanilla, *supra* note 201.

d) *Anti-Terrorism Law*

On July 6, 2006, ARENA legislators formed a commission to study an anti-terrorism bill that had been languishing in the Legislative Assembly since its introduction in 2005.[389] Spurred by student protests on July 5, 2006, that left two policemen dead and eight others injured,[390] El Salvador's Congress passed an updated version of the legislation in September 2006.[391] The legislation criminalizes membership in a terrorist organization.[392] It also provides for five-to-ten year prison sentences for those who "simulate" terrorism,[393] issue public statements in "defense of" terrorism, or "incite"[394] terrorism. Rights groups assert that the concepts of "terrorism" and "terrorist organization" that appear in the law are vague, and they express further concern that the Act

---

[389] Wilfredo Salamanca, *Sin aprobarse ley contra terrorismo*, EL DIARIO DE HOY, July 7, 2006.

[390] The July 5, 2006, events involved a student protest outside the University of El Salvador (UES) and are discussed in greater detail, *infra*, Part C 1. They are credited with accelerating the passage of the anti-terrorism law and with pervading discussions about the adequacy of such a law during legislative debates. Rodrigo Baires Quezada, *Debate abierto por la ley antiterrorista*, EL FARO, July 17, 2006, http://www.elfaro.net/secciones/observatorio/20060717/observatorio1_20060717.asp (Ulises del Dios Guzmán, Supreme Court Justice in the Penal Chamber, told the press: "this proposal [the antiterrorist law] got a jump start after the July 5 events outside the UES, and their reprehensible nature may influence any discussion surrounding the antiterrorism law.").

[391] Decreto [Decree] No. 108/2006, Ley Especial Contra Actos de Terrorismo [Special Anti-Terrorism Law] [hereinafter Special Anti-Terrorism Law] (2006).

[392] *Id.* at art. 13. (In Spanish: *"Los que formaren parte de organizaciones terroristas, con el fin de realizar cualquiera de los delitos contemplados en la presente Ley, serán sancionados con prisión de ocho a doce años. Las organizadores, jefes, dirigentes o cabecillas, serán sancionados con prisión de diez a quince años."*)

[393] *Id.* at art. 9. (In Spanish: *"El que simulare la realización de cualquiera de los delitos contemplados en la presente Ley o cualquier tipo de prueba en apoyo a tal simulación, será sancionado con prisión de cinco a diez años."*)

[394] *Id.* at art. 8. (In Spanish: *"El que públicamente hiciere apología del terrorismo o incitare a otro u otros a cometer cualquiera de los delitos previstos en la presente Ley, será sancionado con prisión de cinco a diez años."*)

could be used to persecute political opponents of the government.[395] According to Jaime Martínez:

> On the pretext of combating terrorism and harmonizing national law with inter-American directives, the government enacted a law that, on the one hand, incorporated international prescriptions against terrorism, and on the other, includes provisions that in practice could be used to squelch public protest—as has in fact been the case.[396]

Indeed, since its enactment, prosecutors have invoked the anti-terrorism law against public demonstrators in three circumstances. First, in February 2007, prosecutors charged Vicente Ramírez, the president of a national small businesses association, and two other leaders of the organization for allegedly causing physical damage to the property of the Municipality of Apopa. These small business owners had participated in a demonstration against the dismantling of the stalls of informal

---

[395] IDHUCA, *La Ley contra el terrorismo*, Proceso, Aug.16, 2006, at 15; IDHUCA, El ID-HUCA Ante la Ley Anti-terrorismo (2006), *available at* http://www.uca.edu.sv/publica/idhuca/leyanti.pdf; *see also PGR espera que no se cometan abusos al aplicar Ley Antiterrorismo*, Diario Co Latino, Sept. 26, 2006, *available at* http://www.diariocolatino.com/es/20060926/nacionales/nacionales_20060926_13930/?tpl=69 (quoting Human Rights Ombudswoman Beatrice de Carrillo describing the law as unnecessary and inconsistent with human rights standards). The term "terrorism" is not defined in the law, though the concept of terrorism is laid out in broad terms in article 1, which states that the law applies to acts whose objective is to provoke fear among the population, such as by placing individuals in danger or threatening the democratic system, state security, or international peace. (In Spanish the full text reads: "*La presente Ley tiene como objeto prevenir, investigar, sancionar, y erradicar los delitos que se describen en esta, así como todas sus manifestaciones, incluido su financiamiento y actividades conexas, y que por la forma de ejecución, medios y métodos empleados, evidencien la intención de provocar estados de alarma, temor o terror en la población, al poner en peligro inminente o afectar la vida o la integridad física o mental de las personas, bienes materiales de significativa consideración o importancia, el sistema democrático o la seguridad del Estado o la paz internacional; todo lo anterior, con estricto apego al respeto a los Derechos Humanos.*") Special Anti-Terrorism Law, *supra* note 391, at art. 1.

[396] Interview with Jaime Martínez, Coordinador, Oficina de Justicia Juvenil, Corte Suprema de El Salvador [Coordinator, Office of Juvenile Justice, Supreme Court], in San Salvador (Mar. 25, 2008).

street vendors.[397]   The second use of the anti-terrorism law against
public demonstrators occurred on May 12, 2007, after a demonstration
organized by street vendors in San Salvador to protest the government's
seizure of their allegedly illegal merchandise.   Finally, prosecutors
invoked the anti-terrorism law a third time on July 2, 2007, in response
to protests in the town of Suchitoto against the enactment of a national
policy to decentralize water services.[398] These three protests, and the
State's application of the anti-terrorism law to those who participated in
them, are explored in more detail in part C. of this chapter.

e) *Organized and Complex Crimes Law*

Enacted on January 22, 2007, the Organized and Complex Crimes
Law states that its purpose is to create a specialized and efficient
procedure to prosecute two different classes of crimes: (1) those
orchestrated by structures of organized crime; and (2) "grave" crimes—
homicide, kidnapping and extortion—when carried out by groups of
two or more, when resulting in two or more victims, or when causing
alarm or social commotion.[399] The law creates specialized tribunals,
staffed by a cadre of specialized judges, with jurisdiction over these two
classes of crimes.[400] Specialized tribunals are located in the capital city
of San Salvador, the eastern city of San Miguel, and the western city of
Santa Ana. Two *jueces de instrucción* (judges who conduct preliminary
hearings to determine whether a case should advance to trial) and two
jueces de sentencia (judges who preside over the trial and sentencing
phases) have been assigned to the San Salvador tribunal. A single *juez*

---

[397] *See, e.g.,* Douglas González, *Confirman cargos contra Ramírez,* EL DIARIO DE HOY,
May 23, 2007, *available at* http://www.elsalvador.com/mwedh/nota/nota_completa.
asp?idCat=2892&idArt=1405188.

[398] *See, e.g.,* Rodrigo Baires Quezada, *Manifestantes de Suchitoto a prisión por "actos de
terrorismo."* EL FARO, July 9, 2007, http://www.elfaro.net/secciones/Noticias/20070709/noti-
cias4_20070709.asp.

[399] Decreto [Decree] No. 190/2007, Ley Contra el Crimen Organizado y Delitos de Realización Compleja, [Organized and Complex Crimes Law], art. 1 (2007).

[400] *Id.* at art. 3.

de instrucción and a single *juez de sentencia* have been assigned to each of the eastern and western district tribunals. All appeals are handled by two *magistrados* (appeals judges).[401]

President Saca described the new law as a "fundamental" and "modern tool" to combat organized crime.[402] However, rights groups, several judges, and independent experts have sharply criticized it as misguided, because it focuses solely on reforming the judicial process, despite the fact that most crimes in El Salvador never reach the courts.[403] In fact, a report authored by the National Commission for Citizen Security and Social Peace (a multi-sectoral, indepedendent commission appointed by the executive branch to evaluate legislative policies)[404] concluded that the specialized tribunals would provide no advantage over the current ordinary justice system.[405] That report emphasized that deficient criminal investigations, rather than an inefficient judiciary, were to blame for rising crime rates.[406] The Commission recommended

---

[401] Ruth Melany Cruz & Gabriel Labrador Aragón, *Toman posesión jueces especiales*, LA PRENSA GRÁFICA, Mar. 31, 2007, *available at* http://archive.laprensa.com.sv/20070331/lodeldia/20070331/9487.asp; *see also*, interview with Chicas Rivas, *supra* note 375.

[402] President Saca, Remarks at the Swearing-in Ceremony of Specialized Judges (Mar. 30, 2007), *available at* http://www.casapres.gob.sv/presidente/discursos/2007/03/disc3001.html.

[403] *See, e.g.*, Jaime Martínez Ventura, Anteproyecto de la ley contra el crimen organizado y delitos de realización compleja, Observaciones presentadas a la Comisión Nacional de Seguridad Ciudadana y Seguridad Social, *available at* http://edgardo.amaya.googlepages.com/CrimenOrganizado_AnteproyectodeLey_O.pdf.

[404] The National Commission for Citizen Security and Social Peace (*Comisión Nacional para la Seguridad Ciudadana y Paz Social*) was created by Legislative Decree 110/2006. The decree provides that the Commission should be an independent body composed of representatives from different segments of society. Commission members are appointed by the President and tasked with providing recommendations and monitoring strategies designed to combat crime, in particular in the area of gang violence. Decreto [Decree] 110/2006 (2006).

[405] COMISIÓN NACIONAL PARA LA SEGURIDAD CIUDADANA Y PAZ SOCIAL [NATIONAL COMMISSION FOR CITIZEN SECURITY AND SOCIAL PEACE], ANÁLISIS Y REVISIÓN DE LA LEY CONTRA EL CRIMEN ORGANIZADO Y DELITOS DE REALIZACIÓN COMPLEJA 3 (2006), *available at* http://edgardo.amaya.googlepages.com/PROPUESTASECRETARIATECNICA.pdf.

[406] *Id.* at 2.

strengthening the investigative capacity of the Office of the Prosecutor, as well as the PNC, as the best means of addressing organized crime.[407] Critics have also stressed that the new law erodes due process rights by allowing the use of hearsay testimony at trial. They also stress that the law violates the principle of *juez natural*[408] by creating a judicial appointment process that disregards the requirement of judicial independence and by giving the prosecution unbounded discretion to choose whether to file a case before an ordinary or a special tribunal.[409] In addition, the law has been criticized for its incomplete definition of "complex crimes" that fails to include money laundering, tax evasion, corruption, and other paradigmatic complex crimes.[410] The Commission's report echoed these criticisms.[411]

In practice, the new law has been employed to prosecute gang members. The specialized tribunals' dockets consist predominantly of cases against gang members, a fact that has earned specialized judges the name of "anti-gang judges."[412] Specialized Judge Lucila Fuentes de

---

[407] *Id.* at 3; *see also CSJ estudiará reforzar jueces especializados*, EL DIARIO DE HOY, Sept. 15, 2007, *available at* http://www.elsalvador.com/mwedh/nota/nota_completa. asp?idCat=6329&idArt=1703337 (quoting Supreme Court Justice Mirna Antonieta Perla Jiménez, who told the press: "Organized crime requires the training of those who prosecute and investigate those crimes.").

[408] The Inter-American Court of Human Rights has explained that "the principle of the competent, independent and impartial court [*juez natural*] . . . requires a case to be heard by the appropriate judge and, in tandem, the right to due process and judicial access." Case of the Rochela Massacre v. Colombia, 2007 Inter-Am. Ct. H.R. (ser.C) No. 163, at para. 204 (May 11, 2007).

[409] Interview with Nelson Rauda, Especialista en Derecho Penal y Asesor del Departamento de Prueba y Libertad Asistida (DEPLA) [Criminal Law Specialist and Aide to the Department of Probation and Parole], in San Salvador (Jan. 20, 2009); interview with Edgardo Amaya, independent consultant and former lawyer with FESPAD, in San Salvador (Mar. 26, 2008).

[410] Martínez Ventura, *supra* note 403.

[411] COMISIÓN NACIONAL PARA LA SEGURIDAD CIUDADANA Y PAZ SOCIAL, *supra* note 405, at 1.

[412] Interview with Durán Ramírez, *supra* note 76 (noting that the specialized judges are informally called *jueces anti-maras* (anti-gang judges)).

Paz told our research team that approximately 95 percent of all crimes prosecuted in the specialized tribunals, both in the capital and the provincial jurisdictions, are gang-related.[413] Specialized Appeals Judge Sandra Luz Chicas Rivas calculated that all but two or three of the 350 cases that had reached the appellate level of the specialized court system as of October 2008—99 percent—involved gang violence.[414]

f) *Reform of the Criminal Process Code*

Enacted on January 16, 2009, the revised Criminal Process Code was among the last major efforts of the departing Saca Administration to address rising crime rates.[415] The version of the bill that was signed into law, however, bears little resemblance to the draft introduced to Congress by the Justice Sector Coordinating Commission (*Comisión Coordinadora del Sector Justicia* or CSJ).[416] The controversy over the draft bill provides another illustration of the tensions between the executive and legislative branches on the one hand, and the judicial branch on the other.

On November 27, 2007, the CSJ introduced a draft bill to the Legislative Assembly to amend the Criminal Process Code.[417] Reform efforts were aimed at reducing docket processing times and increasing judicial efficiency. The authors of the draft bill emphasized several specific advantages over the Criminal Process Code then in effect, including the adoption of features of an adversarial system; the clear delineation of investigative and judicial roles; the granting of exclusive jurisdiction to investigate crimes to the Office of the Prosecutor (*Fiscalía General*

---

[413] Interview with Fuentes de Paz, *supra* note 72.

[414] Interview with Chicas Rivas, *supra* note 375.

[415] Decreto [Decree] No. 733/2009, Código Procesal Penal [Penal Process Code] (2009).

[416] Press Release, Ministerio de Seguridad Pública y Justicia, Se Presenta a la Asamblea Legislativa el Proyecto de Nuevo Código Procesal Penal (Nov. 27, 2007), *available at* http://www.seguridad.gob.sv/Web-Seguridad/Noticias/codigoprocesal.htm.

[417] *Id.*

de la República); and the overall increase in investigative efficiency that would result from giving prosecutors broader authority to carry out investigations without immediate judicial oversight.[418] In spite of these advertised advantages, the proposed bill drew strong opposition from a broad array of actors, including rights groups, academics and members of the judiciary. These analysts criticized the bill as having been drafted in secret and without meaningful participation from the judicial branch.[419] In addition, academics, rights groups, and members of the judiciary disagreed strongly with the proposed code's core, substantive provisions, arguing that expanding prosecutorial powers was irresponsible in light of the political character of the Office of the Prosecutor and the demonstrated lack of investigative capacity and inefficiencies that plague that office.[420]

The Legislative Assembly responded to mounting pressure to reject the proposed draft code[421] by convening a workshop and establishing an ad-hoc legislative commission, that relied on a three-judge panel to make changes to the draft bill.[422] The Legislative Assembly ultimately set aside the original draft in favor of an alternative proposal drafted by

---

[418] *Id.*

[419] Suchit Chávez & Gregorio Morán, *Jueces piden detener entrega de proyecto de Código Procesal*, La Prensa Gráfica, Nov. 27, 2007, *available at* http://www.laprensagrafica.net/nacion/931577.asp (noting that seven associations of judges criticized the drafting process, calling for "broader analysis and discussion" of the proposed code before its adoption).

[420] *See, e.g.,* Jaime Martínez Ventura, *La inminente aprobación del Código Procesal Penal*, Diario Co Latino, Sept. 16, 2008, *available at* http://www.diariocolatino.com/es/20080916/opiniones/58847/ (noting that the process code drafted by the CSJ "attempted to turn the Office of the Prosecutor into the lord and master of the country's penal process."); Edward Sidney Blanco Reyes, Comentarios al Proyecto del Código Procesal Penal (emphasizing that the Office of the Prosecutor is not an independent entity, but rather, favors political commitments to the party in power over technical knowledge and capacity) (on file with authors); Rodrigo Baires Quezada, *Los baches del nuevo Código Procesal Penal*, El Faro, Jan. 28, 2008, http://www.elfaro.net/secciones/Noticias/20080128/noticias2_20080128.asp.

[421] The March of Judges described in Chapter II *supra*, for example, was one of the many demonstrations of public discontent with the proposed draft.

[422] Leonor Cárdenas & Iván Escobar, *Juristas piden estudiar proyecto de Código Procesal Penal*, diario Co Latino, Sept. 16, 2008, *available* at www.diariocolatino.com/es/20080916/nacionales/58874/.

the three-judge panel. President Saca signed this alternative bill into law on January 16, 2009.[423] Although the consultation process adopted by the Legislative Assembly was also criticized for its "hermetism" and failure to represent a plurality of opinions,[424] most judges, academics, and rights groups interviewed for this book agreed that the alternative bill cured the major shortcomings of the initial draft.[425]

There is a growing consensus among many observers, including law enforcement officials, that the *Mano Dura* policies and legislative reforms described above have been ineffective or even counter-productive.[426] This view was widely shared by representatives of civil society organizations interviewed by our researchers in El Salvador. However, with the exception of the underfunded *Mano Amiga* and *Mano Extendida* plans cited above, the Salvadoran government has failed to develop robust alternatives to *Mano Dura*-style strategies for addressing the gang phenomenon. A police official who told our researchers that *Mano Dura* policies were widely recognized as a failure also acknowledged that PNC officers on the ground continue to employ *Mano Dura* practices of mass arrests and raids because of institutional inertia and the lack of a coherent alternative approach.[427] The following sub-chapters explore the effects of these state responses on various sectors of Salvadoran society.

---

[423] Amadeo Cabrera, *Asamblea aprueba nueva legislación procesal penal*, LA PRENSA GRÁ-FICA, Oct. 23, 2008, *available at* http://www.laprensagrafica.net/nacion/1163098.asp.

[424] Martínez Ventura, *supra* note 420.

[425] *See, e.g.*, interview with Edward Sidney Blanco Reyes, Juez Quinto de Instrucción de San Salvador [Judge in the First Instance, Fifth Instruction Tribunal in San Salvador], in San Salvador (Oct. 21, 2008); interview with Rogel Zepeda, *supra* note 45.

[426] In an interview with our researchers, Hugo Ramírez, PNC Subcommissioner and Head of the Juvenile and Family Services Division, stated: "The strategies of *Mano Dura* and all that stuff have weakened our position [that of the PNC] with respect to institutions.... It has been openly admitted that the Plan *Mano Dura* has been a failure." Interview with Ramírez, *supra* note 126.

[427] *Id.*

2. *Institutionalized Discrimination Against Targeted Groups, Including Tattooed Persons and Youth*

> *Youth are trapped in this country. They are imprisoned in their own homes, or in their communities, or in jail. And they are stigmatized by all governmental institutions. In El Salvador, to speak of youth is to speak of violence, to speak of crime.*
>
> - Aída Luz Santos de Escobar, San Salvador Juvenile Sentencing Judge, in San Salvador (Oct. 22, 2008)

One primary consequence of the *Mano Dura* laws and policies has been the institutionalization of police profiling of certain groups.[428] The focus in the first and second Anti-Gang Laws on appearance and tattoos as identifiers or proxies for unlawful gang membership or "illicit association,"[429] combined with generalized law enforcement strategies that de-emphasize investigation and prioritize arrest of alleged gang members, have nurtured a climate in which police target certain sectors of Salvadoran society for stops and arrests on the basis of social characteristics, age, and background. For example, youth with tattoos, gang-related or not, often fear being targeted for arbitrary arrests and detentions in El Salvador.[430] At the Goodbye Tattoos (*Adiós Tatuajes*)

---

[428] *See generally* interview with Aguilar, *supra* note 157; interview with Perla Jiménez, *supra* note 150; interview with Durán Ramírez, *supra* note 76.

[429] Discussed in Part A 1. of this Chapter.

[430] Interview with R.S.A., in San Salvador (Mar. 29, 2006) (describing how police officials arbitrarily arrested and detained her son, who has tattoos but who asserts that he has not been a member of any gang, and two of his friends for twenty-four hours; authorities later dropped vandalism charges against her son, which she asserted were unfounded. She and her son believe that the police arrested him on account of his tattoos); interview with Morales, *supra* note 230 ("Most clients come because of the persecution they face for having tattoos....The police harass people too just for having tattoos. They stop them on the street, and they beat them. That's happened to lots of our clients. And to get a job, employers make you take off your shirt to see if you have tattoos, especially anything in the government/pub-

program, a tattoo removal clinic run by a parish in San Salvador, clinicians told our researchers that their clients arrive to remove tattoos of all sorts because of discrimination and targeting they experience from police and society at large.[431] One administrator at the program recalled an incident in which a client ran into the clinic and begged her to come outside to confirm to the police that he was in the midst of the tattoo-removal process. When she went outside, the police were there waiting.[432] Other clients report that the police beat them for having tattoos, even when they know that they are in the process of having them removed. In addition to police violence, clients of the clinic reported schools denying them admission on the basis of tattoos (even artistic tattoos) and employers that refuse to hire without first checking the prospective employee for tattoos.[433]

Our researchers interviewed other former gang members who reported experiencing state or private discrimination or harassment on account of their tattoos.[434] For example, one former gang member who had been deported from the United States told our researchers that he had serious difficulties finding a job because of his tattoos. Though he was able to get a job with a moving company, he was fired after a

---

lic sector."); Interview with R.E., *supra* note 272 (reporting that he was anxious traveling in public transportation because of his tattoos and describing efforts to begin to remove them).

[431] Interview with Morales, *supra* note 230.

[432] *Id.*

[433] *Id.*

[434] Interview with W.M., *supra* note 248 ("Another time I was walking with co-workers and we all have artistic tattoos. We were waiting for the bus. Cops were staring at us. One co-worker had his young son with him. The cops put us against the wall and searched us, searched our stuff, opened our sterilized tattooing equipment. We told them not to because they would contaminate it. They pushed me around, but eventually they let us go."); interview with M.P., *supra* note 272 (describing difficulties finding work due to his tattoos); interview with E.C.C., *supra* note 239 (reporting being stopped for having tattoos and being arrested for illicit association during one of these stops); interview with J.R.T., *supra* note 272 (describing how the police stop young men (even in the absence of any illicit behavior) and have them lift their shirts to check for tattoos, frequently abusing those who turn out to be tattooed).

week on the job when his boss caught a glimpse of a tattoo.[435] In light of this stigmatization of tattoos and persecution of the tattooed, gangs increasingly discourage the use of tattoos among their members.[436] In spite of this shift in gang behavior, our interviews in El Salvador indicate that targeted harassment and social discrimination of tattooed individuals has continued.

Our researchers in El Salvador found that the *Mano Dura* policies have fostered state and societal discrimination against other sectors of the Salvadoran population as well. For example, our researchers found evidence that in certain neighborhoods in El Salvador, the simple facts of being young, male, and in a public space were sufficient to trigger frequent police suspicion and arrest.[437] These findings are discussed in greater detail in the next chapter on arbitrary arrests and police violence. Those deported from the United States, who were explicitly singled out in the original Anti-Gang Law for arrest and detention upon arrival in El Salvador, constitute another group frequently subject to social discrimination and police abuse in El Salvador. Politicians and the media also tend to depict deportees as dangerous gang members and criminals,[438] though statistics indicate that between 1998 and 2004, only

---

[435] Interview with J.R.T., *supra* note 272.

[436] Interview with Hernández Portillo, *supra* note 156 (noting that a gang leader who was recently put in jail did not have any tattoos); interview with Aguilar, *supra* note 157.

[437] *See, e.g.,* interview with T.C., *supra* note 200 (T.C. is an 18-year-old man from Soyapango who asserts that he has never been a member of a gang. He described to us how, beginning when he was fourteen, the police in his neighborhood frequently stopped, arrested, and beat him, accusing him of "illicit association" without further evidence than having seen him near other young men in the street.); *see also* interview with A.F., *supra* note 310 (A.F. is a 24-year old man from Mejicanos who asserts that he has never been a member of a gang. He stated to us that the police stop him one or two times each week.).

[438] *See, e.g.,* Jaime García, *Deportados por delitos en EE.UU. llegan a 1,515*, EL DIARIO DE HOY, Aug. 20, 2006, *available at* http://www.elsalvador.com/noticias/2006/08/30/nacional/nac4.asp; Katlen Urquilla, Enrique Miranda & Liz Hidalgo, *Preocupa a Gobierno que lleguen mareros*, EL DIARIO DE HOY, Mar. 16, 2005; Enrique Miranda & Nelson Dueñas, *País propone cárcel para los deportados convictos*, EL DIARIO DE HOY, Apr. 1, 2005; Edward Gutiérrez & David Marroquín, *Saca preocupado por deportaciones*, LA PRENSA GRÁFICA, Mar. 16, 2005; *Maras deportados, peligro en El Salvador*, UNIVISIÓN NEWS ONLINE, Sept. 20, 2006, *available at* http://www.univision.com/content/content.jhtml?chid=3&schid=181&secid=10

about one-third of those deported from the United States to El Salvador had a criminal conviction.[439]

3. *Police Violence and Arbitrary Arrests*

A primary aim of Salvadoran law enforcement initiatives since 2003 has been to capture and detain as many gang members as possible.[440] International and domestic civil society organizations have suggested that this emphasis on mass detentions—carried out by police-military forces with limited investigative capacity and poor human rights records—has resulted in troubling patterns of arbitrary stops and arrests by Salvadoran police.[441] Based on interviews of youth and community members carried out by our researchers in El Salvador in 2006, 2007,

---

984&cid=967427.

[439] According to statistics from the Department of Homeland Security (DHS), of the 72,452 Salvadorans deported from the United States between 1998 and 2007, in only 25,464, cases the Department had evidence that the deportee had a criminal conviction. *See* DEPARTMENT OF HOMELAND SECURITY, YEARBOOK OF IMMIGRATION STATISTICS tbl.37 (2007).

[440] *See, e.g.,* statement of former President Flores in announcing the first *Mano Dura* plan in the summer of 2003, emphasizing the government's determination to capture gang members throughout the country; Calderón, *supra* note 318; *see also Aplicación de la ley Combate a las pandillas: una Mano Dura y otra suave, supra* note 153 (describing the government's emphasis on arrest and capture of suspected gang members in its *Mano Dura* and *Súper Mano Dura* strategies); INFORME ANUAL JUSTICIA JUVENIL, *supra* note 123, at 27 (including a graphic display of statistics from the PNC regarding annual numbers of detention of juveniles for illicit association: the number jumped from 98 to 1,462 from 2002 to 2003).

[441] *See, e.g.,* Red para la Infancia y la Adolescencia de El Salvador (RIA) [El Salvador Network for Children and Youth], *Informe Ejecutivo de la RIA El Salvador en el Marco de Reunión con la Comisión Interamericana de Derechos Humanos (CIDH), sobre el tema de pandillas o maras en El Salvador, Audiencia y Reunión de Trabajo realizado en la sede de la CIDH*, Washington, DC, Oct. 26-27 2004 (reporting unlawful detention of children in El Salvador under the 2003 and revised versions of LAM I); INFORME ANUAL JUSTICIA JUVENIL, *supra* note 123, at 25.

2008 and 2009,[442] as well as observations by human rights advocates,[443] it appears that the police practice of stopping, searching, and arresting individuals based solely on their appearance continues in spite of the formal expiration of the 2003-04 Anti-Gang Laws.

FESPAD and the El Salvador Center for Penal Studies (*Centro de Estudios Penales de El Salvador* or CEPES) conducted a quantitative review of police arrest and prosecution statistics after the first year of the *Mano Dura* policies. The results were disturbing: between July 2003 and August 2004, police detained 19,275 people on grounds that they belonged to gangs, according to police statistics published in the Salvadoran daily *El Diario de Hoy*. Police released 84 percent of those arrested because there were no cognizable grounds for their arrest, and prosecutors dropped charges against another 7 percent, or nearly half of those not yet released, due to a lack of evidence. As of August 2004, only 5 percent of accused gang members arrested after July 2003 were being held by judicial order while criminal proceedings against them were underway.[444] Summing up the results of this analysis, FESPAD and CEPES concluded that "more than ninety percent of [suspected gang members arrested between July 2003 and August 2004] were arrested because of their appearance, their dress, or because they had tattoos or used 'signs', reasons that are insufficient to establish criminal responsibility in court."[445]

Interviews conducted by our researchers in poor neighborhoods on the outskirts of San Salvador suggest that these patterns of profiling and arbitrary arrest have continued. Most of the boys and young men from

---

[442] *See, e.g.,* interview with C.A., *supra* note 143; interview with T.C., *supra* note 200; interview with E.R.M., *supra* note 214; interview with P.V., in Santa Ana (Oct. 19, 2007); interview with members of the Comité de Madres Pro-Reo [Committee of Mothers for Detainee Rights], in San Salvador (Oct. 19, 2008); interview with members of the Comité de Derechos Humanos de la Parroquia de San Bartolo [Human Rights Committee of the San Bartolo Parish], in San Salvador (Oct. 21, 2008); interview with J.T., *supra* note 211.

[443] Interview with Alemanni de Carrillo, *supra* note 119; interview with Salazar Flores, *supra* note 91; interview with B.E., *supra* note 119.

[444] *See* INFORME ANUAL JUSTICIA JUVENIL 2004, *supra* note 123, at 25.

[445] *Id.*

poor and marginalized areas in and outside San Salvador interviewed by our researchers reported having been stopped and patted down by police on a regular, often weekly or even daily, basis.[446] Several of these reported having been wrongfully accused by police of being gang members.[447] Many reported having been subjected to arbitrary arrest and detention by the police.[448] In some instances, these interviewees informed our researchers that the police explained that they were being detained for "illicit association."[449] Young people who live in areas with a gang presence described being stopped arbitrarily by police and told to lift up their shirts for a search of gang tattoos as a regular, often weekly, occurrence.[450] One youth described an incident in which he and several

---

[446] *See, e.g.,* interview with C.A., *supra* note 143 (C.A., a 24-year-old former gang member who was living in an urban area on the outskirts of San Salvador, reported that the police stopped and searched him on a near-daily basis.); interview with E.R.M., *supra* note 214 (E.R.M., an 18-year-old former street child, reported that when he lived on the street, he was harassed and sometimes beaten by the police "almost every day."); interview with A.F., *supra* note 310 (A.F., a 24-year-old resident of an urban area on the outskirts of San Salvador who asserted that he had never been involved with gangs, reported that he was stopped and searched weekly by police.); interview with T.C., *supra* note 200 (T.C., an 18-year-old who grew up in a densely populated city near San Salvador and who stated that he was never a gang member, reported that he "always" had problems with police when he was on the streets of his neighborhood and that police had arrested him some ten times for illicit association.); interview with P.V., *supra* note 442 (noting that the police regularly stopped kids whom they presume to be gang members in her neighborhood and asked them to lift their shirts; if they refused, she told us, the police can become violent.)

[447] Interview with A.F., *supra* note 310; interview with T.C., *supra* note 200.

[448] *See supra* notes 430 and 437.

[449] Interview with C.A., *supra* note 143; interview with R.S.A., *supra* note 430 (describing the arrest of her son from his home by fifteen armed policemen who later announced that they had captured dangerous gang members and then detained her son for twenty-four hours); interview with R.E., *supra* note 272; interview with M.P., *supra* note 272.

[450] Interview with C.A., *supra* note 143 (reporting being stopped and searched by police on a near-daily basis); interview with R.E., *supra* note 272 (reporting having been stopped twice since being deported three years ago, taken one time to the police station, and held for five days after the police saw his tattoos under his shirt); interview with M.P., *supra* note 272 (reporting having been detained three times); interview with T.C., *supra* note 200 (T.C. stated that he was not a gang member but lived in an area with a heavy gang presence, and has "always" been stopped and searched by police on leaving his neighborhood.).

friends were driving to a wake. En route, the police stopped them, took them to a police station, and beat them with their rifles.[451] The police officers told them that they were being arrested for "illicit association," but authorities never gave the youths a court date and released them five days later.[452] This young man reported additional police harassment and violence in the weeks following this detention.[453] Yet another youth described being arrested for "illicit association" between six and eight times.[454] Each time, he was held for three to five days and then released.[455] Another reported being arrested eleven times for hanging out with his friends, who were not gang members. The police officers who arrested him, this young man informed our research team, told him that he was being detained for "illicit association" or for walking around at night without any papers.[456]

In July 2006, in a particularly visible illustration of the Salvadoran authority's reliance on mass arbitrary arrests, police stormed a church in a poor neighborhood outside San Salvador during a wake for three young gang members who had been killed.[457] The raid, in which police arrested more than 190 young people, took place several hours after a police officer in the area had been killed.[458] Church officials reported

---

[451] Interview with D.H., in Cabañas (Aug. 25, 2006).

[452] *Id.*

[453] *Id.*

[454] Interview with P.E., in Cabañas (Aug. 25, 2006).

[455] *Id.*

[456] Interview with T.C., *supra* note 200.

[457] Parroquia San Bartolo [San Bartolo Parish], Ilopango, Publicación Especial, Allanamiento 3 (2006). It bears noting that the *modus operandi* by which these youths were killed corresponds highly to a death squad killing. *See* Tutela Legal, Sobre los Actos de Profanación y Allanamiento Ilegal a la Capilla de la Iglesia Católica de la Cima I, San Bartolo, Municipio de Ilopango y las Detenciones Arbitrarias Masivas en el Mismo Lugar, Ocurridas el 12 de Julio de 2006 [hereinafter Tutela Legal San Bartolo Report] 1 (2006).

[458] Tutela Legal San Bartolo Report, *supra* note 457, at 1.

that they had visited the local police station with the families of the boys killed in the days before the wake to notify police officials of their plans for the funeral and to request police protection during the service.[459] (See insert: Mass Arrests at the San Bartolo Parish.)

According to witness accounts compiled and published by church leaders, the funeral was proceeding peacefully when police entered the church after midnight wearing ski masks and bullet-proof vests and carrying high caliber weapons.[460] Once inside, the police forced the boys and men present to strip down to their underwear, opened and searched coffins, and searched everyone inside, before arresting 194 youths.[461] Church leaders and rights groups contend that in the process of conducting the operation, police officers shouted obscenities and beat the young people they searched.[462] According to initial reports, the Office of the Prosecutor intended to charge those arrested in the raid with "illicit association" and resisting arrest, but the office dropped criminal charges against all the young people arrested within six days of the incident.[463] These events prompted significant outcry from Catholic and other religious communities in El Salvador.[464]

---

[459] *Id.*

[460] *Id.* at 2.

[461] *Id.* at 2-3.

[462] *Id.* at 2.

[463] *Id.,* at 3.

[464] Parroquia San Bartolo, *supra* note 457 (reproducing press releases and letters of support from leaders of various religious communities in El Salvador that express concern about the raid and the deteriorating human rights situation in the country).

<u>Mass arrests at the San Bartolo Parish</u>

On July 10, 2006, four teenage boys were killed, execution-
style, by unknown assailants. At least two of them were
members of the Mara 18.[1] The local parish priest, Father
Domingo Solís Rodríguez, offered to hold a wake for three of
the deceased in his church, and opened the doors to family
and friends. Before the wake began, Father Solís Rodríguez
and some family members of the victims went to the police
station to advise the police that the wake would take place that
evening and to ask that police be present at the ceremony for
the safety of those attending. In response to these requests, the
police stationed at least four agents at the church to monitor
the situation.

Approximately 100 family members attended the wake,
along with nearly 200 friends of the deceased—some of whom
were gang members. The mood was sober; the crowd prayed
and sang together until late into the night. By 1:00 A.M., the
crowd had shrunk, and the priest and nuns had gone home.
About half an hour later, the police approached to tell the
remaining mourners that security was being withdrawn.
Shortly thereafter, a new group of police—apparently, members
of the "Police Reaction Group"—descended on the church. The
police forced open the coffins, searching for guns.[2] The special
police forces beat mourners, forced the men to strip, and threw
their clothes on the ground.[3] The police also forced women

[1] Tutela Legal, Sobre los Actos de Profanación y Allanamiento Ilegal a la Capilla de la Iglesia Católica de la Cima I, San Bartolo, Municipio de Ilopango y las Detenciones Arbitrarias Masivas en el Mismo Lugar, Ocurridas el 12 de Julio de 2006 1 (2006).

[2] Marielos Márquez, *Policía interrumpe vela dentro de iglesia para arrestar a pandilleros*, Diario Co Latino, July 12, 2006.

[3] Parroquia San Bartolo [San Bartolo Parish], Ilopango, Publicación Especial, Allanamiento 3 (2006).

> to lift their shirts up to their necks, and beat a 12-year-old boy on the head.[4]
>
> Police forces detained and held as suspected gang members nearly 200 people, including 38 minors.[5] They released them five days later, when the government was unable to produce any evidence that a crime had been committed.[6] - *Virginia Corrigan*
>
> ---
>
> [4] *Id.*
>
> [5] Márquez, *supra* note 2.
>
> [6] *Liberan a pandilleros tras la megarredada*, EL DIARIO DE HOY, July 18, 2006.

Interviews conducted by our researchers in El Salvador indicate that the arbitrary stops and arrests of Salvadoran youths are often accompanied by police abuse and physical violence, including beatings on the street or in police detention centers.[465] These first-hand reports of abuse came from active gang members, former gang members, and non-gang members alike.[466] One 24-year-old man, interviewed in on the outskirts of San Salvador, described a recent interaction with police on his street:

---

[465] Interview with C.A., *supra* note 143; interview with R.E., *supra* note 272 (both reporting having been beaten by police); *see also* interview with E.C.C., *supra* note 239 (reporting having been stopped by police three times in the year since he was deported; the third time he was charged with illicit association); interview with D.H., *supra* note 451 (describing an incident in which he was beaten by ten or eleven police officers over a two-hour period of interrogations); interview with J.L., in Cabañas (Aug. 25, 2006) (describing an incident in which a group of police officers and soldiers shoved a gun against his chest, held a grenade up to his head, and told him they were going to kill him).

[466] *See, e.g.,* interview with A.F., *supra* note 310 (not a member of a gang); interview with E.R.M., (not a member of a gang), *supra* note 214; interview with C.A., *supra* note 143; interview with D.H., *supra* note 451; interview with L.F.G., *supra* note 233.

> There were seven of us sitting on a bench outside a store.
> None of us are gang members. We were drinking there.
> Then four police officers [approached us and searched
> us] and told us to open up our legs more, they pushed
> us and then kicked us. We didn't have any drugs or any
> weapons, they didn't find anything on us. They told us
> that only "whores, thieves, and fags" were outside at
> night and then they left.[467]

An 18-year-old male who became a street child in San Salvador at
the age of thirteen reported that when he lived on the streets, he was
repeatedly subjected to physical abuse by police:

> I had a lot of problems with police on the streets.
> Sometimes they grabbed me and beat me up hard,
> sometimes because they saw me rob something. They
> would hit me really hard, they would take me to dark
> areas . . . They would hit me with guns and sticks . . .
> Sometimes when I was asleep in the street they would
> wake me up to beat me up . . . Sometimes they beat me
> up and just left, sometimes they brought me into the
> police station.[468]

Other young people interviewed by our researchers described being
subjected to even more serious instances of physical abuse and violent
threats by police.[469] Similarly, residents of marginalized neighborhoods
reported witnessing the systematic harassment and physical abuse of
young men and women from their communities by police. For example,
a woman who lived in Colonia Majucla, a poor neighborhood on the
outskirts of San Salvador, described witnessing the following incident:

---

[467] Interview with A.F., *supra* note 310.

[468] Interview with E.R.M., *supra* note 214.

[469] *See, e.g.,* interview with L.F.G., *supra* note 233 (describing having part of his earlobe
ripped off by police officers).

A policeman grabbed a young boy by the hair, put a gun to his face, and hit him with the butt of the gun. The boy worked at the local supermarket and was just hanging out with two of his friends. When his mother, who was nearby, tried to defend her son, the policeman told her "what are you complaining about, you're just like those boys."[470]

Police brutality is directed not only at youth who live in blighted communities. Entire families may be subjected to abuse, especially if the police suspect that a family member has ties with local gangs. For example, a female member of the Committee of Mothers for Detainee Rights (*Comité de Madres Pro-Reo*, a group of mothers who came together to protest deplorable living conditions in prison) told our researchers that police officers had entered her home to conduct searches without a warrant on a number of occasions. Police incursions into her home had happened so frequently that she remarked: "It has become a hobby for the police to raid my home."[471]

In addition, we heard testimonies from several community members who recounted that police officers often cover their badges or wear ski masks while patrolling their neighborhoods.[472] A volunteer who works with the San Bartolo Parish Human Rights Committee (*Comité de los Derechos Humanos de la Parroquia de San Bartolo*) told our researchers that she lives in constant fear of the police because she has witnessed repeated instances of police violence. For example, she stood five to ten meters away from a group of youths while they were brutally beaten

---

[470] Interview with a resident of Colonia Majucla and member of the Comité de Madres Pro-Reo [Committee of Mothers for Detainee Rights], in San Salvador (Oct. 19, 2008). San Bartolo Parish's Human Rights Committee meets every Tuesday afternoon to conduct intake interviews of community members who believe their rights have been violated. The all-volunteer committee includes lawyers, non-legal advocates, and local community members.

[471] Interview with a member of the Comité de Madres Pro-Reo [Committee of Mothers for Detainee Rights], in San Salvador (Oct. 19, 2008).

[472] *Id.*; interview with members of the Human Rights Committee of the San Bartolo Parish, in San Salvador (Oct. 21, 2008).

by police and witnessed two young men being dragged out of their homes by two policemen and three others in civilian dress, all of whom were wearing ski masks.[473] Father Domingo Solís Rodríguez similarly emphasized that communities are afraid of the police: "People are afraid. They come to me for help because they don't know who else to turn to. But I am also afraid and where do I go for help?"[474] Because of this generalized atmosphere of fear and distrust of police forces, many instances of police abuse go unreported.

Salvadoran human rights organizations have also documented cases of severe physical abuse and killings committed by PNC officers in recent years. The National Human Rights Ombudsperson's Office reports that complaints of human rights violations committed by the police constitute the single largest category of denunciations that the office receives (see Figures 6, 7a, and 7b).[475]

---

[473] Interview with a member of the Human Rights Committee of the San Bartolo Parish and resident of the Cimas I de San Bartolo neighborhood, in San Salvador (Oct. 21, 2008).

[474] Interview with Solís Rodríguez, *supra* note 202.

[475] Interview with Alemanni de Carrillo, *supra* note 119; interview with Salazar Flores, *supra* note 91; *see also* Procuraduría para la Defensa de los Derechos Humanos, Actuaciones de la Inspectoría General y las Secciones Disciplinarias de la PNC en el Departmento de San Salvador 12-13 (2005), *available at* http://www.pddh.gob.sv/docs/informeinspectoriaconanexos.pdf ; Informe de Labores de la Procuraduría 05-06, *supra* note 102, at 46; Informe de Labores de la Procuraduría 07-08, *supra* note 131, at 168.

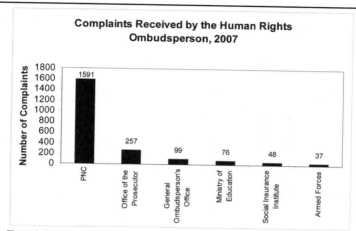

Figure 6. Complaints Received by the Human Rights Ombudsperson in 2007
Source: PROCURADURÍA PARA LA DEFENSA DE LOS DERECHOS HUMANOS [OFFICE OF THE NATIONAL
HUMAN RIGHTS OMBUDSPERSON], INFORME DE LABORES DE LA PROCURADURÍA PARA LA DEFENSA DE LOS
DERECHOS HUMANOS JUNIO 2007-MAYO 2008 [REPORT ON THE WORK OF THE NATIONAL HUMAN RIGHTS
OBUDSPERSON].
(Note: The General Ombudspersons' Office (*Procuraduría General de la República*) safeguards the rights
and interests of the family, minors, and the handicapped, and provides legal aid to people of limited
means.)

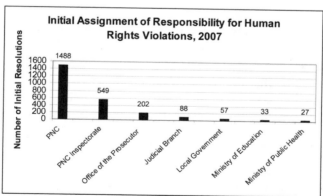

**Figure 7a. Initial Assignment of Responsibility for Human Rights Violations by the Office of the
National Human Rights Ombudsperson**
Source: PROCURADURÍA PARA LA DEFENSA DE LOS DERECHOS HUMANOS [OFFICE OF THE NATIONAL
HUMAN RIGHTS OMBUDSPERSON], INFORME DE LABORES DE LA PROCURADURÍA PARA LA DEFENSA DE LOS
DERECHOS HUMANOS JUNIO 2007-MAYO 2008 [REPORT ON THE WORK OF THE NATIONAL HUMAN RIGHTS
OMBUDSPERSON].

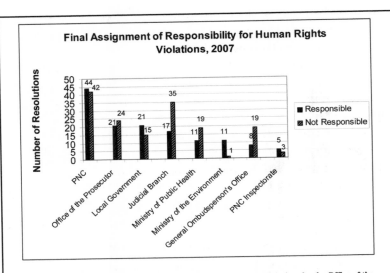

Figure 7b. Final Assignment of Responsibility for Human Rights Violations by the Office of the National Human Rights Ombudsperson
Source: Procuraduría para la Defensa de los Derechos Humanos [Office of the National Human Rights Ombudsperson], Informe de Labores de la Procuraduría para la Defensa de los Derechos Humanos Junio 2007-Mayo 2008 [Report on the Work of the National Human Rights Ombudsperson].

Tutela Legal investigated in-depth nine incidents of killings by PNC officers in 2004, 2005, and 2007, and ten such incidents in 2006.[476] Lissette Miranda, the National Director of the Pro-Youth Program, told our researchers that she has seen police officers harass Pro-Youth Program participants on a number of occasions. She described a particular case in which a policeman held the flame of a lighter very

[476] Tutela Legal del Arzobispado de San Salvador, Informe de Tutela Legal del Arzobispado de San Salvador Sobre la Situación de los Derechos Humanos en El Salvador a partir de la defensa de los mismos y de las investigaciones de violaciones a estos derechos, ocurridas durante el 2004 74-89 (2004) [hereinafter La Situación de los Derechos Humanos en El Salvador 2004]; Tutela Legal del Arzobispado de San Salvador, Informe Anual de Tutela Legal del Arzbobispado de San Salvador: La Situación de los Derechos Humanos en El Salvador 2005 16-17 (2005) [hereinafter La Situación de los Derechos Humanos en El Salvador 2005]; La Situación de los Derechos Humanos en El Salvador 2006, *supra* note 173, at 20; La Situación de los Derechos Humanos en El Salvador 2007, *supra* note 173, at 22.

close to a youth's face. She also emphasized that good preventive work was carried out by a small segment of the police forces, but that lack of communication and coordination between and among different branches of the police, as well as insufficient funding, undermined much of their work.[477] Assistant Police Inspector Amaya Márquez, who works in crime prevention, underscored that some police officers are still influenced by their previous military training, which makes them more likely to resort to physical violence.[478]

The Salvadoran state's decision to involve military agents in civil policing activity discussed in Chapter II is a particularly troubling aspect of its crackdown on youth gangs.[479] The militarization of Salvadoran policing activities poses serious human rights concerns for several reasons. As international organizations such as the Washington Office on Latin America have noted, the separation of military and police functions and the establishment of a civilian police force constituted one of the major accomplishments of the Peace Accords.[480] The use of joint patrols undermines that achievement and exposes civilians to a heightened risk of abuse by members of the Armed Forces,[481] an

---

[477] Interview with Miranda, *supra* note 220.

[478] Interview with Amaya Márquez, *supra* note 179.

[479] *See* INFORME ANUAL JUSTICIA JUVENIL 2004, *supra* note 123, at 29.

[480] *See* WASHINGTON OFFICE ON LATIN AMERICA, YOUTH GANGS IN CENTRAL AMERICA: IS-SUES IN HUMAN RIGHTS, EFFECTIVE POLICING, AND PREVENTION (2006), *available at* http://www.wola.org/gangs/gangs_report_final_nov_06.pdf.

[481] For example, our researchers spoke separately with two gang members in a small city in central El Salvador who reported being subjected to serious rights violations by joint police-military patrols. L.F.G. told our researchers that one day while he was eating in a local store/restaurant, he was called out to the street by two police officers and two soldiers, who told him to lift up his shirt (revealing a large gang tattoo). The officers placed a gun and a knife to his chest, then forced him into a car and then to an area just outside of town where they interrogated him about a recent incident in which a police officer had been shot. He denied knowing about the incident and was placed back in the police car and taken to another area. Again the officers placed a gun to his chest and then ripped off the lower part of his earlobe. A police officer placed a grenade to his head and told him 'you're going to pay for this; I'm going to kill you (plural) one by one.' The officers and soldiers left him in this area and told him to wait for them to return; he fled instead. Interview with L.F.G., *supra* note 233. P.E. told our researchers: "The last time I had an encounter with the police was on

institution whose historic human rights record is extremely poor, as discussed in Chapter I.

4. *Prison Overcrowding and Violence*

The massive number of arrests under the anti-gang crackdown since 2003 has placed a severe burden on El Salvador's prison system, exacerbating the conditions of overcrowding and violence that became a central national concern in the 1990s. In 2001, there were 7,500 detainees in Salvadoran prisons. By the end of 2008, this number had soared to 19,814, though the national system had an operating capacity for only 8,227 prisoners.[482] According to the Director General of Penal Centers, as of mid-2006, most of the increase in the national prisoner population since 2001 could be attributed to the arrest and incarceration of gang members.[483]

The rapid growth in El Salvador's prison population and the increased incarceration of gang members have been accompanied by increasingly poor and dangerous conditions within prisons.[484] In recent years there have been dozens of killings[485] in the Salvadoran

---

Monday. I was going back after getting medicine for my mother. A girl was with me. There were two police officers and two soldiers. They hit me in the street and I left running. The police officers were the ones who hit me, the soldiers were there as guards. They chased me until I got home." Interview with P.E., *supra* note 454.

[482] *See* BUREAU OF DEMOCRACY, HUMAN RIGHTS, AND LABOR, *supra* note 125.

[483] Interview with Villanova, *supra* note 124.

[484] *See* INFORME ANUAL JUSTICIA JUVENIL 2004, *supra* note 123, at 44-47.

[485] Statistics released by the Ministry of Public Security and Justice show that eleven inmates died in 2005, twenty in 2006, and twenty-four in 2007 as a result of prison violence. MINISTERIO DE SEGURIDAD PÚBLICA Y JUSTICIA [MINISTRY OF PUBLIC SECURITY AND JUSTICE], VIOLENCIA CARCELARIA, http://www.seguridad.gob.sv/Web-Seguridad/Centros%20 penales/logros-2.htm; *See also Muertos y heridos en el penal*, EL DIARIO DE HOY, Mar. 2, 2004; *Dos muertos en una riña dentro de centro penal*, EL DIARIO DE HOY, Mar. 16, 2004; *Confirman muerte de reo en Mariona y nuevos túneles de escape en Penal de Cojutepeque*, EL DIARIO DE HOY, Mar. 7, 2006; *Identifican a recluso ultimado en el penal*, EL DIARIO DE HOY, Apr. 21, 2006; *Prisiones están en alerta*, EL DIARIO DE HOY, Nov. 15, 2006 (all reporting killings of prisoners).

prison system, including a massacre in January 2007 that left twenty-one detainees dead in the Apanteos prison in the city of Santa Ana in western El Salvador.[486] The massacre took place several days after one hundred prisoners who were not gang members were transferred to the prison, which predominantly housed members of the M-18.[487] According to press reports, Human Rights Ombudswoman Beatrice de Carrillo attributed the massacre to the transfer of non-gang members into the prison.[488] Another massacre in August 2004 at the *La Esperanza* detention facility outside San Salvador in which thirty-one prisoners were killed also generated international attention and condemnation.[489] Salvadoran authorities blamed gang disputes for that massacre, and subsequently stepped up efforts to segregate rival gang members into separate detention facilities.[490] However, violence in the Salvadoran prison system has continued, as evidenced by the 2007 Apanteos massacre and other incidents,[491] including six apparently coordinated killings in two separate facilities on a single day in March 2006[492] and the

---

[486] David Marroquín, *21 reos asesinados en riña en Apanteos*, LA PRENSA GRÁFICA, Jan. 7, 2006.

[487] *Id.*

[488] *Id.*

[489] *See* AMNESTY INTERNATIONAL, EL SALVADOR REPORT 2005, *available at* http://web.amnesty.org/report2005/slv-summary-eng.

[490] *Saca's anticrime plan bets on specialization*, LATIN AMERICAN WKLY. REP., Sept. 7, 2004 ("In mid-August a fight between gang members and other criminals left 31 dead and 30 injured at the La Esperanza prison in Mariona, just outside San Salvador. Last week a similar confrontation was averted at the Apanteos penitentiary in Santa Ana by transferring 702 gang members to two other prisons. Saca intends to make segregation of gang members a keystone of his prisons policy.").

[491] The January 2007 killings prompted the Inter-American Comission on Human Rights to release a statement urging the Salvadoran government to address overcrowding and other dangerous conditions in the nation's prison system. *See* Press Release, Inter-American Commission on Human Rights, The Inter-American Commission Expresses its Concern over Violent Deaths in a Prison in El Salvador (Jan. 9, 2007), *available at* http://www.cidh.org/Comunicados/English/2007/2-07eng.htm.

[492] *Muertos en Quezaltepeque y Ciudad Barrios*, EL DIARIO DE HOY, Mar. 22, 2006.

killings of four youth in two Juvenile Detention Facilities, in incidents just days apart in January 2009.[493]

Human rights organizations and law enforcement officials agree that the prison system is severely overburdened and that serious challenges exist to ensuring security and the rule of law within many Salvadoran prisons.[494] However, rights groups criticize the repressive measures the Salvadoran state has taken to address the situation—such as limitations on access to visitors, unannounced transfer of prisoners, and the construction of a new maximum security facility—as ineffective, and sometimes in contravention of Salvadoran law and international human rights principles.[495]

---

[493] Luna, *supra* note 128; interview with Salazar Flores, *supra* note 91; interview with Rivas Galindo, *supra* note 68. Detention center authorities had reportedly received warnings from the Transnational Anti-Gang Center (TAG) that specific individuals within those two detention centers were in danger of being killed. Although these warnings included physical descriptions of the likely targets, prison authorities failed to take necessary action to prevent the killings. The TAG is an agreement between El Salvador and the United States "to share intelligence information on gang activities across Central America and the U.S." Press Release, Federal Bureau of Investigations, Going Global on Gangs: New Partnership Targets MS-13 (October 10, 2007), *available at* http://www.fbi.gov/page2/oct07/ms13tag101007. htm; *see also* David I. McKeeby, *Merida Initiative Takes Aim at Transnational Crime*, U.S. State Dep't, May 9, 2008, http://www.america.gov/st/peacesec-english/2008/May/2008050 8174708idybeekcm6.284732e-02.html.

[494] *See, e.g,* FESPAD & CEPES, Estado de la Seguridad Pública y la Justicia Penal en El Salvador Enero-Agosto 2005 66-67 (2005) [hereinafter Estado de la Seguridad Pública y la Justicia Penal en El Salvador 2005]; interview with Ramírez, *supra* note 126.

[495] Estado de la Seguridad Pública y la Justicia Penal en El Salvador 2005, *supra* note 494, at 66-67; *see also* Procuraduría para la Defensa de los Derechos Humanos [Office of the National Human Rights Ombudsperson], Informe Preliminar de la Señora Procuradora Sobre el Traslado de Miembros de las Maras "MS y XVIII" de los Centros Penales de Chalatenango y Quezaltepeque hacia el Centro de Seguridad de Zacatecoluca, el 7 de Febrero del 2005 (2005), *available at* http:// www.pddh.gob.sv/docs/ResEjTrasladosinternos15feb05.pdf (criticizing the sudden transfer of gang members from the Chalatenango and Quezaltepeque prisons to the maximum security Zacatecoluca facility as unlawful under El Salvador's Prison Law (*Ley Penitenciaria*) and its Constitution); interview with Nelson Rauda, *supra* note 409 (criticizing Salvadoran maximum security prisons as inimical to human dignity, and emphasizing that inmates in these facilities are often tied at their wrists and ankles and kept in complete isolation).

Our researchers interviewed Dany Balmore Moreno, a former inmate who had been transferred to six different detention facilities during his fifteen years in prison. He described enduring deplorable living conditions and physical abuse by prison guards in all six detention centers. For example, at the Apanteos prison, guards forced him to strip down and beat him; at the Chalatenango prison, he lived through a tuberculosis outbreak in an extremely crowded cell with only one bathroom for 106 people. The brutal beating and ensuing death of a close friend by prison guards motivated Moreno to start lodging complaints about these inhumane conditions of detention to prison authorities and to the Human Rights Ombudsperson. He also organized other inmates to do the same. As a consequence, prison authorities regularly transferred Moreno from one detention center to another and ultimately labeled him a "high security risk" detainee, eventually sending him to the Zacatecoluca maximum security prison.[496] Interviews with relatives of detainees revealed that prison guards often also mistreat visitors. Women in particular report having been subject to extremely degrading body searches.[497]

The director of a social service NGO and a government employee who work with prisoners both told our research team of frequent rights violations in Salvadoran prisons.[498] In particular, these sources told our researchers that abuses frequently occur in the context of mass searches of the prisons (carried out in conjunction with members of the PNC) following the declaration of a state of emergency by prison officials.[499] Although regulations require that the judge charged with

---

[496] Interview with Dany Balmore Moreno, in San Salvador (Mar. 23, 2008).

[497] Interview with members of the Comité de Madres Pro-Reo [Committee of Mothers for Detainee Rights], *supra* note 471.

[498] Interview with Rikkers, *supra* note 151 ("[The] PNC has participated in many violent, illegal, provocative situations while supposedly conducting searches."); interview with Torres, *supra* note 126. Ms. Torres, whose job entails monitoring the treatment of and advocating for prisoners in the Quetzaltepeque prison, told our researchers that prison guards commit abuses, including verbal provocations and taunting as well as physical abuse, and that judges are frequently reluctant to respond to allegations of abuse.

[499] Interview with Rikkers, *supra* note 151; interview with Torres, *supra* note 126.

oversight of the prison be called before these mass searches begin, a source who is familiar with the Salvadoran prison and judicial systems told our researchers that judges frequently learn of these mass searches only *after* they have begun. According to this source, prison directors often declare a state of emergency to justify these crackdowns and searches, which sometimes involve physical abuse. This source also told our researchers that when judges arrive at the prisons seeking to get the names of officers who have engaged in abuses, they are thwarted because the officers involved wear masks and do not have any visible identification.

Although our on-site research did not focus on abuses in prison, our visits to detention centers allowed us to confirm that inmates lived in extremely overcrowded conditions. During our visits, we also heard numerous complaints of guard-on-prisoner and prisoner-on-prisoner violence. The recent and unprecedented peaceful protests across all Salvadoran detention centers spotlight the continuous and widespread nature of human rights violations in Salvadoran prisons. (See insert: A Peaceful Riot.)

A Peaceful Riot

We are asking for nothing but respect for our dignity . . .[1]

Detainees in El Salvador's overcrowded and oppressive prisons are routinely deprived of access to adequate sanitation and essential health care. Inmates and their visiting family members are frequently subject to abuse and mistreatment at the hands of prison officials. Even putting to one side the massacres that have taken place in El Salvador's overburdened detention centers, detainees are subject to conditions that deprive them of their basic human dignity, as we have documented based, in

---

[1] E-mail from Rosa Anaya Perla, Colectivo Derechos Humanos, San Salvador (Feb. 22, 2009, 11:09 EST) (on file with authors).

part, on our own visits to detention centers.[2]

In February 2009, the desperation of El Salvador's detainees was starkly illustrated in an historic nation-wide protest led by the inmates. Detainees across the country—including members of both M-18 and MS-13—conducted a peaceful sit-down strike in eleven of El Salvador's nineteen penitentiaries.[3] A petition signed by some 11,000 prisoners set out the detainees' requests, which ranged from an end to the systematic torture of inmates to the provision of adequate medical care and extensions of visitation rights for family members.[4] The protest was remarkable for several reasons, including the scale of the coordination and the unprecedented cooperation between members of the M-18 and MS-13.[5]

The Government's response was mixed: on the one hand, they agreed to the petition's main request, establishing a round-table discussion with prisoners and NGOs to address the detainees' requests. On the other hand, reports have emerged of police investigations into the coordinators of the strike and political attempts to discredit the organizers.[6] Suspicion and

---

[2] *See, e.g.,* interview with Jaime Roberto Villanova, Director General, Centros Penales de El Salvador [Director General of Penal Centres], in San Salvador (Mar. 28, 2006); interview with Jeanne Rikkers, then-Program Director, Christians for Peace in El Salvador (CRISPAZ), in San Salvador (Aug. 21, 2006); interview with Dany Balmore Moreno, in San Salvador (Mar. 23, 2008); visit to the Chalatenango prison (Mar. 28, 2006).

[3] Raúl Gutiérrez, *El Salvador: Masiva y pacífica protesta de presos*, INTER-PRESS SERVICE (IPS), Feb. 17, 2009.

[4] Petición de Familiares de los/as Privados de Libertad de El Salvador [Petition by the families of El Salvador detainees], Feb. 16, 2009 (on file with authors).

[5] E-mail from Rosa Anaya Perla, Colectivo Derechos Humanos, San Salvador (Feb. 22, 2009, 11:09 EST) (on file with authors).

[6] *See, e.g., Presos de diez penales realizan protesta en El Salvador,* AGENCE FRANCE PRESSE (AFP), Feb. 15, 2009; Lissette Ábrego, *Grupos externos instigan a reos a generar desorden en varios penales,* EL NUEVO DIARIO, Feb. 15, 2009.

distrust of detainees distort public discussion of this issue in El Salvador: even the peaceful protest was sensationally reported by the media as "rioting,"[7] a "prisoner uprising,"[8] and "a rebellion,"[9] and even, paradoxically, a "peaceful riot."[10] The difficulties faced by both detainees and their advocates remain acute. - *Natalie Zerial*

---

[7] Carlos Montes & Ernesto Pérez, *Penales en alerta por protesta de reos*, LA PRENSA GRÁFICA, Feb. 15, 2009.

[8] Carlos Montes, *Se extiende la rebelión en los centros penales*, LA PRENSA GRÁFICA, Feb. 16, 2009.

[9] *Protesta masiva de presos salvadoreños por malos tratos*, RADIO LA PRIMERÍSIMA, Feb. 16, 2009.

[10] Blanca Abarca, *Reos de nueve penales se declaran en rebeldía*, LA PRENSA GRÁFICA, Feb. 14, 2009.

5. *Targeted Law Enforcement Efforts Aimed at Deportees*

Finally, it is important to take note of one other effect of the government's policies of the past several years: increased law enforcement and media attention on Salvadorans deported from the United States. As noted in the discussion of anti-gang legislative initiatives, *supra*, LAM I included a provision that specifically provided for the detention of suspected gang members upon arrival in El Salvador. The Supreme Court ruled that provision unconstitutional in April 2004. Conversations with civil society advocates and deportees indicate, however, that the reception of hundreds of Salvadorans deported weekly from the United States, which until 2005 included robust participation from civil society groups concerned with protecting the rights and safeguarding the well-being of the deported population,[500] has been a process dominated largely by law enforcement interests.[501] While the Salvadoran state has legitimate interests in monitoring and registering the arrival of deportees, rights groups in El Salvador are concerned that violations of deportees' rights occur during the interrogations and searches that appear to be a standard element of the reception process.[502]

---

[500] Interview with Pérez, *supra* note 242; interview with Luis Fernando Trujillo, Director Nacional [National Director] of CARITAS (a Catholic social services organization), in San Salvador (Mar. 29, 2006). Both IDHUCA and CARITAS were involved in providing humanitarian and legal assistance to deportees upon arrival at the airport in El Salvador until oversight of the program changed hands from a joint civil society-government task force to the Ministry of the Interior (*Ministerio de Gobernación*) in 2005. In 2007, the program changed hands once again to the National Immigration Office (*Dirección General de Migración y Extranjería*). CARITAS offered a shelter for deportees who had arrived in the country with no immediate prospects for lodging until 2005; *see also* IDHUCA, BALANCE DE LOS DERECHOS HUMANOS DEL 2005, *supra* note 203, at 3-4 (noting the change in management of the Welcome Home (*Bienvenidos a Casa*) program and lamenting what it perceived as a decline in the quality of the services provided to deportees); Luis Alvarado & Jesús Hernández, *Migración toma control de Bienvenido a Casa*, LA PRENSA GRÁFICA, July 31, 2008.

[501] INFORME DE LABORES DE LA PROCURADURÍA 07-08, *supra* note 131, at 44 (noting that "Salvadorans [who are deported] are not treated with the dignity required to guarantee their rights" because the Welcome Home (*Bienvenidos a Casa*) program is subordinated to PNC policies); interview with Pérez, *supra* note 242. In 2006, our researchers also interviewed deported Salvadorans who described intense law enforcement screenings and limited or non-existent offerings of social services or assistance. *See* interview with W.M., *supra* note 248 (W.M., who was deported in December 2005, told us that during his reception process at the airport, he did not interact with anyone from the "Welcome Home" humanitarian program, only law enforcement officials, who took pictures of all his tattoos); interview with R.Z., in Mejicanos (Aug. 28, 2006) (R.Z., deported in early 2006, told us that he was interrogated twice when he arrived at the airport upon deportation and that law enforcement officials took pictures of all his tattoos and his face); interview with M.A.H., in Ilobasco (Sept. 1, 2006). (M.A.H., deported in early 2006, told our researchers that contrary to what he had heard from other Salvadorans deported in earlier years, there were no *pupusas* (traditional Salvadoran stuffed flatbread) or coffee waiting for him in the airport, "only police officers." He reported that police officers took many close-up pictures of his tattoos with multiple cameras and that they asked him questions about his criminal history in the United States (according to him, they had his criminal record in front of them while they interrogated him) and about his plans for life in El Salvador.)

[502] INFORME DE LABORES DE LA PROCURADURÍA 07-08, *supra* note 131, at 44 (noting that the PNC treats virtually all deportees as putative gang members and that PNC policies emphasize registration and search procedures over measures to promote successful reinte-

These concerns arise at least in part from rights groups' past experience: staff of civil society organizations that provide services to deportees told our researchers of several instances in which law enforcement officials targeted deportees with no criminal record in El Salvador for investigation and arrest.[503] Changes in 2005 to the administration of the "Welcome Home" airport reception program for deportees were accompanied by restrictions in access to deportees upon their arrival in El Salvador. Representatives of several civil society organizations that have historically provided legal and humanitarian services to the deported population told our researchers that they no longer enjoyed access to the airport reception process.[504]

In sum, the Salvadoran state's direct responses to the phenomenon of youth gangs have primarily involved the use of repressive law enforcement tactics targeting particular sectors of Salvadoran society, including those with tattoos, youth, and deportees. These tactics have failed to stem gang-related or other forms of violence in El Salvador. The next part of this chapter explores what we have termed the Salvadoran state's secondary responses to the gang phenomenon. Specifically, it examines the ways in which the state has *failed to respond* effectively, in accord with its international obligations, to gang-related and other forms of violence in the country.

---

gration into Salvadoran society); interview with Pérez, *supra* note 242; interview with Ale-manni de Carrillo, *supra* note 119; interview with Gerardo Alegría, Procurador Adjunto de los Derechos Civiles e Individuales, Procuraduría para la Defensa de los Derechos Huma-nos [Adjunct Ombudsperson for Civil and Individual Rights, Office of the National Human Rights Ombudsperson], in San Salvador (Aug. 29, 2006) (describing an alleged instance of a deported woman who was inappropriately strip-searched as part of the reception process).

[503] For example, Gilma Pérez of the Migration Program of IDHUCA described several cases in late 2003 in which she defended young men with no criminal records in El Salvador who had been arrested and taken into custody, solely on the basis of their appearance and tat-toos, upon arrival in El Salvador under Article 29 of LAM I, discussed in Part A1 (legislative responses) of this chapter, *supra*. Interview with Gilma Pérez, *supra* note 242. Additionally, staff of CARITAS, which ran a shelter for deportees until 2005, told our researchers that staff of the shelter had clashed on several occasions with police who asked the shelter to investigate deportees staying there and who sometimes monitored the comings and goings of deportees who stayed at the shelter. Interview with Trujillo, *supra* note 500.

[504] Interview with Gilma Pérez, *supra* note 242; interview with Trujillo, *supra* note 500.

B. *Secondary State Responses to the Gang Phenomenon: Impunity*

In addition to its direct role in the commission of human rights abuses against actual or alleged gang members or other criminal suspects, the Salvadoran government also regularly fails to uphold its obligation to ensure the security of its population and to investigate and prosecute those responsible for violence. The Salvadoran justice system as a whole is considered weak and ineffective (see Chapter II), but the state's failure to protect the poorest and most vulnerable of its citizens— those most likely to be victims or perpetrators of violence—is especially pronounced.[505] International human rights norms impose affirmative obligations on states to ensure the protection of fundamental rights and to provide public security.[506] The government's failure to protect certain classes of Salvadoran citizens thus constitutes a serious violation of the most basic international human rights standards, including the rights to life and physical integrity.

In El Salvador, the lack of protection for presumed or future victims of gang and other violence takes a number of forms, including failure to ensure the security of potential victims of violence; a lack of effective witness protection; and inadequate or non-existent criminal investigations into alleged or presumed inter- or intra-gang violence.[507]

---

[505] *See, e.g.,* the WORLD BANK ET AL., *supra* note 117, at 6 (reporting that the most vulnerable sectors of the Salvadoran population suffer the consequences of violence, including death, in part due precisely to their low socioeconomic status). Additionally, the Research Director of El Salvador's National Institute of Forensic Medicine told our researchers that the amount of time government investigators spend collecting evidence at the scene of a homicide "sometimes depends . . . on how important the victim is." Interview with Molina Vaquerano, *supra* note 173. Dr. Molina also told our researchers that "homicides are increasing, especially among young people."

[506] Velásquez-Rodríguez Case, 1988, Inter-Am. Ct. H.R. (ser. C) No. 4 (July 29, 1988). JAMES CAVALLARO, INTERNATIONAL COUNCIL ON HUMAN RIGHTS POLICY, CRIME, PUBLIC ORDER, AND HUMAN RIGHTS 16-19 (2003) (discussing states' obligation under international norms to provide "basic security to the people they govern.").

[507] Interview with Torres, *supra* note 126; interview with Martínez Ventura, *supra* note 117; interview with F.R., *supra* note 200 (describing the lack of investigation and follow-up in the cases of her two brothers, who were associated with gangs and were killed within the past

The Salvadoran state's failure to protect, investigate, and prosecute violence is especially pronounced in cases of possible extra-judicial killings linked to state actors.[508] This chapter will discuss each of these issues in turn.

1. *Failure to Ensure Public Security/Provide Effective Protection*

Actual and threatened victims of violence interviewed by our researchers in El Salvador—including suspected or imputed gang members and residents of areas with a heavy gang presence—reported that Salvadoran police were unwilling or incapable of providing citizen protection.[509] A resident of a poor urban region outside San Salvador, emphasizing the ineffectiveness of police presence in the area, told our researchers that police abandon their posts and disappear when gang members take to the streets in her area, leaving citizens vulnerable to extortion, threats, and violence.[510] Another resident of that region told us that the two major gangs' geographic control was so complete that residents of an area controlled by one gang could not go into the area controlled by the other gang. "There is no freedom of movement here," she explained.[511]

Our researchers encountered another sad illustration of the Salvadoran state's failure to ensure citizen security in an interview

---

several years).

[508] *See* Estado de la Seguridad Pública y la Justicia Penal en El Salvador 2005, *supra* note 494, at 102-103 (describing the results of a 2001-2005 study in which it identified 622 possible instances of extrajudicial killings, based on Salvadoran media reports).

[509] *See, e.g.,* interview with X.D.H., *supra* note 314 ("There is one man who was in Mariona who has threatened me. I could file a complaint but why? It won't do any good and I don't want to put my children in danger. Even when walking in the park with my daughters I have been approached by people [threatening me]. I've been followed while going on the bus route. I've been told my throat would be cut.").

[510] Interview with F.R., *supra* note 200.

[511] Interview with D.L., *supra* note 305.

with a 17-year-old male in a juvenile detention facility, also featured in Chapter III, Part (C)(2). The adolescent grew up in a densely populated, poor neighborhood just outside San Salvador with his family, in an area controlled by a *clika* of the M-18. Members of the M-18 charged *renta* to families in the area, demanding money and threatening them if they did not comply.[512] The youth, the oldest male in his family, increasingly became a target for M-18 members, who harassed him, threatened him, and stole from him when he left his house.[513] According to the version told us by the adolescent, instead of providing protection to the adolescent or his family, police in the area regularly stopped and searched the boy, and sometimes arrested him on illicit association charges.[514] After resisting the gang's extortion attempts for two years, the adolescent "lost control" one day when the leader of the M-18 *clika* came to the house threatening to "do away" with his family if they did not give him money. The youth fought with and killed the *clika* leader, thus becoming a perpetrator as well as a victim of the violence that has come to define life in marginalized Salvadoran neighborhoods over the past several years.[515]

In addition to failing to protect many victims of gang violence, including other gang members and residents of poor neighborhoods in which gangs exercise significant power, the Salvadoran state frequently fails to investigate and prosecute violence in which the victim is a member of a marginalized or powerless social group—or presumed to be a gang member.[516] The sister of two young brothers who had been killed in the past several years spoke to our researchers near her home in a poor area on the outskirts of San Salvador. Both brothers allegedly had been connected to gangs, and as far as the woman knew, neither brother's death had been investigated by the police:

---

[512] Interview with T.C., *supra* note 200.

[513] *Id.* (describing the gang's harassment of him and his family).

[514] *Id.*

[515] *Id.*

[516] Interview with Torres, *supra* note 126; interview with Molina Vaquerano, *supra* note 173.

> After my first brother was killed, there was no investigation. My mother asked about it in the hospital but they didn't tell her anything. After my second brother was killed, they called us to come into the Criminal Investigation Division, but we didn't go. We never heard anything after that.[517]

Several other witnesses and victims interviewed reported that governmental authorities display a cavalier attitude toward presumed inter-gang violence. For example, one 18-year-old current gang member told our researchers that police who stopped him near his home invoked the threat of inter-gang violence to taunt him:

> [The police] told me that someone from the other gang was nearby, that I was going to pass by him. They told me his name and that he was armed. They told me, "you're crying, you're scared."[518]

Attorneys at IDHUCA shared with our researchers several case files from 2003 and 2004 involving Salvadorans deported from the United States who had sought governmental assistance in securing protection from threats of gang violence. These documents, which include attorneys' files and interview notes as well as copies of communications with the police and Office of the Prosecutor, suggest that law enforcement authorities failed to respond to appeals for protection from deportees formerly associated with gangs.[519]

2. Lack of Effective Witness Protection

Another related factor that plays an important role in the Salvadoran government's failure to provide meaningful protection to certain sectors

[517] Interview with F.R., *supra* note 200.

[518] Interview with L.F.G., *supra* note 233.

[519] IDHUCA, *supra* note 248.

of society is the absence of an effective witness and victim protection program. Many of the witnesses, victims, and experts interviewed by our researchers emphasized that victims and witnesses in criminal cases in El Salvador become targets for retaliation and violence. Dr. Carlos Henríquez Hernández Ávila, of the University of El Salvador School of Medicine, spoke with our researchers about the challenges he and his team faced in forming local citizen-police committees for a Pan-American Health Organization-funded project to reduce homicide levels in El Salvador. According to Hernández Ávila, "There is citizen distrust of the police . . . because oftentimes if citizens report crimes to the police, they will be killed."[520] The mother of a young woman allegedly killed by gang members in a poor neighborhood outside San Salvador told our research team that she regularly sees the people she believes killed her daughter, but that she has not reported them to the police:

> What am I going to do . . . my son told me not to report [the murder] because the police don't do anything and then [the people who killed my daughter] would come after us.[521]

Academic researchers examining the phenomenon of violence and citizen insecurity also point to the lack of protection for witnesses and victims of crime as a significant contributing factor to the sense of public insecurity that pervades El Salvador.[522]

The program created by the 2006 Witness and Victim Protection Law is severely underfunded and has so far been unable to provide effective witness protection—giving rise instead to the over-reliance on *testigos*

---

[520] Interview with Dr. Carlos Henríquez Hernández Ávila, Centro de Investigación, Facultad de Medicina, Universidad de El Salvador [Research Center, School of Medicine, University of El Salvador], in San Salvador (Aug. 29, 2006).

[521] Interview with A.M., in San Salvador (Aug. 31, 2006).

[522] Aguilar & Miranda, *supra* note 157 (describing how pervasive impunity and lack of witness protection contribute to the environment of public insecurity and reporting that witnesses refrain from testifying for fear of retaliation).

criteriados and the accompanying violation of defendants' due process rights described below. A 2007 study of homicide investigations in the municipalities of San Salvador, Santa Ana, and San Miguel concluded that "in many of the cases investigated, the witness protection program did not operate adequately: in spite of being under a protection regime, numerous witnesses were murdered or could not be located to testify at trial."[523] Rights groups and members of the judicial branch have also called into question the effectiveness of the 2006 protection regime. For example, David Morales, a lawyer at FESPAD, told our researchers that "witnesses run grave risks" because the program is backed by insufficient resources and is thus unable to provide effective protection in practice.[524] Likewise, Judge Edward Sidney Blanco Reyes, author of the report on police, prosecutorial and judicial deficiencies described in Chapter II, emphasized that the witness and victim protection program is poorly funded and ineffective. "As a judge, I cannot tell the difference between the old and the new victim and witness protection regime. We still have cases in which witnesses are murdered both before and after they testify."[525] Mauricio Rodríguez, Director of the UTE (the Technical Unit tasked with administering the Witness and Victim Protection Program), confirmed that funds earmarked for the program are often insufficient to cover even the basic needs of individuals under its care.[526] Special prosecutor Alan Edward Hernández Portillo attributed some of the shortcomings of the protection program to its relatively recent creation.[527] Nevertheless, even if program operations are streamlined in the near future, it will be difficult to provide effective protection absent

---

[523] Blanco Reyes & Díaz Rodríguez, *supra* note 118, at 63.

[524] Interview with David Morales, Coordinador del Área de Seguridad Ciudadana y Justicia Penal, FESPAD [Coordinator of the Citizen Security and Penal Justice Unit of FESPAD], in San Salvador (Oct. 23, 2008).

[525] Interview with Edward Sidney Blanco Reyes, ex-Juez Quinto de Instrucción de San Salvador [Judge in the First Instance, Fifth Instruction Tribunal of San Salvador], in San Salvador (Mar. 25, 2008).

[526] Interview with Rodríguez, *supra* note 379.

[527] Interview with Hernández Portillo, *supra* note 156.

adequate funding and a concurrent investment in police training and professionalism, which should include resources to strengthen technical capacity and increase institutional focus on community policing.

The story of 18-year-old A.P. discussed in Chapter III, Part (B)(3) (c) is a poignant illustration of the Salvadoran government's failure to provide effective witness protection and to conduct an adequate technical investigation.[528] A week after a brutal attack, and while A.P. was still in the hospital, news of the attempt on A.P.'s life and her friend's death were published in a local newspaper. The news story all but revealed A.P.'s identity: it mentioned where she went to school, her friend's full name, and the hospital where she was recovering. It also noted that, if A.P. survived, she would be a key witness. The publication of this story could well have placed A.P.'s life in danger if the perpetrators, who had taken pictures of her and her friend, realized she was still alive and could identify them. Prosecutors returned A.P. to her house, located in a small neighborhood, promising only that they would withhold her identity at trial. "People talk and soon the entire neighborhood knew [what had happened to me]," A.P. told our researchers.[529] Soon thereafter, A.P. left her house and, as of March 2009, was living in hiding.

The investigation into the attack on A.P. and L.R.'s murder also suffered from several deficiencies. First, the police did not arrive promptly at the crime scene after receiving a phone call from a neighbor who had seen the perpetrators leave with A.P. and L.R. Second, the IML waited four days after the attack to conduct a physical exam. Third, the Office of the Prosecutor took fifteen days after the attack to collect her bloody clothes, which the police had placed in a bag and returned to A.P.[530] The Ombudsperson's Office issued a resolution in A.P.'s case, assigning responsibility to the Office of the Prosecutor for failing to

---

[528] Interview with K.H.D., *supra* note 304.

[529] Interview with A.P., in San Salvador (Oct. 28, 2008); Procuraduría para la Defensa de los Derechos Humanos [Office of the National Human Rights Ombudsperson], resolution on A.P.'s case (on file with authors).

[530] Procuraduría para la Defensa de los Derechos Humanos [Office of the National Human Rights Ombudsperson], resolution on A.P.'s case (on file with authors).

provide A.P. appropriate protection, and to the PNC for failing to take appropriate measures to safeguard A.P. and L.R's rights.[531]

3. *Persistent Impunity: The State's Failure to Investigate and Prosecute*

Finally, in spite of the repressive law enforcement strategies employed by the Salvadoran state in recent years, the rates of investigation and prosecution of homicides in El Salvador remain extremely low. As discussed in Chapter II, a 2007 report authored by Edward Sidney Blanco Reyes and Francisco Díaz Rodríguez revealed that just 14.21 percent of all homicides registered by the Institute of Forensic Medicine between January 1 and December 31, 2005, had been forwarded for judicial processing, and that only 3.8 percent had resulted in a conviction by May 2007. The causes of this persistent impunity are complex, but can be grouped in three general categories. First, and most basically, Salvadoran police and justice institutions still lack the capacity to investigate and prosecute crimes effectively.[532] As criminality in El Salvador becomes increasingly organized and complex, these institutional weaknesses have translated into deep limitations in the state's ability to control violence and bring perpetrators to justice.[533]

---

[531] *Id.*

[532] Blanco Reyes & Díaz Rodríguez, *supra* note 118, at 62. This assertion is also made repeatedly by Salvadoran rights groups and policy research institutions, as well as by members of the judiciary. *See, e.g., Gregori Morán, 984 delincuentes libres por delatar a sus complices,* La Prensa Gráfica, Apr. 15, 2006 (reporting that the police rely on confessions as a primary crimefighting tool while neglecting the need to conduct effective criminal investigations); *see also* IDHUCA, Editorial, Tras la guerra, catorce años de violencia e impunidad, (Jan. 16, 2006), http://www.uca.edu.sv/publica/idhuca/ar_editoriales06.html#16012006 (citing ineffective and even counterproductive police investigations and lack of a clear crimefighting strategy, as well as a refusal to acknowledge and correct these shortcomings, as among the main factors impeding the state's attempts to control crime); interview with Martínez Ventura, *supra* note 117.

[533] *See, e.g.,* The World Bank, et al., *supra* note 117 (reporting that investigations of serious crimes such as murder, rape, organized crime, and corruption are ineffective and that state authorities clarify the circumstances of these crimes in only a small percentage of cases).

Second, political will to dedicate police, investigatory, and prosecutorial resources to cases in which the victims are poor and marginalized and/or seen as gang members or criminals themselves has been lacking.[534] There is a widespread perception in El Salvador that gangs constitute the primary threat to public security and necessitate a tough response from the government.[535] This is the case even though estimates from the National Institute of Forensic Medicine indicate that, in 2006, gangs had been responsible for fewer than one in five homicides in the country.[536] Similarly, *Tutela Legal* annual reports for 2005, 2006, and 2007 assign responsibility for fewer than 30 percent of all homicides to gangs.[537] People who work in the criminal justice system in El Salvador told our researchers that the perception that gangs are responsible for most of the violence in El Salvador, which is often encouraged by the police,[538] can serve to legitimate the under-investigation of homicides that are superficially dismissed as gang killings.[539] The director of *Tutela Legal*,

---

[534] *See, e.g.,* interview with Molina Vaquerano, *supra* note 173; Blanco Reyes & Díaz Rodríguez, *supra* note 118, at 62.

[535] A 2006 national survey by IUDOP found that 82.9 percent of Salvadorans supported or strongly supported the *Mano Dura* Plan. IUDOP, *Los salvadoreños evalúan la situación del país a finales de 2005 y opinan sobre las elecciones de 2006*, Proceso, Dec. 7, 2005, *available at* http://www.uca.edu.sv/publica/proceso/proc1173.html. A separate IUDOP survey found that more than 90 percent of the Salvadoran population believed that gangs constitute a "major problem." This survey is cited in Central America and Mexico Gang Assessment, *supra* note 6, at 10-11.

[536] Interview with Aguilar, *supra* note 157; interview with Henríquez Hernández Ávila, *supra* note 520; interview with Molina Vaquerano, *supra* note 173.

[537] La Situación de los Derechos Humanos en El Salvador 2005, *supra* note 476; La Situación de los Derechos Humanos en El Salvador 2006, *supra* note 173; La Situación de los Derechos Humanos en El Salvador 2007, *supra* note 173.

[538] *See, e.g., Los homicidios en El Salvador aumentaron: en lo que va del año suman más de 800*, Univision.com, Apr. 3, 2006 (quoting a high-ranking police official stating that gang members are the "principal cause" of murders in the country); *see also* Aguilar & Miranda, *supra* note 157, at 52 (stating that available statistics do not support the PNC's assertion that gangs are responsible for 60 percent of killings in El Salvador).

[539] Interview with Torres, *supra* note 126.

told our researchers that police rarely investigate the killings of gang members.[540] In an interview with our researchers in August 2006, Dr. Fabio Molina Vaquerano, Research Director of the National Institute of Forensic Medicine, also noted the discrepancy between the figures from his office and those of the police regarding homicides attributed to gangs. He suggested that the quality of police homicide investigations are sometimes determined by the "importance" of the victim.[541]

Third, as discussed in Chapter V, there are indications that some Salvadoran state and law enforcement authorities may be complicit in, or at least consciously and deliberately indifferent to, extrajudicial killings and social cleansing. This is perhaps the most worrisome factor contributing to high levels of impunity and a widespread sense of public insecurity in El Salvador. Salvadoran rights groups link the current failures of the Salvadoran state to investigate homicides, including possible extrajudicial and death squad killings, to the legacy of impunity for the grave abuses of the civil war and the decades of authoritarianism that preceded it.[542]

C. Relationship between Political Polarization and Violence in El Salvador

The recent growth in the gang phenomenon, rising levels of criminality, and increased human rights violations in El Salvador must be understood in the context of the country's deeply polarized political

---

[540] Interview with María Julia Hernández, *supra* note 303; *see also* LA SITUACIÓN DE LOS DERECHOS HUMANOS EN EL SALVADOR 2006, *supra* note 173, at 33; LA SITUACIÓN DE LOS DERECHOS HUMANOS EN EL SALVADOR 2007, *supra* note 173, at 33 (describing systematic impunity for the groups and people responsible for extrajudicial killings).

[541] Interview with Molina Vaquerano, *supra* note 173; *see also* ESTADO DE LA SEGURIDAD PÚBLICA Y LA JUSTICIA PENAL EN EL SALVADOR 2004, *supra* note 52, at 88.

[542] FESPAD, LOS ACUERDOS DE PAZ, SU AGENDA PENDIENTE, Y LOS DERECHOS HUMANOS EN EL SALVADOR DE HOY (2006), *available at* http://fespad.org.sv/portal/html/Archivos/Descargas/LAP.pdf; *see also* IDHUCA, Editorial, Herederos de la impunidad (Aug. 24, 2006) (identifying impunity as the unifying characteristic of violence in El Salvador both during and following the civil war and stating that the current lack of criminal investigations is the "legacy" of this longstanding climate of impunity).

climate. In recent years, international and domestic human rights advocates have frequently criticized the Salvadoran government for what they characterize as political manipulation of public insecurity and gang violence.[543] According to these critiques, Salvadoran political leaders have taken advantage of widespread insecurity and fears of criminality to legitimize repressive law enforcement strategies, to consolidate electoral power, and to justify legislative initiatives aimed at suppressing dissent, such as the anti-terrorism law introduced in the summer of 2006.[544] Because the aim of our investigation was to research allegations of human rights abuses associated with gang violence, we did not document political exploitation of criminality and public insecurity in an exhaustive or systematic manner. However, this issue arose repeatedly in our research and interviews in El Salvador, and it became clear that no documentation of gang violence and related abuses would be complete without an acknowledgment of the complex ways in which violence is refracted through, and amplified by, deep political divisions and power struggles in the country. This chapter addresses two specific examples of patterns or incidents of violence directly linked to the country's growing political polarization and highlights the role the media have played in shaping public perceptions of and policy responses to violence.

---

[543] For an example of a representative domestic critique, see IDHUCA, *Estado en Crisis* (2006), *available at* http://www.uca.edu.sv/publica/idhuca/articulos.html#espacio_tres (describing former President Flores' launch of the *Mano Dura* plan as a strategy with "clear electoral purposes"). For an example of a representative international critique, *see* Memorandum from Geoff Thale, Washington Office on Latin America, to Colleagues, International Assistance in Responding to Youth Gang Violence in Central America 2 (Sept. 30, 2005), *available at* http://www.wola.org/gangs/international_coop_memo.pdf ("In Central America, everyone agrees that the problem is serious, but there are clearly both press and political agendas at work.").

[544] *See, e.g.,* IDHUCA, Editorial, *Terror ante la nueva ley*, May 11, 2006, http://www.uca.edu.sv/publica/idhuca/ar_editoriales06.html#24082006 (criticizing the government's evident use of the deaths of state agents to justify the implementation of authoritarian and unconstitutional measures).

1. July 5, 2006 Protests, the Anti-Terrorism Law, and its Aftermath: The Apopa, San Salvador, and Suchitoto Cases

a) *July 5, 2006 Protests*

In July 2006, violent clashes between civilian protesters and the national police in downtown San Salvador highlighted the fragility of El Salvador's democratic transition and the intersection of political polarization, governmental responses to violence, and public perceptions of criminality. Throughout the first half of 2006, transportation workers, students, and other sectors of society frequently took to the streets of San Salvador to protest economic policies, generally, and planned increases in bus fares in particular. On July 5, 2006, university and secondary school students gathered for another protest in the area surrounding the General Francisco Menéndez Institute near the National University in San Salvador.[545] As tensions between police and protesters mounted that morning,[546] several special police forces (including the Maintenance Order Team [*Unidad de Mantenimiento del Orden* or UMO] and the Police Reaction Group [*Grupo de Reacción Policial* or GRP]), as well as an armed police helicopter, were mobilized in the area.[547] Witnesses and television crews reported seeing police snipers stationed on the roof of the nearby Bloom Hospital.[548] The tense confrontations between

---

[545] Procuraduría para la Defensa de los Derechos Humanos [Office of the National Human Rights Ombudsperson], Informe Preliminar de la Señora Procuradora para la Defensa de los Derechos Humanos, sobre los Hechos de Violencia Acaecidos en los Alrededores de la Universidad de El Salvador Durante Actividades de protesta Estudiantil ante el Incremento de las Tarifas al Transporte Público de Pasajeros, Ocurridos el día 5 de Julio del 2006 (2006) [hereinafter Procuraduría 5J Report] paras. 13, 15.

[546] *Id.* at para. 18. (According to the National Human Rights Ombudswoman, the police used tear gas and rubber bullets to control protesters, who threw objects–including rocks and Molotov cocktails–at police officers.)

[547] *Id.* at para. 22.

[548] *Gobernación Acepta que Segundo Helicóptero voló sobre UES*, La Prensa Gráfica, July 11, 2006.

police officers and protesters that morning came to a violent end when snipers—apparently firing from the University of El Salvador—shot and killed two police officers. The next day, government officials named two students, who were also low-level FMLN party activists, as suspects in the killings.[549]

In the days following the July 5 protests, government officials and opposition party leaders engaged in heated rhetorical battles that evoked the polarized discourse of the 1980s and revealed the fragility of the country's democratic transition. During a legislative session held several days after the events, legislators from the ARENA and FMLN traded insults that harkened back to the country's civil war. ARENA legislator Norman Quijano called FMLN a party of "terrorists, kidnappers, and murderers" and FMLN legislator Calixto Mejía characterized ARENA as the party of *escuadronistas* [death squad members].[550] On July 6, 2006, President Saca was quoted in the national media as saying:

> I think very few people in the country doubt that the FMLN is linked with these front groups that, sheltered in the guise of protesters, commit acts of terrorism. . . . the country should know that we are dealing with people who signed the Peace Accords and now are laughing at them.[551]

Government officials initially denied that police had fired live ammunition at protesters, that snipers had been positioned on rooftops, or that military helicopters had been sent to the scene of the protests. After the publication of media reports and photographs contradicting these denials, officials retracted their earlier statements.[552]

---

[549] David Marroquín & Ruth Cruz, *Terrorismo Urbano*, LA PRENSA GRÁFICA, July 26, 2006.

[550] Milton Grimaldi, Alexandra Bonilla & Amadeo Cabrera, *Comisión Especial por Actos Terroristas*, LA PRENSA GRÁFICA, July 7, 2006.

[551] Bernardo Valiente, *El FMLN está vinculado con estos grupos de fachada*, LA PRENSA GRÁFICA, July 7, 2006.

[552] *Gobernación Acepta que Segundo Helicóptero voló sobre UES*, supra note 548.

The July 5 protests played a key role in the enactment of the anti-terrorism law: they provided a reference framework and set the tone of the debate. Proponents of the law advocated for the proposed legislation by implying that such a law could have been used to prosecute July 5 demonstrators and by depicting protesters as a terrorist threat to democracy. For example, Rodrigo Ávila, Director of the PNC, emphasized that "the law forbids covering one's face and carrying weapons during public demonstrations, but these provisions are dead-letter law. We need a [new] instrument [to prosecute these crimes] that cannot be open to differing interpretations. . . . The antiterrorism law is one such instrument."[553] Likewise, Félix Garrid Safie, Director of the Office of the Prosecutor, called for urgent reform and emphasized the need for a law that would effectively criminalize disguising one's face while participating in a public protest.[554] In contrast, opponents of the bill saw the July 5 events as an example of how an anti-terrorism law could be misapplied to squelch public demonstrations and target political dissidents.[555] For example, Beatrice de Carrillo, National Human Rights Ombudswoman, remarked:

> When terrorism is defined so broadly, any act that may prove a nuisance to society or that may be construed as an attack on public property could be considered terrorism. [The anti-terrorism law], besides being unnecessary, is a law that attempts to exert social control, to intimidate the public from participating in public protests.[556]

Indeed, the anti-terrorism law has been invoked at least three times in the context of public demonstrations: to prosecute informal street

---

[553] Rodrigo Baires Quezada, *Debate abierto por la ley antiterrorista*, EL FARO, July 17, 2006, http://www.elfaro.net/secciones/observatorio/20060717/observatorio1_20060717.asp.

[554] *Id.*

[555] *Id.*

[556] *Id.*

vendors in Apopa (first); and San Salvador (second); and to prosecute organizers and demonstrators in the city of Suchitoto (third). The charged political climate that pervaded debates about the passage of the anti-terrorist law has similarly influenced its application to political demonstrations.

b) *The Anti-Terrorism Law: Street Vendors in Apopa and San Salvador*

On February 10, 2007, Vicente Ramírez led a protest against the dismantling and relocating of the stalls of street vendors in the city of Apopa. The protest turned violent when some of the participants started throwing stones and bricks at municipal property and set a government vehicle on fire. A municipal worker was also reported to have been injured. The Office of the Prosecutor accused Vicente Ramírez, Suyapa Martínez, and Luis Contreras of having participated in these attacks and, interpreting their actions to constitute "acts of terrorism," pressed charges against all three under Articles 15 and 34 of the new anti-terrorism law.[557] Ramírez was placed in provisional detention while the Office of the Prosecutor gathered evidence in its case against him. Ultimately, the judge would drop the terrorism charges, noting that destroying municipal property was an act of vandalism that should be

---

[557] *See* International Labour Organization (ILO), Committee on Freedom of Association, *Complaint against the Government of El Salvador presented by the Latin American Central of Workers (CLAT)*, Report No. 348, Case No. 2551 (2007), *available at* http://www.ilo.org/ ilolex/english/caseframeE.htm; *see also* Ruth Melany Cruz, *Capturan a Ramírez por actos terroristas*, La Prensa Gráfica, Feb. 18, 2007, *available at* http://www.laprensagrafica.net/ nacion/719196.asp. Article 15 provides for the application of the anti-terrorism law to individuals who use "weapons, flammable artifacts or substances . . . or similar articles, in a public space . . . causing death or physical or psychological harm to one or more persons." The government argued that the three defendants had violated sections (a), (c), (g), (h) and (j) of Article 34 of the anti-terrorism law. Article 34 provides for an aggravated sentence when, among other circumstances, the crime (a) is committed by two or more people; (c) involves an attempt against public property; (g) disrupts public services or normal traffic in the main points of entry to the national territory, or in governmental buildings; (h) involves physical, psychological, or sexual violence; (j) causes death or physical harm or endangers the life or physical integrity of the victims. Special Anti-Terrorism Law, *supra* note 391, at arts. 15, 34.

prosecuted as such under the Penal Code.[558] The judge also emphasized that the interpretation of the anti-terrorism law advocated by the Office of the Prosecutor was impermissibly broad, as it encroached on the jurisdiction of the penal code to encompass "almost any crime."[559] Human rights practitioners and analysts interviewed for this book agreed with the judge's opinion and similarly disapproved of the application of the new law to simple acts of vandalism.[560]

The Office of the Prosecutor employed the anti-terrorism law a second time against street vendors. Following a police operation that confiscated allegedly pirated goods, street vendors staged a large street demonstration on May 12, 2007. Protesters burned cars and vandalized and looted several local businesses. The Office of the Prosecutor charged twenty-seven people, two of them juveniles, with having committed acts of terrorism under Articles 15 and 34 of the anti-terrorism law.[561]

President Saca defended the broad application of the anti-terrorism law to acts of vandalism, emphasizing that "a person who flips a car, burns it, attacks businesses, destroys them, [and] commits acts of vandalism"

---

[558] Diego Murcia, *Juez no aplica ley antiterrorista*, La Prensa Gráfica, June 7, 2007, *available at* http://www.laprensagrafica.net/nacion/796823.asp.

[559] *Id.*

[560] *See, e.g.,* interview with Martínez, *supra* note 396 ("It seems impossible that, based on the language of article 15, the Prosecutor arrested the demonstrators in Apopa. The sticks and stones they were carrying were considered 'weapons' under article 15."); interview with Amaya, *supra* note 409 ("The anti-terrorism law has ambiguous provisions, which can lead to the arbitrary application of the law in the context of public demonstrations."); interview with Maria Silvia Guillén, Directora Ejecutiva de FESPAD, in San Salvador, (Mar. 26, 2008) ("Every nation has the right to issue an anti-terrorism law, but this particular law criminalizes social protest. The language [of article 15] "similar weapons" allowed the Prosecution to argue that the protesters' sticks and stones were terrorist weapons. The law has too many ambiguities, it is too broad.").

[561] *Vendedores crean pánico en el Centro*, El Diario de Hoy, May 12, 2007, *available at* http://www.elsalvador.com/mwedh/nota/nota_completa.asp?idCat=2892&idArt=1369727; Suchit Chávez & Amadeo Cabrera, *Saca: son actos terroristas*, La Prensa Gráfica, May 14, 2007, *available at* http://www.laprensagrafica.com//nacion/778826.asp; *Vendedores provocan saqueos e incendios de vehículo*, Diario Co Latino, May 12, 2007, *available at* http://www.diariocolatino.com/es/20070512/nacionales/nacionales_20070512_16590/?tpl=69.

is a terrorist who should be prosecuted under the new law.[562] He also illustrated the charged political context in which the anti-terrorism law operates when he warned the public that street vendors who participate in public demonstrations are nothing other than "radical groups dressed like vendors who are looking to kill someone."[563]

c) *The Anti-terrorism Law and Suchitoto's Water Rights Protest*

On July 9, 2007, the Office of the Prosecutor charged fourteen leaders of social organizations with having committed acts of terrorism, and in particular with having endangered the life and integrity of the President of El Salvador and other government officials. The fourteen had gathered in the town of Suchitoto and environs to participate in a series of peaceful protests and teach-ins regarding President Saca's initiative to privatize water services. The President himself was scheduled to give a talk in Suchitoto that day.

According to the Office of the Prosecutor and the PNC, protests were organized to carry out violent attacks against the police.[564] Nevertheless, rights groups who have investigated the case, including Amnesty International and *Tutela Legal*, found that police officers used disproportionate force against the protesters. Moreover, Amnesty International and local rights defenders charged that police officers had been the principal instigators of violence in several instances, had indiscriminately arrested people not even present at the site of the confrontations, and had physically abused detainees.[565]

---

[562] Chávez & Cabrera, *supra* note 561; *see also* President Saca, Press Conference (Feb. 19, 2007), *available at* http://www.casapres.gob.sv/presidente/declaraciones/2007/02/dec1901. html (noting that the terrorism law should be applied to those street vendors who destroy or break property, as well as "those who block off streets or burn buses in front of the National University"–a clear allusion to the July 5 events.).

[563] Chávez & Cabrera, *supra* note 561.

[564] Rodrigo Baires Quezada, *Manifestantes de Suchitoto a prisión por 'actos de terrorismo,'* EL FARO, July 9, 2007.

[565] Press Release, *Tutela Legal* del Arzobispado, Pronunciamiento Público ante los sucesos

The Suchitoto prosecution was filed in a specialized tribunal under the Organized and Complex Crimes Law. The specialized judge who heard the case, Lucila Fuentes de Paz, would ultimately find she did not have jurisdiction to try the protesters, but only after the prosecutor had decided to substitute the terrorism charges with the charge of disorderly conduct. The case against the protesters was dismissed six months later by a judge in the ordinary justice system when the prosecution failed to appear at the trial. As was the case with the Apopa and San Salvador street vendors' protests, President Saca and other government officials in several public remarks sought to link Suchitoto protesters with clandestine armed groups.[566] (See insert: "The Suchitoto Case.")

de violencia acaecidos en la población de Suchitoto, el pasado día 2 de julio de 2007 (July 12, 2007), *http://www.tutelalegal.org/paginas/suchitoto.htm;* Public Statement, Amnesty International, El Salvador: Demonstrators Victims of Anti-terrorist Legislation (July 13, 2007), http://www.amnesty.org/en/library/info/AMR29/002/2007/en.

[566] *Saca vincula grupos armadas con ataque en Suchitoto,* El Diario de Hoy, Dec. 28, 2008; *Golpe incipiente a guerrilla,* El Diario de Hoy, July 2, 2007.

The Suchitoto Case

On July 2, 2007, President Antonio Saca was scheduled to visit the town of Suchitoto to announce the launch of a water decentralization program, which many feared would lead to water privatization. Both protestors and riot police began preparing for the visit the previous evening. Local community organizations, joined by several NGOs including El Salvador Christian Committee for Displaced Communities (*Comité Cristiano Pro Desplazados de El Salvador or CRIPDES*), planned a forum on water issues to be held at the same time as the President's visit in Suchitoto's central square.[1]

According to *Tutela Legal* and IDHUCA, two reputable Salvadoran rights organizations, both police and military personnel were deployed to the Suchitoto area in the early morning hours of July 2, 2007.[2] By 9:30 A.M., demonstrators had gathered on the road to Suchitoto reportedly blocking a section of the road. Anti-riot police reacted by firing rubber bullets and tear gas into the crowd.[3] According to reports, police forces also indiscriminately beat and used pepper spray on members of the crowd, in what then-Human Rights Ombudsperson Beatrice de Carrillo characterized as "an abuse of force against civilians."[4] Several demonstrators explained that this indiscriminate use of force triggered a confrontation in which protesters threw rocks at the police and burned tires

---

[1] *See generally* Rodrigo Baires Quezada, *Manifestantes de Suchitoto a prisión por "actos de terrorismo,"* EL FARO, July 9, 2007; Katlen Urquilla & Julio Mejía, *Grupos de izquierda boicotean visita Saca,* EL NUEVO DIARIO, July 2, 2007.

[2] Press Release, *Tutela Legal* del Arzobispado, Pronunciamiento Público ante los sucesos de violencia acaecidos en la población de Suchitoto, el pasado día 2 de Julio de 2007 (July 12, 2007), *available at http://www.tutelalegal.org/paginas/suchitoto.htm*; Press Release, IDHUCA, ¡Salvar a El Salvador! (July 18, 2007).

[3] *See, e.g.,* Urquilla & Mejía, *supra* note 1.

[4] Baires Quezada, *supra* note 1.

by the side of the road. Similar attacks occurred elsewhere, with several police groups pursuing community members into the surrounding hills, where they beat and arrested several demonstrators. Among those arrested were four leaders of the CRIPDES delegation who were driving into the city to take part in the forum, and who denied having participated in any confrontation with police forces. Police allegedly beat several protesters as they were taken into custody.[5]

The Director of the Office of the Public Prosecutor charged thirteen with having committed acts of terrorism under Article 5 of the Special Anti-Terrorism Law, which carries a penalty of up to 60 years in prison. The government maintained that the events at Suchitoto constituted organized acts of terrorism against government officials, including President Saca.[6] In contrast, national and international rights organizations regard the detainees as political prisoners, and have widely decried their arrest. Rights groups, including *Tutela Legal*, the Human Rights Institute at the University of Central America, and Amnesty International, have criticized the government's excessive and arbitrary use of force, conflation of political demonstration with violent crime, physical and psychological ill-treatment at the time of arrest, and the use of anti-terrorism legislation to incarcerate domestic protestors without due process of law.[7]

Although authorities eventually dropped the terrorism charges, the Suchitoto arrests remain emblematic of governmental misuse of "anti-terrorism" legislation to clamp down on demonstrators and stifle public protest. - *David Carpman and Dustin Saldarriaga*

---

[5] *See Tutela Legal, supra* note 2; Public Statement, Amnesty International, El Salvador: Demonstrators Victims of Anti-terrorist Legislation (July 13, 2007), *available at* http://www.amnesty.org/en/library/info/AMR29/002/2007/en

[6] *See, e.g.,* Baires Quezada, *supra* note 1.

[7] *Tutela Legal, supra* note 2; Amnesty International, *supra* note 5; *Organizaciones marchan en San Salvador para exigir libertad de 14 activistas,* LA PRENSA GRÁFICA, July 7, 2007.

2. *Conflating political opposition, gangs, and terrorism*

The violence on July 5 and the government's efforts to deploy the anti-terrorism law against public demonstrators reveal the extent to which the ideological and political battles of the 1980s still shape Salvadoran society and public institutions. Appreciating the dynamics of this polarized climate is critical to understanding gang violence and associated rights violations in El Salvador for several reasons. First, the Salvadoran state has increasingly linked political opposition, gang members, and terrorism in an explicit fashion. The anti-terrorism law represents a particularly vivid example of the conflation of these groups, as does the rhetoric employed by government officials following the events of July 5. This rhetoric is illustrated by President Saca's statements to the press noted above. Likewise, Rodrigo Ávila portrayed the July 5 protests, as well as the demonstrations spearheaded by street vendors and by activists at Suchitoto, as grave threats to democracy, orchestrated by "communist urban guerrillas," with the participation of gang members.[567] He warned the public: "We are in imminent danger and cannot rule out another July 5."[568] Indeed, opposition political activists interviewed by our researchers reported having been targeted by police and falsely accused of gang association.[569] In August 2006, the Director General of Penal Centers in El Salvador, Dr. Jaime Roberto Villanova, told our researchers that he had reason to believe Salvadoran gangs had ties to international terrorist organizations, including Al Qaeda.[570]

---

[567] *Golpe incipiente a guerrilla, supra* note 566.

[568] *Id.*

[569] Interview with N.O., activist with the Bloque Popular Juvenil [Popular Youth Bloc, hereinafter BPJ], in Ciudad Delgado (Aug. 31, 2006) (describing an incident in which police pulled him off a bus and beat him); and with other activists from the BPJ, including D.R.O., who told us that his picture was published in the media along with accusations that he was a member of the M-18, limiting his ability to travel in certain areas for fear of the MS-13 and the police.

[570] Interview with Villanova, *supra* note 124 ("We have information, about this international terrorism. Especially Al-Qaeda. . . . We have a newly created department which is the Service of Penitentiary Intelligence. It detects the sort of elements that could be operating in the prisons.").

He provided no evidence of this connection beyond the assertion itself. In a contradiction that may reveal the politicized nature of these allegations, the Director of the National Council for Public Security told our researchers in March 2006 that reports of a relationship between Al Qaeda and Central American gangs were untrue and nothing more than "an invention of a Honduran legislator."[571] More generally, the polarization of the Salvadoran government and public life fosters a climate in which the rule of law is subordinated to political power struggles and in which rights abuses flourish.

3. Pre-Election Violence

While in El Salvador, our researchers heard from a range of experts and observers that the periods preceding major Salvadoran elections since 2003 have been marked by spikes in media attention to violence and in actual violence, often imputed to gangs.[572] These observations— which came from sources as varied as academic researchers, government employees, and human rights activists and which have also been documented to some extent in published reports—include two components. First, sources noted a shift in media coverage of homicides and gang violence in the months prior to elections. Generally, this coverage increased and intensified, helping to fuel the centrality of violence and criminality as issues in electoral campaigns.[573] Second, we also heard widespread anecdotal reports of an increase in the number of homicides prior to elections, particularly in gruesome killings that bear the hallmarks of death squad murders from the civil war years.[574] These

---

[571] *See* interview with Bonilla, *supra* note 134.

[572] *See* interview with Cruz, *supra* note 145; *see also* interview with Henríquez Hernández Ávila, *supra* note 520; Aguilar, *supra* note 100.

[573] *See* interview with Torres, *supra* note 126 ("There is manipulation before elections. In the newspapers, there are lists of the dead. And people say automatically, oh, that's a gang killing.").

[574] *See* interview with Cruz, *supra* note 145; interview with Astrid Torres, *supra* note 126; interview with Eisen, *supra* note 208; interview with Anaya Perla, *supra* note 227.

observations, even if only partially true, suggest that any depiction of violence in El Salvador as common or apolitical criminality is seriously incomplete.

Recent election cycles in El Salvador have been characterized by particular emphasis on the gang phenomenon and the threat of gang violence in the country. Political candidates in El Salvador have invoked criminality and violence, frequently in a sensationalized fashion, for political gain. Media coverage of gang violence fuels this phenomenon. Public security has been a central theme in recent election cycles, and the ARENA party—which held the presidency from 1994 to 2009—was successful at winning elections by emphasizing its tough approach to crime.[575] Jeannette Aguilar, of the University Institute for Public Opinion Research (IUDOP), wrote in 2004 that:

> The manipulation of the feelings of citizen security, through the deliberate exploitation of citizen fear for political-electoral ends, has been recurrent. In this way, the incapacity of the governing party to control criminal violence and resolve the structural problems that generate and reproduce it has been hidden.[576]

A related but distinct question is whether there has been an actual increase in violent crimes before elections. José Miguel Cruz, former director of the IUDOP, told our researchers in March 2006 that:

> In the last three elections, there have been very brutal crimes. When we start to investigate, this issue remains very gray. The information is very inconsistent . . . So it makes us think that although there are certainly gang members behind these crimes, there must be some other factors involved, groups with political interests.

---

[575] Aguilar & Miranda, *supra* note 157, at 61 (noting that despite its poor results, the *Mano Dura* plan has served as a successful and central campaign platform for the current administration).

[576] Aguilar, *supra* note 100.

> Gang members often act as paid assasins (*sicarios*); these could be crimes that aren't instigated by gangs themselves.[577]

In an effort to investigate further this widely-reported phenomenon, our researchers reviewed homicide statistics from the IML for 2004. (The most recent presidential election took place on March 21, 2009 but no statistics are yet available for that year.) We also reviewed newspaper reports of killings for the one-month period prior to presidential elections on March 21, 2004, and compared that information to newspaper reports of killings for the one-month period between May 21 and June 21, 2004. Quantitatively, we found that March was the bloodiest month in El Salvador in 2004: there were 291 homicides reported by the IML for that month, compared to a rough monthly average of 244.[578] We also found a clustering of particularly brutal killings—in particular, those of unidentified women whose bodies were found dismembered— in the one-month period prior to the elections on March 21, 2004, as compared to the month May 21 through June 21, 2004.[579] The media sometimes attributed these killings to gangs. However, many experts in the country note that these killings are inconsistent with the *modus operandi* of gangs and suggest that political forces interested in instilling fear in the population prior to the elections could be behind them.[580]

The legacy of the civil war and a halting transition toward democracy have impeded the development of judicial and police institutions needed

---

[577] Interview with Cruz, *supra* note 145.

[578] CORTE SUPREMA DE JUSTICIA, INSTITUTO DE MEDICINA LEGAL [National Institute of Forensic Medicine, Supreme Court], DEFUNCIONES POR HOMICIDOS, EL SALVADOR, AÑOS 2003, 2004 [HOMICIDE FATALITIES, EL SALVADOR, YEARS 2003, 2004] 165 (2004).

[579] For purposes of this comparison, we looked for "particularly brutal killings," which according to experts like José Miguel Cruz of IUDOP do not bear the markings of gang murders. Specifically, we looked for killings that involved unidentified victims and dismemberment or other visible signs of torture. We found six such killings reported in *La Prensa Gráfica* from February 21-March 21, 2004, and five such killings reported in *El Diario de Hoy*. From May 21-June 21, 2004, *La Prensa Gráfica* reported three such killings, as did *El Diario de Hoy*.

[580] *See* interview with Cruz, *supra* note 145; interview with Perla Jiménez, *supra* note 150.

to ensure citizen protection.[581] The information we gathered through interviews and research, however, indicates that powerful political forces in El Salvador—including some possibly connected to the government in power through early 2009—may believe that perceived public insecurity can advance their political or electoral interests. This information also suggests that, when it suits their interests, these political forces may directly or indirectly participate in perpetrating violence. The polarization of Salvadoran society and government constitutes a serious impediment to the state's capacity to provide security and ensure the protection of its citizens.

D. Victims' Narratives of State Violence

1. *Targeting of Actual and Alleged Gang Members*

> *I get hit from all angles. The . . . gangs, organized crime groups, the cops . . . Everyone who sees me, the first thing they say to me is, "Wow, you're still alive? I can't believe you're still alive!"*[582]
>
> - A former gang member in San Salvador, who planned to flee the country for fear of being killed, in San Salvador (August 30, 2006)

Those presumed, rightly or wrongly, to be gang members constitute the group most likely to be subjected to abuse by agents of the Salvadoran state. Some of these individuals are actual or former members of gangs; however, others are targeted simply for looking suspicious, a term which, in certain urban neighborhoods, requires nothing more than being young and male.[583] There was overwhelming agreement

---

[581] *See* Chapters I and II, *supra*.

[582] Interview with W.M., *supra* note 248.

[583] *See, e.g.*, interview with Perla Jiménez, *supra* note 151; interview with A.Y., *supra* note 277.

among those interviewed for this book that having one or more tattoos renders a person suspicious in the eyes of the police and of society at large; tattooed youths in particular face discrimination and run a high risk of being attacked as gang members.[584] In other cases, people may perceive someone to be a gang member solely because he or she lives in a neighborhood known to be the territory of a certain gang.[585]

Those presumed to be gang members face danger and stigmatization from all sides. They are blamed by government representatives and much of the public for the high level of violent crime in the country,[586] demonized in the media,[587] harassed and physically abused by the police,[588] and targeted for assassination by rival gangs and by death squads engaged in social cleansing.[589]

The police rarely, if ever, provide protection to presumed or former gang members facing any of the foregoing threats.[590] By contrast, the police themselves generally view these individuals as enemies[591] rather than citizens whose rights they should protect. Indeed, some PNC officers are thought to be complicit in the targeted killings and abuse of members of this population.[592] In this manner, tattooed youth and

---

[584] *See, e.g.,* interview with Alemanni de Carrillo, *supra* note 119; interview with Jeanne Rikkers, *supra* note 151; interview with Aguilar, *supra* note 157; interview with Morales, *supra* note 230; interview with M.A.H., *supra* note 501; interview with R.Z., *supra* note 501; interview with V.R., in San Salvador (Aug. 28, 2006).

[585] *See, e.g.,* interview with F.R., *supra* note 200; interview with A.F., *supra* note 310.

[586] *See, e.g.,* interview with Torres, *supra* note 126; interview with Flores, *supra* note 153.

[587] *See, e.g.,* interview with Perla Jiménez, *supra* note 150; interview with Torres, *supra* note 126; interview with W.M., *supra* note 248.

[588] *See* interview excerpts below in Part a) of this Chapter.

[589] *See, e.g.,* interview with Alemanni de Carrillo, *supra* note 119; interview with Martínez Ventura, *supra* note 117; interview with Aguilar, *supra* note 157; interview with A.Y., *supra* note 277.

[590] *See, e.g.,* interview with Alemanni de Carrillo, *supra* note 120; interview with Alegría, *supra* note 502.

[591] *See* Part a) of this Chapter.

[592] *See, e.g.,* interview with Alegría, *supra* note 502; Press Release, *Tutela Legal* del Arzo-

others presumed to be affiliated with gangs—a class already targeted for severe human rights violations—cannot reasonably depend on the government of El Salvador for protection against such violations.

The excerpts that follow provide a more detailed picture of the pervasive human rights violations facing Salvadoran youth who are presumed—rightly or wrongly—to be affiliated with gangs. In particular, these narratives illustrate four main problems facing this population: police harassment and violence, killings by rival gang members, extrajudicial execution by death squads, and discrimination in areas such as employment and school enrollment.

a) Police Harassment and Violence Against Suspected Gang Members

Nearly all those interviewed for this report spoke of targeted harassment and violence against gang members, tattooed youth, or young males in general by the police. In the words of Gilma Pérez, Director of the Migrants Program at IDHUCA, gang members and ex-gang members are "under siege" by authorities.[593] Further, the PNC's use of repressive tactics against suspected gang members increased with the implementation of the *Mano Dura* policies.[594] Members of one community youth group observed in 2006 that, "for the police, every group of young people is an illicit association."[595]

Public officials and NGO workers interviewed for this report discussed several deaths thought to constitute summary executions and unjustified killings by the police. For example, an NGO coordinator

---

bispado, Ejecución arbitraria de cuatro jóvenes en San Bartolo, Ilopango (July 19, 2006), *available at* http://www.tutelalegal.org/paginas/prensa.htm#ejecucion; Leonel Herrera, *PDDH insiste en investigar a grupos de exterminio*, Diario Colatino, Aug. 30, 2006, *available at* http://www.diariocolatino.com/nacionales/detalles.asp?NewsID=13629.

[593] Interview with Pérez, *supra* note 242.

[594] Interview with Martínez Ventura, *supra* note 117; interview with Hernández, *supra* note 303; interview with A.F., *supra* note 310; interview with A.Y., *supra* note 277.

[595] Interview with A.Y, *supra* note 277.

working in a poor neighborhood outside San Salvador told our researchers about an incident in December 2005. According to this source, police arrested more than a dozen youths attending a Christmas party at which members of the M-18 were present and then summarily shot them to death, blaming the massacre on gangs.[596] In another case reported to the National Human Rights Ombudswoman on June 6, 2006, witnesses asserted that two police officers unnecessarily shot and killed a 17-year-old member of the M-18 from behind; according to the complaint filed with the Ombudswoman's Office, a preliminary investigation was opened against the officers, but after the witnesses decided not to testify out of fear for their safety, the case was dropped.[597] In 2007, it was discovered that a large, clandestine extermination group had been operating within the San Miguel police department. Sixteen members of the Criminal Investigation Unit were implicated in the murder of 46-year-old farmer Amado García Amaya.[598] The group was also suspected of involvement in several other killings in the area.[599] Between 2001 and 2005, FESPAD monitored media reports of homicides for possible instances of extrajudicial killings, using a methodology similar to that applied by the United Nations Joint Group for the Investigation of Politically Motivated Illegal Armed Groups in El Salvador in 1994.[600] FESPAD identified 622 cases of possible extrajudicial killings during that period.[601] The issue of clandestine

---

[596] Interview with McConville, *supra* note 209.

[597] Procuraduría para la Defensa de los Derechos Humanos [Office of the National Human Rights Ombudsperson], *Resumen de Expediente [File Summary], Complaint filed June 6, 2006* (on file with authors).

[598] Amado García Amaya's murder is reported to have been a contract killing. Elder Gómez, *Más policías vinculados a grupo de sicarios que operaba en PNC*, DIARIO CO LATINO, Sept. 11, 2007, *available at* http://www.diariocolatino.com/es/20070911/nacionales/47031/.

[599] Jorge Beltrán & Carlos Segovia, *Investigarán a ex policías por 31 casos de homicidios*, EL DIARIO DE HOY, Aug. 8, 2007, *available at* http://www.elsalvador.com/mwedh/nota/nota_completa.asp?idCat=6329&idArt=1617024.

[600] ESTADO DE LA SEGURIDAD PÚBLICA Y LA JUSTICIA PENAL EN EL SALVADOR 2005, *supra* note 494, at 104.

[601] *Id.*

violence, including an in-depth discussion of the case of Amado García Amaya, and an analysis of other evidence of police involvement in extra-judicial killings is explored in Chapter V, Part A.

The excerpts below illustrate a more frequent pattern of human rights violations against suspected gang members (mostly tattooed youth), involving police stops and searches on the street. These stops often include threats, beatings, and other forms of abuse. It is striking to note the frequency with which some youth report experiencing such stops, which in some cases were said to occur every few days or even several times per day. Equally or more significant is the fact that in most cases, the police have targeted the youth in question based on appearance, focusing on tattoos or the fact of being outdoors in the company of other young males. Moreover, participation in community youth groups, rehabilitation programs, and even tattoo-removal treatment appears to have little impact on the likelihood of being stopped and abused by police, demonstrating that once a person is considered a "suspected gang member" or is known to have any past affiliation with gangs, his or her efforts at positive engagement in the community generally will not alter the tendency of the police to treat him or her as a gang member.

> 1. *A group of kids was playing on the street when the police arrived. Some of the kids tried to run away, but the police caught them and hit them on the head with a club. Then they lifted their shirts to look for tattoos. You're left feeling very scared. And if you speak you're dead. This is how they [the police] make us feel. This type of thing happens all the time in my neighborhood. The police arrive with ski masks so that you can't see their faces. They don't wear badges, or they cover them. Sometimes their vehicles don't have license plates. Sometimes they wear civilian clothing.*[602]
> - Member of the Human Rights Comittee of the San Bartolo Parish, in San Bartolo (October 21, 2008)

2. The Human Rights Committee of the San Bartolo Parish made

---

[602] Interview with a member of the Human Rights Committee of the San Bartolo Parish, *supra* note 472.

available to our researchers copies of their intake interviews. One of these interviews, labeled as a "community complaint," described the constant harrassment of community youth by the police. Excerpts of this intake interview are reproduced below:

We, in representation of the communities of [a neighborhood in the outskirts of San Salvador], lodge this complaint against members of the National Police. On Saturday, August 30, between eight and ten police officers arrived in our neighborhood and started hitting young members of our community without provocation; the police did not show [the youth] a warrant for their arrest, and gave no explanation for their behavior. . . . The community was forced to intervene so that the police would stop their indiscriminate physical abuse. This is not the first time that police officers have acted with such violence against our community. . . . [The PNC's actions] have generated fear in our community.[603] - Complaint dated September 9, 2008

3. [The police] always beat me up. Sometimes they stop me up to twice in the same day; on Fridays they stop me more often than other days. On Tuesday [two days ago] they stopped me, and on the way back they stopped me a second time . . . They still beat me up [though I am no longer in any gang]. . . . [One time] they asked me where I was coming from, told me they were going to search me, asked me if I was in a gang, made me lift up my shirt. They're corrupt: they tried to plant marijuana in my pocket. Thank God a man witnessed it from behind. These types of encounters can last from five to thirty minutes. There are two or three police. At times they punish you when they stop you. One time when I was [still] in the gang, they found a knife on me and they made me do push-ups in the street. When you get too tired, they hit you. These things normally happen at night. . . . Even though your tattoo may not be from a gang, if you have one, the police think

---

[603] Human Rights Committee of the San Bartolo Parish, *Community Complaint*, Sept. 9, 2008 (on file with authors).

that you're suspicious.[604] - 24-year-old former gang member, in San Salvador (March 30, 2006)

4. *There's one policeman who would always follow and harass us. When he would see us in the street, he would always come to search us. One time my friend opened his garage because he knew that this policeman was going to follow us. The policeman followed us and we ran to the garage and went inside. The policeman said that he would be back, that when we left the garage he would get us. This was four months ago. This kind of thing happens to us all the time. The police have searched me about three times this month . . . They started to stop me and search me more in the street in 2003-2004; this was when the situation worsened and they started to search us more.*[605] - 24-year-old resident of San Salvador, who told our researchers that he was not a member of any gang, in Mejicanos (August 27, 2006)

5. *The Police patrol my neighborhood every day. If they don't like the way you look, they'll stop you. I've been stopped three times since May. They asked for my identity card and made me lift my shirt. I have no tattoos.*[606] - U.B., 19-year-old youth, who stated he was not a member of any gang, in Santa Ana (October 20, 2007)

6. *One time there was a group of twenty of us hanging out and drinking in the street. Five police officers arrived and told us, "everyone against the wall." They have this tactic where they hit you on the legs to get you scared. They took one guy's finger and bent it over backwards. Then a patrol showed up with four more police. The owner of the house had to come out and look at us; he told the police that we weren't gang members and that he knew*

---

[604] Interview with C.A., *supra* note 143.

[605] Interview with A.F., *supra* note 310.

[606] Interview with U.B., in Santa Ana (Oct. 20, 2007).

us.[607] -26-year-old male resident of San Salvador, who stated he was not a member of any gang, in San Salvador (August 30, 2006)

7. *I see the police almost every day hitting the people they have stopped. They hit them with a club. They use something that gives you an electric shock.*[608] - C.B., 16-year-old youth, who told our researchers that he was not a member of any gang, in Santa Ana (October 20, 2007)

8. *If [the police] see you on a bus, even though you're minding your own business, they tell you to lift your shirt up, and if they see tattoos, it's* Mano Dura *for you. I've served time in prison, but I've also been picked up for nothing more than having tattoos and detained for three to five days. They put me under investigation, put my name in the system. One day I was moving into a new house, my television broke, the police were coming by, and they detained me. If you tell the police, I'm rehabilitating myself through* Homies Unidos, *they say,* "Homies Unidos—*that means nothing to us!*" *And you can say, I'm employed now, but they say,* "But *you're not working now—you're in the street, so let's go inside*"—*and they arrest you.*[609] - 28-year-old former gang member, in San Salvador (March 28, 2006)

9. *The police arrive at the communities and often beat the young people there. A friend of mine was horribly beaten when I know he's not involved with gangs. I don't know what kind of methodology they [the police] use to do this, what criteria they employ, but they just arrive, take some people into custody, hold them for two or three days, and then release them. Because of this, the community does not trust the police. Their impression is*

---

[607] Interview with T.V.L., in San Salvador (Aug. 30, 2006).

[608] Interview with C.B., in Santa Ana (Oct. 20, 2007).

[609] Interview with J.R.T., *supra* note 272.

that the police destroy things, that they are violent, that they take their children away, lock them up and mistreat them.[610] - B.E., staff of a youth center, outside San Salvador (January 21, 2009)

10. *When I would walk around in my neighborhood, every time the police saw me, they would take me into custody and beat me. . . . They've detained me maybe ten or eleven times. . . . They would always say I was guilty of illicit association, but I wasn't going around with gang members, I would just wave to other guys in the street and the police said that I was with them, that that was illicit association. All of this started when I was maybe fourteen years old. Sometimes they would also say that they were arresting me for not having papers, for being out at night without papers. . . . They would take me to a police lockup; normally I was there for only three days, but sometimes I was there for six or seven days. . . . One time they wanted to send me to an adult prison, but I told them I was a minor. They took my [identity] card from me and tore it up; they said that I was an adult.*[611] - 17-year-old from Soyapango, who stated he was not a member of any gang, in Ilobasco (August 25, 2006)

11. *Victor was walking with his friend at 9:30 A.M. when the police told them to stop. They ran instead and the police pursued Victor. It was one policeman and three soldiers. They said that they have orders to shoot if people do not stop. They shot and they missed, but Victor got tired and fell. Then the police beat him to death.*[612] - Testimony of Victor Alexander López's mother, in Tonacatepeque, Distrito Italia (March 23, 2008). Victor's story was covered in the news media, which reported discrepancies between the story as told by witnesses and by members of the GTA (the joint police-army unit involved in the case). While

---

[610] Interview with B.E., *supra* note 119.

[611] Interview with T.C., *supra* note 200.

[612] Interview with Victor Alexander López's mother, in Tonacatepeque (Mar. 23, 2008).

the GTA alleged Victor had died suddenly of a heart attack, witnesses told the press, "The policeman and the soldiers beat him to death. I saw the footprint of a boot on his chest; it was as if they had stood on it."[613]

12. *A month ago the police [arrested me]. . . . I was going to a friend's wake. There were four of us. We were driving to the wake, and there was a team of police. They told us to get out of the car. . . . They put us in their car and took us to the police station. In the station they beat us up. They hit us with guns. They beat all of us for like two hours; there were ten or eleven police officers. They were asking us questions about past cases. [Then] they put us in a jail cell for five days. . . . They told us they had arrested us for illicit association, but they never gave us any court date. . . . One time, here near the chapel, the police got me. I was walking from the chapel after a meeting of my [youth group]. When I reached this isolated part, they approached me. They told me to come with them. . . . We walked to an isolated place and they tore out my eyebrow-ring and beat me. They left me there and I went home. . . . Since then I've stayed indoors. . . . [During my lifetime] they've stopped me to search me like one hundred times.[614]* - 17-year-old gang member, in Cabañas (August 25, 2006)

13. *The police do not help. They stop kids around here all the time. They say they are part of the gang and they don't respect the kids, but they won't do anything to help them. There is no opportunity here, only masses of murdered sons and daughters, and mothers without children . . . who are dying for no reason.[615]* - Mother

---

[613] Enrique Carranza, *Muere menor tras ser perseguido por policías y soldados,* EL DIARIO DE HOY, Mar. 10, 2008.

[614] Interview with D.H., *supra* note 451.

[615] Interview with murdered gang member's mother, Tonacatepeque, Distrito Italia (Mar. 23, 2008).

of a 14-year-old murdered gang member, in Tonacatepeque, Distrito Italia (March 23, 2008)

14. *One Saturday about a month and a half ago, I was eating in a shop when some police came and told me to go outside. They lifted up my shirt; they put a gun to my chest; this was two police and two soldiers. They took me in their car . . . they told me that it was me that shot another police officer. Supposedly someone had shot a police officer and they said it was me, but it wasn't me. They took me to the other side [of this area] and put a gun to my chest. They tore the lower part of my ear and put a grenade up against my head to threaten me. The police told me, "You'll pay for this, we're going to kill you slowly." . . . When they left me there, they told me, you have to wait here until 7 P.M., we're going to come back and if we don't find you here, we'll kill you. But when they left I went home. . . . The neighbors in that place told me later that the police had come back looking for me. . . . They've taken me to a jail cell twice, but they've searched me a ton of times, more than I can even tell you. . . . Since the last time that I got out of a jail cell, I don't leave my house much.*[616] - 18-year-old gang member, in Cabañas (August 25, 2006)

---

[616] Interview with L.F.G., *supra* note 233.

b) *Targeting of Suspected Gang Members for Discrimination in School Enrollment and Employment*

Finally, those who are presumed by others to be gang members (e.g. people with tattoos) face pervasive social discrimination even apart from the violence and threats described above. Indeed, such discrimination is often institutionalized in the form of rules (whether official or unofficial) prohibiting their attending school or obtaining jobs solely because they are tattooed. Even those with artistic tattoos report pervasive discrimination and violence. We spoke with one man who had a tattoo of his wife's name who reported being turned away from jobs on account of this tattoo.[617]

1. *It's very difficult to get a job, they ask you if you're in any gang, and if they see tattoos on you they won't hire you. I was working about two weeks ago, unloading trucks. But they saw my tattoos and they let me go. They told me that I couldn't work with them any more. . . . I want to work but can't.*[618] - 28-year-old former gang member, in San Salvador (March 28, 2006)

2. *Most clients come [to this tattoo removal clinic] because of the persecution they face for having tattoos. . . . We have people come who have artistic tattoos, because for instance one man worked at a business and they told him to have his tattoo removed or he couldn't come back to work. Some schools won't enroll kids who have tattoos, even if they're only artistic. And to get a job, employers make you take off your shirt to see if you have tattoos, especially any jobs in the public sector.*[619] - Olga Isabel Morales, Administrator, Goodbye Tatoos Program, in San Salvador (August 25, 2006)

---

[617] Interview with W.Z.H., in San Salvador (Aug. 31, 2006).

[618] Interview with J.R.T., *supra* note 272.

[619] Interview with Morales, *supra* note 230.

c) *Persons Deported from the United States*

As deportations from the United States have transformed the gang phenomenon in El Salvador and gang violence has intensified in correlation with the increase in deportations, deportees have become scapegoats for worsening crime and other societal problems.[620] Our interviews revealed that deportees, whether tattooed or not, are widely treated as gang members,[621] which leads to stigmatization by society and abuses by the police. Gabriel Trillos, editor-in-chief of *La Prensa Gráfica*, one of El Salvador's main newspapers, told us that the the police assert that the strengthening of the gangs is due to the deportations from the United States, although officials have provided scarce information to support this proposition.[622] Trillos asserted that deportees are stigmatized, citing arrests of deportees who have no relation to gangs whatsoever.[623]

The view of deportees as presumptively dangerous is shared and advocated by high government officials. For example, as president of El Salvador, Antonio Saca referred to deportees coming from the United States in general as "extremely dangerous people that have to be watched."[624] Then Director of the National Civil Police, Rodrigo Ávila, told us that deportees are "a problem for public security."[625] Chief Prosecutor for the Special Extortion Unit Alan Edward Hernández Portillo explained to us that "those who return [to El Salvador from the United States] return as gang members."[626] This perception of deportees

---

[620] *See* Chapter IV.A.5., *supra*.

[621] *See* interview with Alegría, *supra* note 502.

[622] Interview with Gabriel Trillos, Editor-in-Chief, La Prensa Gráfica, in San Salvador (Mar. 28, 2006).

[623] *Id.*

[624] *Saca Preocupado por Deportaciones*, La Prensa Gráfica, Mar. 16, 2005.

[625] Interview with Ávila, *supra* note 155.

[626] Interview with Hernández Portillo, *supra* note 156.

as a menace to society, in conjunction with law enforcement and anti-gang crackdowns, has exposed many deportees to abuse and persecution. Across the board, members of El Salvador's civil society, as well as the National Human Rights Ombudsperson, emphasized to our researchers that the government has failed to provide deportees appropriate protection, as well as the means to reintegrate into Salvadoran society.[627]

The problem for deportees is that, as José Miguel Cruz from the IUDOP explained to our researchers, they are victims of a cycle that seems to leave them with few options.[628] As violence has increased in El Salvador, the press and government officials increasingly blame and demonize gangs and deportees, which in turn leads to fear and reproach among the population, making it harder for former gang members to reintegrate into society by finding jobs.

1. *Deportees are thought of as criminals by Salvadoran society. [People blame deportees for] having brought gangs [to El Salvador]. But many deportees have no ties to gang members.[629]*
- Edgardo Amaya, independent consultant and former lawyer with FESPAD, in San Salvador (October 22, 2008)

2. *I've been unemployed since I got back. I do tattoos in the tattoo parlor but I can't make a living just from that. When I came back I also had no place to stay. I can't live with my baby's mom's family because they're in La Campanera, and that's too dangerous a place for people like me. . . . Since returning I have wanted to leave, not back to the States, just anywhere other than here. I can't rent many places to live because of my tattoos. They turn you away or charge you very high rent. So I've already spent all my savings on high rent.[630]* - 32-year-old former gang member

---

[627] *See* interview with Perla Jiménez, *supra* note 150; interview with Alemanni de Carrillo, *supra* note 119; interview with Rikkers, *supra* note 151.

[628] Interview with Cruz, *supra* note 145.

[629] Interview with Amaya, *supra* note 409.

[630] Interview with W.M., *supra* note 248.

and deportee, in San Salvador (August 30, 2006)

2. It's a problem to have tattoos here, they don't want to give you a job, I can't find a job.[631] -31-year-old former gang member and deportee from Ilobasco (September 1, 2006)

3. Deportees are stigmatized, whether they have committed a crime or not. They are heroes when they are away and sending remittances and ostracized when they are deported to El Salvador.[632] - Jeanne Rikkers, Program Director, CRISPAZ, in San Salvador (March 25, 2008)

4. I tried to get a job but nothing. . . . Reintegration to society is costly. . . . Here the situation is ugly. When I go to the beach I cannot take off my shirt. I cannot go out freely.[633] -22-year-old former gang member and deportee, in San Salvador (March 28, 2006)

5. Deportees try to remain unnoticed. They are treated badly by the government and by society. Everyone assumes they were deported because they committed a crime, even though this is not true for the vast majority of deportees. And the stigma of being a gang member attaches indiscriminately to all deportees.[634] - B.F., Director, CFO, in Mejicanos (October 21, 2008)

---

[631] Interview with M.A.H., *supra* note 501.

[632] Interview with Rikkers, *supra* note 151.

[633] Interview with R.E., *supra* note 272.

[634] Interview with B.F., *supra* note 119.

CHAPTER V:
CLANDESTINE VIOLENCE

"Organized crime acts with impunity and counts on the cooperation of existing power structures."

- Jaime Martínez Ventura, October 23, 2008, Coordinator, Office of Juvenile Justice, Supreme Court of El Slavador

Although the international community singled out death squads as perhaps the most troubling feature of El Salvador's socio-political system throughout the war and during the early post-war period,[635] national authorities have failed to eradicate extrajudicial violence, which has become increasingly prevalent in the years after the peace accords.[636] As detailed in Chapter I, death squads with varying levels of association with the state have been a part of Salvadoran life for decades and were responsible for thousands of killings between 1980 and 1991. In 1992, the Truth Commission called forcefully on the Salvadoran government to investigate "the structural connection . . . between death squads and state bodies."[637] The next year, the U.N. continued to emphasize the danger that death squads posed to the nascent Salvadoran democracy.[638] In particular, the United Nations Observer Mission in El Salvador (ONUSAL) reported extrajudicial killings of both FMLN and ARENA party leaders, as well as human rights activists during the two years immediately following the Peace Accords, and urged the Salvadoran government to investigate death squad activities.[639]

---

[635] *See, e.g.,* COMISIÓN DE LA VERDAD PARA EL SALVADOR, *supra* note 6; *see also Report of the Secretary-General 1994, supra* note 101, at ¶ 4 (reiterating concerns expressed in an earlier report that "so-called death squads" were re-emerging).

[636] For accounts of post-war extrajudicial violence in the 1990s generally, *see* AMNESTY INTERNATIONAL, EL SALVADOR: THE SPECTRE OF DEATH SQUADS (1996), *available at* http://web.amnesty.org/library/pdf/AMR290151996ENGLISH/$File/AMR2901596.pdf. *See also* POPKIN, *supra* note 10, at 186-87. Numerous sources whom our researchers interviewed in El Salvador told us that extrajudicial violence had increased in recent years. Interview with Alegría, *supra* note 502; interview with Cruz, *supra* note 145; *see also* WASHINGTON OFFICE ON LATIN AMERICA, *supra* note 480, at 16 (noting that "social cleansing"-style killings have increased in Guatemala, El Salvador, and Honduras in recent years).

[637] COMISIÓN DE LA VERDAD PARA EL SALVADOR, *supra* note 6, at 144.

[638] The Secretary General, *Further Report of the Secretary-General on the United Nations Observer Mission in El Salvador,* ¶ 11, *delivered to the Security Council,* U.N. Doc. S/26790 (Nov. 23 1993).

[639] *Id.* at ¶ 11 ("In recent weeks, a number of murders and assaults have raised fears about the possible resurgence of illegal armed groups with political objectives, including the so-called death squads. In October, the Division of Human Rights of ONUSAL alerted the Government to this danger and stressed the usefulness of establishing an autonomous mechanism for the investigation of these incidents. The subsequent killings of two senior

The U.N. Special Rapporteur on Extrajudicial, Summary or Arbitrary Executions reported that death squad activities were still occurring and were "apparently connected to the [upcoming] March 1994 elections."[640] Moreover, the Special Rapporteur noted that "no investigations were said to have been opened into most of the extrajudicial killings attributed to such groups."[641] Thus, even as the international community urged the Salvadoran government to take the opportunity afforded by the peace accords to bring an end to extrajudicial violence, death squads continued to operate, targeting political and human rights activists. The post-war situation was so serious that in December 1993, the U.N. formed a special commission, composed of representatives of the Salvadoran government and staff of ONUSAL, to investigate continued post-war death squad activity.[642]

As a sense of public insecurity and fear of crime emerged in the years following the peace accords, death squads began to target those suspected of involvement in ordinary crime, as well as political activists. In 1994, a group calling itself the *Sombra Negra* ("Black Shadow") appeared in the eastern city of San Miguel, purportedly to combat crime. The *Sombra Negra* targeted alleged criminals for extrajudicial

---

FMLN leaders, a member of the governing party (ARENA) and two former municipal officials belonging to that party, brought this issue into sharper focus. In view of these killings and the ONUSAL position as expressed by its Human Rights Division, the Government created an Interinstitutional Commission to investigate this type of crime."); *see also* The Secretary General, *Report of the Secretary-General 1994, supra* note 101, at ¶ 6 ("Since the establishment of the Joint Group, several acts of violence have been committed against representatives of political or social organizations, including the assassination, immediately after the establishment of the Joint Group, of a member of the highest decision-making body of the FMLN. Investigations are under way in an effort to clarify the motives for these acts and to identify the culprits.").

[640] Special Rapporteur on Extrajudicial, Summary or Arbitrary Executions, Bacre Waly Ndiaye, *Question of the Violation of Human Rights and Fundamental Freedoms, in Any Part of the World, with Particular Reference to Colonial and Other Dependent Countries and Territories: Extrajudicial, Summary, or Arbitrary Executions,* ¶ 278, *delivered to the Commission on Human Rights,* U.N. Doc. E/CN.4/1994/7 (Dec. 7, 1993).

[641] *Id.* at ¶ 277.

[642] POPKIN *supra* note 10, at 187.

killings, justifying its activities with assertions that "the laws of the country were not working," "the PNC did not have sufficient resources to combat crime," and "too many crimes were committed in El Salvador daily."[643]   In 1995, several alleged members of the group, including four officials of the PNC, were arrested and charged with homicide. By 1999, none had been convicted.[644]   The three-time mayor of the city of San Miguel (elected in 2000, 2004, and 2008) was one of those charged in the mid-1990s.[645] According to expert consultant to the U.S. Asylum and Immigration Office, Douglas Payne, "in December 1998 and January 1999 there were at least twelve killings of gang members in the metropolitan San Salvador area with the hallmarks of organized executions."[646]

This chapter focuses on evidence of the re-emergence of death squads that carry out contract killings, social cleansing operations, and, to a lesser extent, political killings. It also provides first-hand accounts from the most common victims of clandestine violence: real or imputed gang members. Finally, it analyzes the actions of clandestine, organized crime networks and their interaction with youth gangs.

A. *Indications of Extrajudicial Killings and the Apparent Re-Emergence of Death Squads*

The emergence of the *Sombra Negra* exemplifies the transformation of Salvadoran death squads from groups seeking to silence political opposition to ones effectuating social cleansing or carrying out contract

---

[643] AMNESTY INTERNATIONAL, EL SALVADOR: THE SPECTRE OF DEATH SQUADS, *supra* note 636.

[644] *Id.;* DOUGLAS PAYNE, EL SALVADOR: REEMERGENCE OF "SOCIAL CLEANSING" DEATH SQUADS 4-5 (1999), *available at* http://www.uscis.gov/files/nativedocuments/QASLV99-001. pdf.

[645] Yurina Rico, *Una Sombra persigue al alcalde de San Miguel,* LA OPINION (Los Angeles), Nov. 20, 2006; *Resurge el fantasma de la Sombra Negra,* EL DIARIO DE HOY, Aug. 2, 2007, *available at* http://www.elsalvador.com/mwedh/nota/nota_completa. asp?idArt=1605218&idCat=6329.

[646] PAYNE, *supra* note 644.

killings. Despite this shift away from an overtly political logic, however, death squads that engaged in social cleansing involved many of the individual and institutional actors linked to death squads during the civil war.[647] Extrajudicial executions of alleged criminals in the 1990s, like those of political activists in prior decades, appeared to be driven by the efforts of powerful actors in Salvadoran society to control the population through fear. Such extrajudicial violence, moreover, was both a cause and a consequence of El Salvador's post-war failure to establish the rule of law through functioning democratic and judicial institutions.

Today, there are strong indications that social cleansing groups that target suspected criminals and gang members have become increasingly active in response to increased levels of violence. International and domestic human rights organizations have documented a spike in unexplained homicides since 2003. Many attribute this increase to the re-activation of death squads.[648] Since 2003, the homicide rate in the country has soared, from 36 per 100,000 residents in 2003 to 60.9 per 100,000 in 2007.[649] Simultaneously, the phenomenon of gang violence has become a central national concern, to which the state has

---

[647] Amnesty International reported that the Sombra Negra likely consisted of former soldiers "with tacit approval of the PNC." AMNESTY INTERNATIONAL, EL SALVADOR: THE SPECTRE OF DEATH SQUADS, *supra* note 636, at 3.

[648] Interview with Cruz, *supra* note 145; interview with Martínez Ventura, *supra* note 117; interview with Alemanni de Carrillo, supra note 119; interview with McConville, *supra* note 209; interview with Mirna Antonieta Perla Jiménez, Magistrada de la Sala de lo Civil de la Corte Suprema de Justicia, Corte Suprema de Justicia de El Salvador [Justice of the Civil Chamber, Supreme Court of Justice of El Salvador], in San Salvador (Oct. 20, 2008). Jeannette Aguilar, Director of the IUDOP, told our researchers that "[t]here is increasing evidence of social cleansing. Faced with a state that is incapable of guaranteeing citizen security, these groups are coming into play. There is an increase in the last several years of homicides of gang members, committed not just by other gang members." Interview with Aguilar, *supra* note 157. In a November 2006 report on Central American gangs, the Washington Office on Latin America noted an increase in unexplained murders in Central America and highlighted as a possible explanation increasing extrajudicial killings of gang members. WASHINGTON OFFICE ON LATIN AMERICA, *supra* note 480; *see also* interview with Alegría, *supra* note 502.

[649] BOLETÍN SOBRE HOMCIDIOS 2007, *supra* note 3.

responded with repressive law enforcement strategies and increasingly harsh rhetoric. Several experts with whom we spoke suggested a link between the re-emergence of death squads and extrajudicial killings, on the one hand, and the repressive *Mano Dura* anti-gang policies that were first implemented in 2003, on the other. According to José Miguel Cruz, former Director of the Institute for Public Opinion Research at the Central American University in El Salvador, these repressive crime-fighting plans have provided "ideological and rhetorical support" for social cleansing groups.[650]

Indeed, in recent years several clandestine groups have distributed pamphlets throughout high-crime areas of El Salvador, accusing the government of being inept and ill-equipped to face rising crime rates and vowing to rid communities of gang members and other criminals.[651] One of these pamphlets, distributed in the eastern city of San Miguel by a group that also called itself *Sombra Negra*, warned: "We are already gathering information to proceed aggressively against extortionists, gangs, kidnappers, criminals and thieves, corrupt judges, defense lawyers who represent gang members, corrupt police officers, and drug traffickers" and gave the government a thirty-day deadline to take aggressive action against crime.[652] It is unclear whether this group is tied to the earlier *Sombra Negra* killers that terrorized the country in

---

[650] Interview with Cruz, *supra* note 145.

[651] Beatriz Castillo, *Asesinan a tres supuestos pandilleros*, Diario Co Latino, Sept. 13, 2006, *available at* http://www.diariocolatino.com/es/20060913/nacionales/nacionales_20060913_13796/; Nicolás Cerón, *"Sombra Negra" amenaza a extorsionistas y pandilleros*, Diario Co Latino, Sept. 1, 2006, *available at* http://www.diariocolatino.com/es/20060901/nacionales/nacionales_20060901_13648/?tpl=69; Rodrigo Baires Quezada, *Un miedo anónimo recorre Chalchuapa*, El Faro, Sept. 17, 2007, http://www.elfaro.net/secciones/Noticias/20070917/noticias7_20070917.asp; Elder Gómez, *Encapuchados piden investigar ola de asesinatos en Chalchuapa*, Diario Co Latino, Aug. 31, 2007, *available at* http://www.diariocolatino.com/es/20070831/nacionales/46667/?tpl=69; Carlos Segovia, *Amenaza presunto grupo de exterminio en San Miguel*, El Diario de Hoy, Jan, 31, 2008, *available at* http://www.elsalvador.com/mwedh/nota/nota_completa.asp?idCat=8613&idArt=2028720; David Marroquín, *Supuesto grupo advierte con azotar a pandilleros*, El Diario de Hoy, Feb. 5, 2009, *available at* http://www.elsalvador.com/mwedh/nota/nota_completa.asp?idCat=8613&idArt=3321435.

[652] Cerón, *supra* note 651.

the early 1990s. Another pamphlet, signed "E.L." and distributed in the western town of Chalchuapa, instituted a curfew (see Figure 8):

> ATTENTION CHALCHUAPANS
> For your own good we recommend that you don't walk on the streets **after 10 p.m.,** given that we will be conducting a campaign to cleanse [our streets] of so many crooks that have robbed us of our tranquility. We recommend that police forces remain in their quarters at night, and that they not interfere with our work. **DO NOT GO OUT** unless you have a real emergency, you may be mistaken for a gang member, etc.
>
> To all the lazy young kids who hang around schools intimidating others, **BE CAREFUL,** the same goes for all the bums who go out on the streets to bother people. Given that the authorities cannot take action, we will take the law into our own hands. [We're taking steps] to bring peace to Chalchuapa. We will be present in colonies, neighborhoods, streets, etc. We will not be stopped.[653]

Community educator Israel Figueroa confirmed that local residents accepted that a de facto curfew was in effect in the town of Chalchuapa. He added that in August 2007 pamphlets instituting a curfew were distributed in the town of Huachapán, and that this practice had spread to other areas with a significant gang presence.[654] R., an 18-year-old male, and U.B., a 20-year-old male, who live in Chalchuapa told us that they could not leave home after 8:30 or 9:00 P.M. because their town had a curfew, though they did not know who had imposed it.[655]

---

[653] EL FARO, Sept. 17, 2007, http://www.elfaro.net/secciones/Noticias/20070917/noticias7_20070917.asp, *supra* note 651.

[654] Interview with Figueroa, *supra* note 297.

[655] Interview with R., in Santa Ana (Oct. 20, 2007); interview with U.R., in Santa Ana (Oct. 20, 2007).

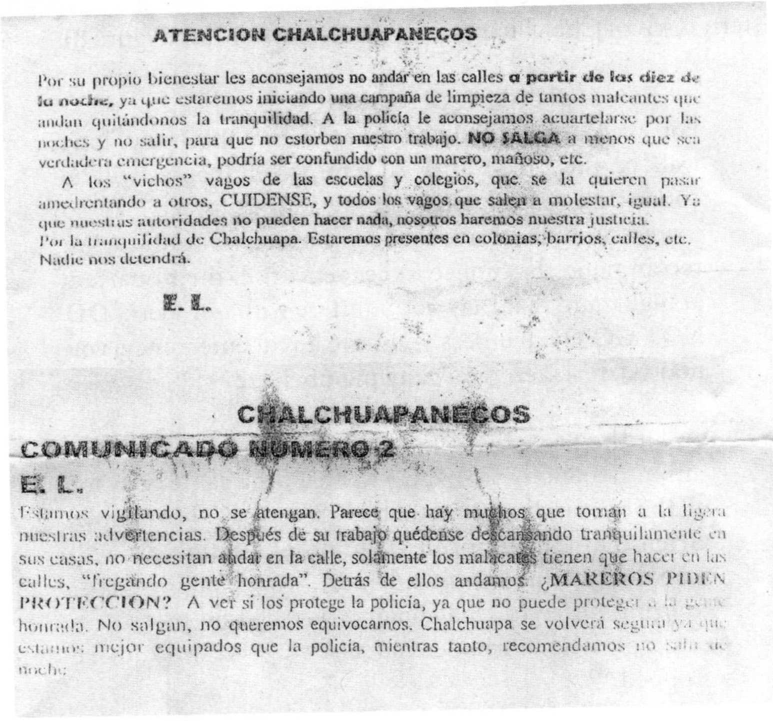

ATENCION CHALCHUAPANECOS

Por su propio bienestar les aconsejamos no andar en las calles **a partir de las diez de la noche,** ya que estaremos iniciando una campaña de limpieza de tantos maleantes que andan quitándonos la tranquilidad. A la policía le aconsejamos acuartelarse por las noches y no salir, para que no estorben nuestro trabajo. **NO SALGA** a menos que sea verdadera emergencia, podría ser confundido con un marero, mañoso, etc.

A los "vichos" vagos de las escuelas y colegios, que se la quieren pasar amedrentando a otros, CUIDENSE, y todos los vagos que salen a molestar, igual. Ya que nuestras autoridades no pueden hacer nada, nosotros haremos nuestra justicia. Por la tranquilidad de Chalchuapa. Estaremos presentes en colonias, barrios, calles, etc. Nadie nos detendrá.

E. L.

CHALCHUAPANECOS
COMUNICADO NUMERO 2
E. L.

Estamos vigilando, no se atengan. Parece que hay muchos que toman a la ligera nuestras advertencias. Después de su trabajo quédense descansando tranquilamente en sus casas, no necesitan andar en la calle, solamente los malacates tienen que hacer en las calles, "fregando gente honrada". Detrás de ellos andamos. ¿MAREROS PIDEN PROTECCION? A ver si los protege la policía, ya que no puede proteger a la gente honrada. No salgan, no queremos equivocarnos. Chalchuapa se volverá segura ya que estamos mejor equipados que la policía, mientras tanto, recomendamos no salir de noche.

Figure 8. Pamphlets Distributed in the Town of Chalchuapa Instituting a 10 P.M. Curfew
Source: El Faro.net

B.F., a priest working in Mejicanos, a poor suburb of San Salvador, told our researchers that notices of a curfew had also appeared in the Mejicanos area, and that community members were unsure whether the police or other armed groups were imposing the curfew.[656]

The *modus operandi* of the death squads that have re-emerged since

---

[656] Interview with B.F., *supra* note 119. Newspaper articles also report that pamphlets imposing curfews have been distributed in Mejicanos and Ayutuxtepeque. The pamphlets, signed by the *Brigada General Maximiliano Hernández Martínez* or B.G.M.H.M., criticized police forces for not fighting crime effectively, and warned gang members and criminals that they would pay a high price for intimidating the population. David Marroquín, *Supuesto grupo advierte con azotar a pandilleros*, EL DIARIO DE HOY, Feb. 5, 2009, *available at* http://www.elsalvador.com/mwedh/nota/nota_completa.asp?idCat=8613&idArt=3321435.

2003 bears a marked resemblance to that of the death squads of the civil war. For example, in its report on "possible extrajudicial, summary, or arbitrary executions in El Salvador in 2004," FESPAD collected media reports of unexplained homicides that may constitute extrajudicial killings. According to FESPAD, these homicides presented a common pattern:

> [the killings are carried out] from cars and bicycles, [with] shots fired to the head at point blank range, bodies [left] face down, with hands and feet tied behind backs, sometimes bound with shoestrings or with barbed wire. . . . Generally [the victims] have been executed by armed men wearing ski masks, and their bodies are left in creeks, rivers, highways. . . . [657]

Other public officials and rights groups in El Salvador also describe current social cleansing operations as bearing striking similarities to the death squad activities of the civil war years.[658] The commonalities

---

[657] Estado de la Seguridad Pública y la Justicia Penal en El Salvador 2004, *supra* note 52, at 85.

[658] Jaime Martínez Ventura, Coordinator, Office of Juvenile Justice, Supreme Court, described the characteristics of current killings he believes to be social cleansing, including deaths in which victims' bodies are found in isolated areas or have been tortured or mutilated. According to Mr. Martínez Ventura, these characteristics are not associated with gang killings, but rather are consistent with killings by groups armed with heavy weaponry and traveling by vehicle. Interview with Martínez Ventura, *supra* note 117. Additionally, National Human Rights Ombudswoman Beatrice Alemanni de Carrillo, speaking to our researchers about the resurgence in death squad activities in recent years, emphasized the brutality and use of heavy weaponry that characterize these killings. Interview with Alemanni de Carrillo, *supra* note 119. Employing criteria developed by the Joint Task Force for the Investigation of Illegal Armed Groups with Political Motives in El Salvador [hereinafter Joint Task Force], *Tutela Legal* concluded that fourteen of 169 homicides investigated by their offices in 2007 "had the factual and operational characteristics of death squads." La Situación de los Derechos Humanos en El Salvador 2007, *supra* note 173, at 14. In 1994, the Joint Task Force (a joint U.N.-El Salvador effort to investigate death squad activity in El Salvador) set forth a set of parameters to evaluate the existence of death squads. These parameters include considering the victim's profile and analyzing the perpetrator's *modus operandi*. See Amnesty International, El Salvador: The Spectre of Death Squads, *supra* note 636.

between these killings and the patterns of death squad activities of the
1980s and early 1990s indicate that some of the same individual or
institutional actors involved in death squads during the civil war may
be linked to current social cleansing activities. Though the level of state
involvement in current social cleansing efforts is unclear, groups acting
with the *modus operandi* characteristic of deaths squads in El Salvador
have operated in recent years with impunity. Human rights groups
and other observers suggest that state actors may be complicit in these
activities.[659]

Our researchers obtained documentation prepared by *Tutela Legal*
regarding an apparent recent example of a death squad targeting gang
members.[660] On July 10, 2006, four suspected members of the M-18
were killed in San Bartolo, Ilopango. The victims (Ricardo Alberto
Álvarez, Manuel Antonio Reyes Góchez, Juan Carlos Cabrera, and
Juan Carlos Dimas Fuentes) were taking shelter from a downpour of
rain on the side of a street when a black vehicle approached them.[661] At
least two armed men emerged from the vehicle, forced the youths to lie
down on the ground, shot them to death, and fled the scene.[662] In this
case, as noted in Chapter IV, the police later staged a late-night raid on
the wake held for the four victims, under the pretext that the wake was
being used to plan a gang attack on the police.[663] Members of the PNC
searched those present for weapons, struck some of the young people
they searched, used abusive language, and allegedly searched the coffins

---

[659] Interview with Alegría, *supra* note 502 (stating that the failure of police and prosecutors
to address the situation of violence suggests not only inefficiency, but also complicity, particularly in light of the climate of impunity for such crimes). Alegría also told our researchers that the Ombudsperson's Office believes that officials of the PNC were responsible for
the extrajudicial killings of suspected gang members in Sonsonate in June 2006. *Id.; see also*
interview with Aguilar, *supra* note 157.

[660] Alegria, *supra* note 659.

[661] *Id.*

[662] *Id.*

[663] Parroquia San Bartolo, *supra* note 457.

of the deceased as well.[664] Police investigation into the killing of the four men had not produced concrete results at this writing. Death squads and state authorities, even if they do not function in explicit cooperation, in practice may operate to reinforce each other and generate a climate of terror for gang members and those who are (rightly or wrongly) presumed to be gang members.

Our researchers also spoke with one youth who had witnessed a death squad killing in his neighborhood and who knew others who had witnessed other death squad killings. He described a group of six men, wearing black ski masks and driving in a large vehicle without license plates, who shot a man in the head.[665] He also described reports from other neighborhood residents of similar targeted killings carried out by groups of men dressed in black.[666]

Thus far, clandestine groups that authored the pamphlets described above, *Sombra Negra* and *E.L.*, have not claimed responsibility for the hundreds of violent homicides whose *modus operandi* resembles that of 1980s and 1990s death squads. Nevertheless, several credible reports indicate that clandestine structures operating within the PNC and in alliance with the private sector have been responsible for at least a portion of these extrajudicial killings. For example, on July 28, 2007, a Joint Task Force (GTC) discovered that an active police officer and a former member of the PNC had participated in the extrajudicial execution of rural worker Amado García Amaya, as noted in Chapter IV. Dressed in black, the officers and a third man drove a black pick-up truck to the victim's house and shot him in the back. Soon after the killing, the victim's family contacted a GTC that was patrolling the area that was able to chase and apprehend the three perpetrators. Prior to their capture, the PNC had expressed no suspicion that captured Sgt. Nelson Antonio Arriaza Delgado and ex-police agent Carlos Geovanni Chávez or any other police officer operated a death squad structure

---

[664] *Id.*

[665] Interview with A.Y., *supra* note 277.

[666] *Id.*

from within the PNC.[667]

Follow-up investigations uncovered a large, illegal framework operating inside the police force in the Department of San Miguel. Sixteen police officers—all members of the Criminal Investigation Unit— were reported to have taken part in Amado García Amaya's murder and to have been part of the clandestine extermination group.[668] The Office of the Prosecutor has also investigated the possible involvement of this group in thirty-one other killings that took place between 2006 and 2007 in eastern El Salvador.[669] Local businessmen are thought to have financed the group's operations. [670]

Established human rights institutions in El Salvador have documented the involvement of PNC officials in other extrajudicial killings in recent years.[671] Gang members have called press conferences to deny

---

[667] Rodrigo Baires Quezada, *San Miguel pone a prueba a la PNC*, EL FARO, Aug. 20, 2007, *http://www.elfaro.net/secciones/Noticias/20070820/noticias6_20070820.asp.*

[668] Amado García Amaya's murder is reported to have been a contract killing. Elder Gómez, *Más policías vinculados a grupo de sicarios que operaba en PNC*, DIARIO CO LATINO, Sept. 11, 2007, *available at* http://www.diariocolatino.com/es/20070911/nacionales/47031/.

[669] Jorge Beltrán & Carlos Segovia, *Investigarán a ex policías por 31 casos de homicidios*, EL DIARIO DE HOY, Aug. 8, 2007, *available at* http://www.elsalvador.com/mwedh/nota/nota_ completa.asp?idCat=6329&idArt=1617024.

[670] Carlos Segovia, *Presunto grupo de exterminio en San Miguel; Ávila: Comerciantes patrocinaban grupos*, EL DIARIO DE HOY, Aug. 1, 2007, *available at* http://www.elsalvador.com/mwedh/nota/nota_completa.asp?idCat=6329&idArt=1602086

[671] *Tutela Legal* documented seven examples of extrajudicial killings committed by members of the PNC in 2007. LA SITUACIÓN DE LOS DERECHOS HUMANOS EN EL SALVADOR 2007, *supra* note 173, at 18. The office documented one such instance of extrajudicial killings committed by members of the PNC in 2005 and eight instances of extrajudicial killings committed by members of the PNC in 2004. LA SITUACIÓN DE LOS DERECHOS HUMANOS EN EL SALVADOR 2005, *supra* note 476, at 10; LA SITUACIÓN DE LOS DERECHOS HUMANOS EN EL SALVADOR 2004, *supra* note 476, at 7. Note that these are not estimates of the incidence of extrajudicial killings by PNC agents in El Salvador, but rather individual cases brought to the attention of *Tutela Legal* and investigated by that organization. Interview with Jeannette Aguilar, Director, IUDOP, in San Salvador (Oct. 18, 2007). According to Aguilar, the country has seen a marked surge of assassinations of gang-involved youth. These killings tend to involve a pattern in which the youth are taken from their homes in the middle of the night and found dead sometime later. There are credible reports that these assassinations are conducted, in part, by off-duty police officers or members of death squads.

responsibility for this type of violent killings[672] and to accuse clandestine groups, such as the *Grupo Omega* (Omega Group) and private security organizations, of targeting gang members.[673]   Independent researcher Sonja Wolf documented claims that such extermination groups operate within El Salvador. According to Wolf, "*Grupo Omega* is managed by various ex-militaries, maintains its intelligence units within some of the Ministries, and receives information and logistical support from senior PNC officials, including [very high-ranking officials]."[674]   She further notes that three extermination groups were embedded within PNC units at the time she conducted her investigation.[675]

In light of these alarming findings, the National Human Rights Ombudsperson's Office, together with national NGOs, have repeatedly called on the PNC, the Office of the Prosecutor, and the Office of the President to launch a comprehensive investigation into the hundreds

---

Id. Ombudswoman Beatriz Carrillo has told the press: "It is almost proven that Sonsonate's PNC harbors extermination groups, this is why my office has requested a special investigation. We have also requested an investigation into death squads that may operate outside police forces." She emphasized that her office had taken the testimony of a young man who had been kidnapped, tortured, and left for dead by a death squad. Leonel Herrera, *PDDH insiste en investigar a grupos de exterminio*, DIARIO CO LATINO, Aug. 30, 2006, *available at* http://www.diariocolatino.com/es/20060830/nacionales/nacionales_20060830_13629/.

[672] Beatriz Castillo, *PNC investigará existencia de grupo de exterminio de mareros*, DIARIO CO LATINO, Aug. 24, 2005, *available at* http://www.diariocolatino.com/es/20050824/nacionales/nacionales_20050824_9023/?tpl=69; Iván Escobar, *Supuestos pandilleros atribuyen violencia a grupos de exterminio*, DIARIO CO LATINO, Feb. 10, 2006, *available at* http://www.diariocolatino.com/es/20060210/nacionales/nacionales_20060210_11218/?tpl=69 (MS members told the press "in light of the propaganda campaign carried out by Mr. Elías Antonio Saca's government and his party, ARENA, who want to blame us for the crime wave that sweeps the country and for all of the resulting deaths, we declare that we are not responsible and denounce those illegal armed extermination groups that exist within the PNC, amongst them the so-called Omega group and private security companies.").

[673] Escobar, *supra* note 672.

[674] Sonja Wolf, The Politics of Gang Control, NGO advocacy in post-war El Salvador 64 n.175 (2008) (unpublished Ph. D. thesis, University of Wales, Aberystwyth), *available at* http://cadair.aber.ac.uk/dspace/bitstream/2160/1258/1/Sonja%20Wolf_thesis.pdf.

[675] *Id.* at 64.

of extrajudicial killings that may implicate illegal structures working
with impunity inside the PNC.[676] The government's reaction has
been to reject allegations that death squads have been operating in
El Salvador, to minimize the gravity of these incidents (calling them
political maneuvers by opposition groups to boycott the *Súper Mano
Dura* Plan),[677] or to hold gang members responsible for the killings.[678]
In spite of these recent discoveries of extensive police involvement in
extrajudicial executions in San Miguel, the PNC and the Office of the
President maintained their position and asserted in August 2007 that
the murder of Amado García Amaya represented an isolated incident
of corruption.[679]

Recent reports also suggest that these clandestine groups, once
again, have begun targeting political activists.[680] In February 2008, a

[676] Gloria Silvia Orellana, *PDDH abrió investigación sobre grupos de exterminio*, Diario Co Latino, Feb. 5, 2005, *available at* http://www.diariocolatino.com/es/20050205/nacionales/nacionales_20050205_6918/; Herrera, *supra* note 671.

[677] Mirna Jiménez, *Investigarán rumor de que grupos políticos están detrás de pandillas*, Diario Co Latino, June 8, 2005, *available at* http://www.diariocolatino.com/es/20050608/nacionales/nacionales_20050608_8231/?tpl=69.

[678] Mirna Jiménez, *Presidente Saca pedirá investigar escuadrones de la muerte*, Diario Co Latino, Aug. 26, 2005, *available at* http://www.diariocolatino.com/es/20050826/nacionales/nacionales_20050826_9054/ (When the press asked President Saca whether he knew of the resurgence of death squads, he said he had only heard about extermination groups within gang structures.); Oscar Iraheta, *Maras son grupos de exterminio*, El Diario de Hoy, Feb. 11, 2006, *available at* http://www.elsalvador.com/noticias/2006/02/11/nacional/nac7.asp ("Death squads exist and are composed of gang members."); Antolín Escobar, *Jefe PNC descarta un "toque de queda,"* El Diario de Hoy, Sept. 23, 2007, *available at* http://www.elsalvador.com/mwedh/nota/nota_completa.asp?idCat=6329&idArt=1719926.

[679] Baires Quezada, *supra* note 651.

[680] Petición de Organizaciones de la Sociedad Civil a la Fiscalía General de la República para que se investiguen asesinatos de activistas de derechos humanos [Petition to the Office of the Prosecutor by Civil Society Organizations to investigate the murders of human rights activists], Feb.12, 2008 (on file with authors); La Situación de los Derechos Humanos en El Salvador 2005, *supra* note 476, at 10 (uncovering evidence of politically-motivated extrajudicial executions in two cases); La Situación de los Derechos Humanos en El Salvador 2006, *supra* note 173, at 8 (uncovering evidence of politically-motivated extrajudicial executions in five cases); La Situación de los Derechos Humanos en El Salvador 2007, *supra* note 173, at 32 (uncovering evidence of politically-motivated

group of civil society organizations urged the Office of the Prosecutor to launch an investigation into the murders of fifteen community leaders. These organizations' formal request accused the authorities in charge of investigating the killings of hastily concluding—without due investigation—that several of the deaths had been perpetrated by gangs or other criminals. It further faulted the government for failing to use guidelines developed by a joint U.N.-El Salvador task force to assess the likelihood of politically motivated killings. The requests argued that use of the task force guidelines would have led to the conclusion that the murders had been carried out by hired gunmen and urged the Office of the Prosecutor to identify those responsible for orchestrating the killings (see Table 4).[681]

---

extrajudicial executions in two cases). Several rights activists and independent experts told our researchers that community leaders and human rights activists had been assassinated in recent years, in a pattern reminiscent of the *modus operandi* of death squads. *See, e.g.,* interview with Perla Jiménez, *supra* note 648; interview with B.F., staff of a youth center, outside San Salvador (Oct. 22, 2007) (noting the targeting of youth who are involved in political organizations associated with the left, and describing one instance in which two masked men broke into the house of one politically active youth who was discovered dead the next day); interview with Elaine Freedman, Educadora Popular, Asociación de Capacitación e Investigación para la Salud Mental (ACISAM) [Community Educator, Association for Training and Research in Mental Health], in San Salvador (Jan. 22, 2009) (describing the abduction and murder of rights activists in 2006, 2007 and 2008; several of these rights activists were reportedly abducted by individuals traveling in pick-up trucks and wearing ski masks).

[681] Petición de Organizaciones de la Sociedad Civil, *supra* note 680. Petitioners relied on the Joint Task Force guidelines to evaluate politically motivated killings, *supra* note 658.

Table 4. Killings with a Possible Political Motive, 2006-2008

Source: *Fundación de Estudios para la Aplicación del Derecho*

No.	Name & Age	Possible Motive	Where & When	How
1	Eligio Ramírez Andrade, 35 yrs. old	Active member of the FMLN and President of the leadership council, Colonia Villa Hermosa, Cuscatancingo.	March 6, 2006 Colonia Villahermosa, Cuscatancingo, San Salvador	Killed by several gunshots, as he returned from the Majucla School where his children went to school.
2	Juana Monjarás, 77 yrs. old	FMLN militants since 1980. Husband and wife and parents of prominent FMLN party militants.	July 2, 2006 In their home in Suchitoto, Cuscatlán	Tortured and then killed with sharp weapons. Afterward, the killers destroyed evidence of the crime by dousing the bodies and the home in oil and setting them on fire.
3	Francisco Manzanares, 77 yrs. old			
4	Lidia Mercedes Pénate, 43 yrs. old	Active members of the FMLN. Husband and wife.	August 23, 2006 San Isidro, Coatepeque, Santa Ana	Assailants intercepted their vehicle, removed them from the car, and shot them in the street. Both were shot in the head.
5	Alex Wilber Flores, 43 yrs. old			

No.	Name & Age	Possible Motive	Where & When	How
6	Jesús Calzada de Carrillo, 57 yrs. old	Pastors from the Lutheran Church and leaders of the Salvation Squad of Jayaque, La Libertad. Husband and wife.	November 4, 2006 Outside the Lutheran Church in Jayaque, La Libertad	Gunned down outside the church as they left a religious service.
7	Francisco Carrillo, 65 yrs. old			
8	Gerson Roberto Alvayero, 32 yrs. old	Member of the FMLN Youth of Cuscatancingo.	January 26, 2007 His decomposing body found on the highway to Santa Ana	Had injuries to his stomach, chest, and neck from a sharp instrument.
9	Oscar Alejandro Franco, 21 yrs. old	Member of the FMLN Youth of Cuscatancingo.	May 1, 2007 Outside his home in Cuscatancingo, San Salvador	Gunned down by a passing vehicle.
10	Miguel Ángel Vásquez, 43 yrs. old	Leader, Electricity Workers' Union (STSEL). Worked for Duke Energy in Soyapango.	July 18, 2007 Found dead in his vehicle in the neighborhood of Mejicanos, San Salvador	Received two gunshots to the head.
11	Salvador Sánchez Roque, 38 yrs. old	Journalist with Maya Visión, Mi Gente, and YSUCA radio stations.	September 20, 2007 Near his home in Soyapango, San Salvador	Killed with a firearm.

Table 4, cont'd: Killings with a Possible Political Motive, 2006-2008

No.	Name & Age	Possible Motive	Where & When	How
12	Wilber Moisés Funes, 41 yrs. old	FMLN Mayor of Alegría, Usulután.	January 9, 2008 On a country road in Alegría, Usulután	Their vehicle was stopped and sprayed with bullets.
13	Zulmar Rivera, 22 yrs. old	Employee of the town of Alegria.		
14	Julio Edgardo Rodríquez Ramírez, 14 yrs. old	Participated in the Network for Childhood and Adolescents. Family part of the Ecclesiastical Base Communities.	April 15, 2008 Community Monte Victor, Ayuntuxtepeque, San Salvador	Assailants hung victim upside down and shot him. Two other youth survived.
15	Omar Huerzo, 26 yrs. old	Security Guard for FMLN representative and founder of the Ita Maura Community Radio.	April 24, 2008 Community of Ita Maura, Town of San Pablo Tacachico, La Libertad	Assailants shot at the youth group as it left the nearby community hall. Three others were injured.
16	Henry Navarrete, 18 yrs. old	Student, member of the FMLN Base Committee, also member of the Ita Maura Community Radio.		

Table 4, cont'd: Killings with a Possible Political Motive, 2006-2008

No.	Name & Age	Possible Motive	Where & When	How
17	Héctor Antonio Ventura Vásquez, 19 yrs. old	One of the fourteen released political prisoners of Suchitoto.	May 2, 2008 Cantón Valle Verde, Suchitoto, Cuscatlán	Attacked in his home while he slept. Fatal knife wound to the heart. Another youth was injured.
18	William Landaverde, 17 yrs. old	Family member of demobilized FMLN combatant, town of Suchitoto.	May 5, 2008 Community of El Barrio, Suchitoto, Cuscatlán	Assailants tortured and destroyed part of his body with rocks.
19	Walter Ayala Ulloa, age n/a	Press Secretary for the FMLN Youth of Santo Tomás Had been publicly threatened days before his death by the ARENA mayor of Santo Tomás, Carlos Sánchez.	Disappeared in San Jacinto on May 21, 2008. His body appeared in the cemetery in Ciudad Delgado the following day.	Died of asphyxiation. Body showed signs of having been handcuffed.
20	Alejandro Portillo, age n/a	President of the community, El Changuitillo.	April 2008	Killed by an axe. Body was mutilated and abandoned.

Table 4, cont'd: Killings with a Possible Political Motive, 2006-2008

No.	Name & Age	Possible Motive	Where & When	How
21	Ángel Martínez Cerón, age n/a	Coordinator of the January 24 Revolutionary Socialist Student Block. He and friends were harassed by police. Police raided his home in May 2008 and detained Cerón, accusing him of illegal possession of firearms.	June 26, 2008 In front of his home in Santa Ana.	Killed by eight shots and one execution-style shot to the head.
22	Bartolo Cerritos, age n/a	Community Organizer, Cantón Comostepeque, Nejapa	Disappeared Saturday, June 28, 2008.	Detained twice by police for unknown reasons.
23	Holman Riva, 39 yrs. old	FMLN Militant and employee of the City of Ilopango.	July 2, 2008	Victims forced from their home and shot nine times each.
24	Walter Alexander Riva, 16 yrs. old			

Table 4, cont'd: Killings with a Possible Political Motive, 2006-2008

In sum, the current resurgence of death squad activities in El Salvador indicates that the government has yet to build public institutions capable of providing for public security in accordance with the rule of law. In the absence of such institutions, historic patterns of clandestine violence aimed at social control persist in their most brutal forms today.

B. *Organized Crime*

Finally, there is a widespread sense in El Salvador that organized criminal networks have grown in the past several years to become powerful clandestine actors in the country. The relationship between the emergence of these networks and the two major gangs in El Salvador is complex and—due to the clandestine nature of both phenomena— uncertain. Academic experts, victims,[682] as well as leaders in the Salvadoran and international law enforcement communities,[683] agree that as gangs have become increasingly organized and well-resourced, the upper echelons of the gang hierarchy seem to be taking on some characteristics of large-scale, organized crime syndicates. Among the indicators of this apparent evolution are the gangs' extortion activities (discussed in Chapter III, Part (B)(2), their access to more sophisticated weapons,[684] reports of their participation in international drug trafficking activities,[685] and their ability to operate in a coordinated

---

[682] Interview with Cruz, *supra* note 145; interview with Aguilar, *supra* note 157; interview with K.H.D., *supra* note 304; Aguilar & Miranda, *supra* note 157, at 51-52; interview with Martínez Ventura, *supra* note 117 (noting in particular the increased levels of organization associated with gang members' participation in trafficking of drugs, arms, and persons); interview with Hernández, *supra* note 303.

[683] Interview with Ramírez, *supra* note 126; *see also* Chris Swecker, Assistant Director, Criminal Investigative Division, Federal Bureau of Investigation, Statement Before the Subcommittee on the Western Hemisphere House International Relations Committee (Apr. 20, 2005) (emphasizing in particular the sophistication and organization of the MS-13 gang and describing a major law enforcement initiative aimed at suppressing further MS-13 development).

[684] Interview with Aguilar, *supra* note 157.

[685] RIBADO, *supra* note 5, at 2.

manner throughout El Salvador.[686] Non-governmental observers note, however, that to the extent gangs are engaging in more lucrative, large-scale criminality, this transformation has been taking place primarily at the top levels of gang hierarchies.[687] Lower-level gang members continue to live in situations of extreme risk and poverty in marginalized neighborhoods as documented and discussed in greater detail in Chapter IV. A report published by the U.N. Office on Drugs and Crime emphasized that, while gang leaders may interact with existing large-scale criminal networks that engage in drug trafficking, they are unlikely to occupy positions of power within these crime syndicates. The report noted:

> It is unclear how the bulk of youth gang members, who live far from the sea and are not known for their maritime skills, would add value to the process of moving drugs northward. Even with regard to traffic along the Pan American Highway, it is unclear how *mareros* could assist. They could be involved in providing some minor logistic or security support, but it is highly unlikely that gang members, who are generally young street kids, are the masterminds behind the movement of cocaine to the United States.[688]

Salvadoran observers also emphasize that the impetus for increased organized criminal activities comes not just from within gang structures themselves, but from other powerful clandestine criminal networks that operate freely in the country.[689] This view is reinforced by U.S.-

---

[686] Aguilar & Miranda, *supra* note 157, at 49.

[687] Interview with Aguilar, *supra* note 157 (contrasting the increasing wealth found in the highest levels of gang hierarchies with the continuing situation of poverty and risk in which "common" gang members live); *see also* Aguilar & Miranda, *supra* note 157, at 57-58 (emphasizing that not all gang members participate in organized crime).

[688] UNODC, *supra* note 153, at 63.

[689] Interview with Aguilar, *supra* note 157 (stating that non-gang actors take advantage of the climate of violence and insecurity to commit violent acts, knowing that such acts will

based organizations such as the Washington Office on Latin America (WOLA), which noted in a recent policy report on Central American gangs that "[t]here is a tendency in much of the discussions about youth gangs to conflate youth gangs with organized crime. While youth gangs can turn into organized crime groups – and some have, sometimes as a response to the *Mano Dura* strategies – the two are separate, and need to be treated separately by police."[690]

While the dynamics of these phenomena are complicated, there is no doubt that the perceived growing power of clandestine networks with the capacity to operate throughout El Salvador has generated a heightened sense of citizen insecurity and a growing lack of public confidence in state institutions. There have been reports of involvement of PNC members with organized crime.[691] Our researchers interviewed one young mother in the midst of her preparations to flee the country due to extortion and threats that her family received from a *banda*, or organized criminal network. She reported that the person behind these threats had told her family members during threatening phone calls: "[W]e are not *mareros* [gang members]. We are professionals."[692] Explaining her decision to

---

likely be blamed on gangs). *See also* interview with Santiago Flores, Religious Worker, in San Salvador (Aug. 22, 2006) (noting that not only gangs, but also organized crime and drug traffickers, are responsible for the situation of violence in the country); interview with Henríquez Hernández Ávila, *supra* note 520 (positing that most homicides are not committed by gang members); interview with Jaime Martínez Ventura, *supra* note 168 ("Some *clikas* interact with organized crime structures, but they do not control them; rather, *clika* members are assigned minor tasks such as local drug distribution. Very litle is known about organized crime syndicates in El Salvador. They are clandestine structures that have been shielded from prosecution by powerful interests.").

[690] WASHINGTON OFFICE ON LATIN AMERICA, *supra* note 480, at 13.

[691] *See* THE WORLD BANK ET AL., *supra* note 117, at 5 (reporting that members of the police are allegedly involved in such crimes as drug trafficking, trafficking in stolen vehicles, and sex trafficking of children). In 2004, Salvadoran media reported that a PNC officer's weapon was found in the possession of a member of the M-18. ESTADO DE LA SEGURIDAD PÚBLICA Y LA JUSTICIA PENAL EN EL SALVADOR 2004, *supra* note 52, at 54; Aguilar & Miranda, *supra* note 157, at 50-51 (reporting that some gang members have been found with heavy weaponry that is exclusively used by the armed forces).

[692] Interview with K.H.D., *supra* note 304.

abandon her home in El Salvador within days of receiving these threats and expressing views common among Salvadoran victims of crime, the young woman told us: "This is organized crime. [The police] capture two people and there are twenty more. The police are [even] involved in it."[693] Increasing levels of organization among gangs themselves have combined with the threat of separate organized criminal networks to exacerbate the climate of public insecurity that already pervades El Salvador.

---

[693] *Id.*

INDEX

List of Proper Names

List of Places

List of Organizations